MARIA EDGEWORTH

MARIA EDGEWORTH

Women, Enlightenment and Nation

+>-<+

Clíona Ó Gallchoir

UNIVERSITY COLLEGE DUBLIN PRESS

PREAS CHOLÁISTE OLLSCOILE
BHAILE ÁTHA CLIATH

First published 2005
by University College Dublin Press
Newman House, 86 St Stephen's Green
Dublin 2, Ireland
www.ucdpress.ie

ISBN 1-904558-45-3 pb
1-904558-46-1 hb

British Library Cataloguing in Publication Data
A catalogue record for this title is available
from the British Library

Typeset in Ireland in Adobe Caslon and Walbaum
by Elaine Burberry, Bantry, Co. Cork
Text design by Lyn Davies
Index by Jane Rogers
Printed on acid-free paper in England by
MPG Books Ltd, Bodmin, Cornwall

For my parents
Máire Hastings and Aindreas Ó Gallchoir

Contents

->-<-

Acknowledgements

->-<-

This book has its origins in research begun more than ten years ago, when I first undertook my doctoral work on Maria Edgeworth at the University of Cambridge. Thanks are therefore due firstly to the supervisor of that doctorate, Nigel Leask. The book has changed in the interim, but he may recognise here some of the things I learnt from him. I would also like to express my thanks to Marilyn Butler, who was very generous in reading some of my work and whose advice and expertise have always been invaluable. The support and enthusiasm of my teachers at University College Dublin, particularly Declan Kiberd, encouraged me to think seriously about doing research in the first place. Friends I met whilst doing my doctorate, including Jacky Cox, Elizabeth Eger, Rebecca Hayward, Christine Kenneally, Susan Manly, Kathleen O'Grady and Eve Regas, made finishing it a lot more enjoyable. The book was completed after my appointment as a lecturer in the Department of English at University College Cork, where I have been fortunate enough to find colleagues whose support made its completion possible. Mary Breen, Valerie Coogan and Lee Jenkins kindly read drafts of various chapters at a number of stages in this process, and thanks are also due to Patricia Coughlan, Alex Davis and (most particularly) Lee Jenkins for very sound advice in the final stages of writing and editing. Anne Mulhall, Moynagh Sullivan and Claire Connolly also read and offered valuable comments on parts of this book and their support in other ways has contributed to its completion. I am particularly grateful to Claire Connolly, who is always generous in sharing her extensive knowledge and insight on Edgeworth and on this period. Special thanks are due to Dr Patrick Crowley, of the department of French at UCC, who offered advice on some issues of translation. In this, as in all cases, any errors are entirely my own responsibility. I would also like to acknowledge the staff of the Boole Library at UCC, whose helpfulness made a real difference to me at a number of stages. The editor at UCD Press, Barbara Mennell, deserves a great deal of thanks for the care and efficiency of her work, as does the reader for the press. I gratefully acknow- ledge the contributions made towards by the cost of publication by the Faculty of Arts at UCC and the publications scheme of the National University of Ireland. My most long-standing debt is however to my family: my sister Bríd, my brother Aindreas and my parents, Máire and Aindreas. I am very grateful to them for listening when I asked them to, and allowing me to forget about research entirely when I needed to.

Clíona Ó Gallchoir
Cork, February 2005

A Note on Texts

→>-<←

Where possible, I have used the Pickering & Chatto edition of the *Novels and Selected Works of Maria Edgeworth*. As *Letters for Literary Ladies* is not included in the *Novels and Selected Works*, the most recent paperback edition has been used. I have also used the most recent paperback edition of *Belinda*, based on the 1802 first edition, as the text in the *Novels and Selected Works* is that of the 1832–3 collected edition, which differs substantially from that of 1802. The practice adopted with French-language texts has been to use the first English translation. The first translation of Germaine de Staël's *De la littérature considérée dans ses rapports avec les institutions sociales* is, however, quite unreliable. For this reason, a recent French edition has been used. I have supplied my own translations.

Italics used in quotations are those of the original author unless indicated otherwise.

Introduction

In the first two decades of the nineteenth century Maria Edgeworth was the most highly regarded Irish writer of the day, as well as being the most highly regarded woman writer in both Britain and Ireland. She began publishing in 1795 and published her last full-length work in 1834, although the period of her greatest productivity and success was in the period 1798–1820. Her career thus coincided with and was engaged with a dramatic period in Irish history, whose repercussions are still felt and which continues to provoke intense debate. Edgeworth's writing has, however, been insistently portrayed within Irish studies as fundamentally out of sympathy with the temper of her times, a lack of fit which is often expressed in terms of the opposition between Enlightenment and Romanticism. Edgeworth is frequently described as an Enlightenment writer, a description that is heavily loaded when one takes into account that the literary-philosophical terms Enlightenment and Romanticism have been pressed into service to describe the transition in Ireland from the eighteenth to the nineteenth century, and the corresponding shift in political and ideological gravity. George Boyce's remark, for example, that 'Romantic Ireland was born as the Irish Enlightenment drew to its close in rebellion'[1] illustrates the marginal position thus accorded to Edgeworth, seemingly anomalous as an Enlightenment writer in a Romantic age. She is positioned on the wrong side of a historical, political, philosophic and aesthetic divide.

The suggestion that Enlightenment is fully coincident with a very specifically designated historical period is, however, questionable. Boyce's remark characterises Enlightenment as redundant and irrelevant following the collapse of the United Irish movement and the subsequent passing of the Act of Union, but a contested and politically located Enlightenment in fact occupies an increasingly pivotal position in Irish historical and cultural debate. A critique of Enlightenment forms part of those strands of Irish literary and cultural criticism which have been influenced by the theoretical schools of postmodernism and postcolonialism. Equally important to readings of Edgeworth, however, are the operations of the concept of Enlightenment in the work of Irish historians. For the past decade and more, the 1790s and 1798 have been the most fiercely debated topic in Irish history, and Enlightenment has emerged as a key factor in competing interpretations of the period. The sometimes heated controversy among historians which has characterised recent discussion of the rebellion can in fact be analysed in terms of their beliefs about Enlightenment, although this is not always explicitly articulated. Enlightenment is clearly a highly contested topic within Irish studies, therefore, but the parameters of the debate have been determined by relatively familiar attitudes towards the nation and nationalism, with the consequent, equally familiar, marginalisation of other discourses, notably gender. One of the central arguments of this book is that the persistent positioning of Edgeworth as a 'belated' Enlightenment figure in a Romantic, nineteenth-century Ireland results from the failure to encompass gender in discussions of Enlightenment in Ireland. The following section gives an account of the main positions on Enlightenment taken both by historians and literary critics and of the points at which the exclusion of women and the category of gender becomes manifest. The dual consideration of literary and historical studies is particularly appropriate in the case of Edgeworth, whose writing is constantly referred to by historians and who has, as I have already noted, been made representative of the passing of a historical period.

CONTESTING ENLIGHTENMENT IN IRISH HISTORY AND CULTURE

The recuperation of Enlightenment as an intellectual and political ideal is explicit in the work of the historian Kevin Whelan on popular politicisation. Whelan celebrates Enlightenment as a means of intellectual liberation at an individual level, thus providing the necessary preconditions for radical political action.[2] His involvement in the commemoration of 1798 which took place in 1998 (in the same year as the signing of the Belfast Agreement) suggested that for Whelan, as for many others in Ireland, 1998 represented the rising of the sun of Enlightenment, the culmination of the long-awaited dawn first glimpsed in 1798. The controversy that greeted Whelan's allegedly politicised linkage of 1798 and 1998 came from historians commonly characterised as 'revisionist',[3] but the source of the disagreement between these two quite clearly opposed groups is paradoxically located in their shared admiration for Enlightenment values and principles. In contrast to Whelan, the revisionist view of 1798 is characterised by a deeply held but implicit sense of the failure of Enlightenment in Ireland, hence the emphasis on 'sectarian atrocities and communal antipathies' as 'a deep-laid and unavoidable theme in Irish history'.[4] The failure of the United Irish movement and the seemingly immediate abandonment of non-sectarian politics in its aftermath has been described very tellingly by Oliver MacDonagh as involving 'reversions to seventeenth-century casts of mind',[5] thus suggesting that Ireland represents one of the 'limits of

Enlightenment'. The revisionist school of history, however, with its focus on 'facts' as opposed to myths, could be described as engaged in an Enlightenment project, an attempt to liberate Ireland from the darkness of unreason. Both these perspectives, whether focused on the possibilities for fulfilling the aspirations of the United Irish project, or emphasising the failure of those aspirations, see Enlightenment as, in Habermas's sense, 'incomplete'.[6]

In spite of the differences between these interpretations of 1798, they represent quite a narrow focus on the implicit promise of Enlightenment that 'everyone' could participate in a 'public' culture. In practice, as we know, a wide range of exclusions operated within this nominally open public sphere which meant that white, middle-class men monopolised the shape and meaning of public participation. The existence in eighteenth-century Ireland of a Penal Code designed to exclude Catholics from property-owning as well as from public offices and most professions has meant that, in Ireland, the study of the practical exclusions from a theoretically open public sphere has focused almost without exception on exclusions based on religious affiliation and sectarian division. Arguments as to whether Enlightenment in Ireland is incomplete, failed (or, as discussed below, exhausted) are therefore carried on with only the most limited consideration given, if any is given at all, to the problematic position of other groups, notably women, with relation to Enlightenment and its liberatory potential. This is symptomatic of the dearth of knowledge about women and gender in earlier periods of Irish history in particular. In the introduction to her recently published survey, *A History of Women in Ireland, 1500–1800*, Mary O'Dowd remarks that, in an international context, her project echoes work carried out in women's history in the 1980s, and that it might appear modest in ambition:

> From the perspective of Irish women's history, however, the aspirations of the volume might be perceived as overambitious, if not foolhardy. Research on women in early modern Ireland has been so sporadic that any attempt at a synthesis might seem premature.[7]

In this context it is highly problematic that historians have for a long time referred to the works of Edgeworth and other women writers, notably Lady Morgan, as 'historical evidence'. The quotation from Boyce's survey of nineteenth-century Ireland with which I opened therefore makes specific reference to Edgeworth and Lady Morgan, and Thomas Moore, to represent the shift from Enlightenment to 'Romantic Ireland', and the practice could be illustrated with any number of other examples. One could almost say that the fiction of both Edgeworth and Morgan has traditionally been regarded as residing almost as much within the field of history as it does within the field of literature. History and literature have periodically defined themselves in terms of their concern with the public and the private respectively. The fiction of Edgeworth and Morgan was pioneering and it commanded attention precisely because it used the 'feminised' form of the novel in order to address 'masculine' topics such as history, politics and, in Edgeworth's case, economics. This of course makes their writing available for mining as 'historical evidence', but the evidence is highly unreliable unless it is informed by an understanding of how the culture of the period both permitted women access to the public sphere in the form of writing and publication, and placed specific, gendered demands on this form of public presence. The fact that historians gather evidence from female-authored texts without considering the role that gender played in their production is symptomatic of a larger issue, and that is the extent to which history in Ireland is to date the history of public events. With one or two exceptions, historians of Ireland in this period have yet to develop methodologies which take them into other areas of experience.[8] Until they do, their use of women's writing as 'historical evidence' is a practice fraught with difficulties.

The limitations of Irish history in this regard have been exacerbated by the way in which the events around 1798 have shaped and dominated historical debate in recent years. Historians of 1798 have made efforts to include women in their considerations, but the attempt has not been entirely successful. The collection of essays edited by Dáire Keogh and Nicholas Furlong, *The Women of 1798*, for example, is on one level very welcome – indeed, invaluable – but the editors' preface reveals that 'adding' women to the picture of 1798 does very little, ultimately, to challenge the bias of history and historians in favour of the political, the military and therefore the masculine. The editors refer to the 'irony' of Enlightenment thinking which perpetuated ideas of female inferiority:

> Definitions of femininity were altered, but the effect remained constant: women were excluded from the public realm. Mary Wollstonecraft compared this denial of rights to the condition of slaves; yet the United Irishmen, for all their lofty talk of liberty, refused to entertain the possibility of the admission of women to the body politic.[9]

In spite of the editors' awareness of the limitations of the bourgeois revolutionary agenda pursued by the United Irishmen, their own continuing preoccupation with admission to the public sphere reveals that they are caught up in the same presumptions, seeing participation in this sphere as the mark of the fully realised subject and citizen. In a very similar vein, writing again of the role of women in the events of 1798, Kevin Whelan has commented that 'from a conservative standpoint, the idea of politically active women, either loyalist or republican, was repugnant, a violation of the concept of separate spheres which regulated thinking about the proper behaviour of women in the eighteenth century'.[10] For Whelan, like Furlong and Keogh, participation in a narrowly defined public sphere is the mark of the fully realised subject. Whelan also implies that the politics of the United Irishmen represents the main or indeed the only path to this form of participation when he says that 'in the aftermath of the rising, women were relegated below the horizon of historical visibility'.[11]

The tendency of many Irish historians to insist on the ideological positioning of women within an inaccessible private sphere is more reflective of their own methodologies than of any immutable division of male and female activity and experience into separate spheres. The 'doctrine' of separate spheres has indeed been increasingly subject to question in recent scholarship, with important implications for how we conceive of 'the nation', amongst other things.[12] This is a topic to which I shall return later. Before turning from history to literary criticism, however, I would also like to note Keogh and Furlong's failure to acknowledge that the republican refusal to admit women to the public sphere is not in any sense 'ironic': on the contrary, the legitimation of bourgeois claims to govern *required* the creation of a public sphere that excluded women. It was not only 'from a conservative standpoint' that women could be censured for appearing to transgress gendered boundaries: the radical critique of *ancien régime* France, by diagnosing the collapse of that society with reference to the corrupting (and implicitly sexualised) role played by women as 'boudoir politicians', implied that politics and the public sphere could only ever be safeguarded in male hands. Edgeworth's response to the exclusionary practices of both Enlightenment and reactionary conservatism alike is a key theme throughout this book, on which I shall comment in more detail in the second part of this introduction.

When it comes to responses to Enlightenment among literary critics, there is evidence of a disciplinary divide: whereas historians by and large remain explicitly or implicitly committed to Enlightenment, literary and cultural critics, less wary of postmodernism, are more likely to regard Enlightenment in an Irish context as 'exhausted', once again to invoke the terms of the Habermas/Lyotard debate. In the work of David Lloyd and Seamus Deane, informed by postcolonial theory and critique, Enlightenment has quite a different face, and the deployment of 'Reason' becomes a means of oppression rather than liberation; in Lloyd's work, as a result, preference is given to a broadly postmodern view of Ireland and Irishness, focusing on its disruptive relation to linear models of progress.[13] Deane's version of postcolonialism, however, as Colin Graham has pointed out, stops short of the radical critique of the nation which a commitment to postcolonialism would seem to imply:

'Deane rebounds postcolonial dissent against nationalism so that it is forced to return to the ethical origins of postcolonialism. "British nationalism", because Irish nationalism copied it (could only copy it) is to blame.'[14] Deane's scepticism as to Enlightenment therefore expresses itself in terms of the equation of Enlightenment and Englishness, and, for Deane, Maria Edgeworth's writing is one of the chief bearers of this oppressive, anglicising Enlightenment. He describes her novels as 'documents in the "civilising mission" of the English to the Irish', and as identifying 'a missionary opportunity to convert [Ireland] to Enlightenment faith and rescue it from its "romantic" conditions'.[15]

Luke Gibbons's *Edmund Burke and Ireland* engages with Deane's characterisation of Enlightenment as inevitably oppressive and specifically anglicising by proposing Edmund Burke as the source of an 'alternative Enlightenment'. He argues that:

> What is often construed as a counter-Enlightenment current in the work of Swift and Burke derives from their determination to reinstate the wounds of history into the public sphere, and, by extension, 'obsolete' or 'traditional' societies into the course of history. For the Enlightenment (particularly in its Scottish variant, as exemplified by Adam Smith), the injured body was incapable of looking beyond itself, and hence of attaining the universal or cosmopolitan stance required to operate in the civic sphere. By contrast, Burke's aesthetics outline an alternative, radical form of sensibility – the 'sympathetic sublime' – in which the acknowledgement of oppression need not lead to self-absorption, but may actually enhance the capacity to identify with the plight of others.[16]

Gibbons's argument is an attractive one, acknowledging the potential of Enlightenment as well as its obvious limitations, and proposing that Enlightenment can be reimagined in a colonial context in such a way as to accommodate what are variously termed 'group rights' or 'cultural rights'.[17] Given Gibbons's interest in Adam Smith and the Scottish Enlightenment, it seems like a missed opportunity that he does not give any consideration at all to Edgeworth, who was one of the major interpreters of the Scottish Enlightenment in Ireland. It may also seem strange that Gibbons adopts the concept of group rights from the feminist philosopher, Iris Marion Young, but does not find a place in his discussion for the most intellectually significant woman writer of the period: it is indicative of the tendency, highlighted by Moynagh Sullivan, to assimilate feminist critiques in Irish studies, without a concomitant consideration of actual women, or feminism.[18] Gibbons's reluctance to address the position of women in Enlightenment is such that it assumes the status of the elephant in the living-room, particularly when, as on a number of occasions, he provides textual examples which foreground gender, but fails to comment on their implications. He discusses, for example, Edward Fitzgerald's sympathetic observations on the advantages in the organisation of society among native Americans without acknowledging their gender politics. Fitzgerald remarks that 'Instead of being served and supported by servants, everything here is done by one's relations – by the people one loves; and the mutual obligations you must be under increase your love for each other.'[19] Gibbons uses this passage in part to comment on its image of an alternative form of freedom, one that 'does not consist in atomised individualism but its opposite, a society permeated by mutual obligations and care for others, as against the instrumental exchanges that pass for civil society in the West'.[20] He ignores the fact that this alternative is predicated on the domestic labour of women. Furthermore he does not acknowledge that the 'western' notion of a freedom based on atomized individualism and instrumental exchange was subject to internal critique, notably by women writers, who, according to the critic Anne Mellor, sought, amongst other things, to 'exten[d] the values and practices of the domestic affections into the public realm'.[21]

Women like Edgeworth were fully aware of the philosophical debates on the superiority of 'natural man', but were necessarily alert to the tendency of new philosophies to continue to imagine women in the same old roles. One of Edgeworth's *Moral Tales*, 'Forester' (discussed further in chapter 1), written in the same year that Edward Fitzgerald died, is an affectionate portrayal of a young man inspired by radical philosophy to live a natural life, who then learns gradually that conformity to some of the norms of society and civilisation does not necessarily corrupt all his noble feelings. This is just one small example of the types of Enlightenment thinking that have so far failed to register in interpretations of Irish history and culture. In both history and literary/cultural criticism, Enlightenment appears increasingly important to interpretations of Irish history and culture, but in spite of the range of attitudes to Enlightenment which we can identify among historians and critics, what unites them is their failure to consider in any depth the impact of Enlightenment on women and discourses of gender. It is the contention of this book that, in the case of Maria Edgeworth, we need to consider the possibility of an Enlightenment other than that which we trace through the revolutionary activities of the United Irishmen, *and* other than the oppressive 'anglicisation' of the Irish postcolonial school. The positions of Irishness and femininity make for an engagement with Enlightenment that is unique and that has so far lacked any form of description. In the post-revolutionary and post-Union period, Irishness and femininity were both unstable positions – together, however, their very instability had the potential to construct a position of unprecedented authority for the woman writer.

NO MAN'S LAND: THE PLACE OF THE IRISH WOMAN WRITER

'Encore *c'est l'Angleterre ou la France. Il n'y a que
ces deux pays en Europe – dans le monde.*'[22]

This statement, attributed to Napoleon, was recorded by Maria Edgeworth in a letter written in 1820. She heard it from Auguste de Staël, the son of Germaine de Staël, during a visit – a literary pilgrimage – to the home of the recently deceased writer in Coppet, Switzerland – a context in which the remark resonates particularly powerfully. Edgeworth underlined these two final sentences in a longer account of Napoleon's conversation, but offers no comment, as if they speak for themselves. They do, but it is in their ambiguity, as addressed to and recorded by Maria Edgeworth, that their power lies. It is of course possible to read the statement and even the intention of its relation by Staël as ironic when directed to Edgeworth, who had after all become famous for her depictions of Ireland and the Irish. The reason that it seized Edgeworth's attention, however, may have been because she perceived it as a truth, one with which she had struggled throughout her writing career. The 'Ireland' of Edgeworth's fiction is located somewhere in the no-man's land between the dominant and oppositionally positioned nations of England and France. As I argue in chapter 2 in particular, the lack of an Irish nation, predicated on an Irish public sphere, facilitated Edgeworth's creation of a public identity as an Irish writer. The situation in which Ireland was placed presented difficulties as well as opportunities for a woman writer, however. Consider, for example, Thomas Moore's satire 'Corruption', in which he imagines Ireland as inevitably embroiled in destructive relationship to either France or Britain:

> All that devoted England can oppose
> To enemies made friends and friends made foes,
> Is the rank refuse, the despis'd remains
> Of that unpitying power, whose whips and chains
> Made Ireland first, in wild, adulterous trance,
> Turn false to England's bed and whore with France.[23]

The 'adulterous trance' to which Moore refers is of course the period of the 1798 rebellion, planned and instigated by the United Irishmen, with French military support in the form of General Humbert's forces. Moore's lines are thus on one level historically specific, but they also have the sweeping time-lessness of Napoleon's reported remarks. The personification of 'Ireland', 'England' and 'France' as participants in a tragic love triangle fixes the relations between them in such a way as to insist on the inevitability of Ireland's status as either good wife or adulterous tramp. The transformation to an existing tradition in which the political relationship between Ireland and Britain is described in marital or sexual terms lies in the crudeness and violence in Moore's image of Ireland as the whore of France, a shift that is attributable to the local impact of 1798, but also to a decisive shift in the perception and self-perception of France and Britain, traditional rivals in Europe whose relations had been transformed by the French Revolution and subsequently by the Revolutionary and Napoleonic wars. Anglo-French rivalry had long roots, but in the period of the French Revolution it acquired political, philosophical and ideological dimensions that changed its nature and elevated it almost to a 'clash of civilisations' – particularly in the minds of British conservatives. The revolution had changed the meaning of fundamental concepts such as Enlightenment, nation and patriotism, destabilising the ideal of universal values and norms and reorienting them in terms of specific national histories. Gender played a critical role in this reorientation, with the new citizen of the French republic constituted as both bourgeois and male, while in Britain the patriarchal family was, in the eyes of conservatives and counter-revolutionaries, the ideal image of the nation. In this context, the casting of treacherous, rebellious Ireland as the whore of France reveals a certain dangerous logic, dangerous in particular if the writer on the subject of Ireland happened to be female, rather than male.

More palatable and politically productive versions of this triangulated relationship were created by Moore himself and by Lady Morgan, who retained the overtones of sexuality and eroticism in the British view of France, but translated them into the alluring but chaste figure of the 'wild Irish girl', Glorvina, who captures the heart of the handsome English traveller. *The Wild Irish Girl*, which has been identified as the emblematic text of 'romantic Ireland', gestures in the direction of the love triangle so crudely depicted in Moore's poem, but, having flirted with its more lewd and subversive potentialities, it ultimately reassures readers that Ireland represents a very domestic form of the gothic and the exotic. This romantic Ireland is an intriguing paradox: a construct designed to reveal the injustice of British treatment of Ireland along with its foundation in hostile prejudice, it won an audience for this criticism by appealing to the tastes and desires of the establishment – to the extent that women at the viceregal court in Dublin Castle wore specially commissioned 'Glorvina brooches', while readers in Britain apparently could not get enough of Morgan's mixture of history, romance and landscape.[24] All of this suggests that the version of Irish identity created in Morgan's texts is responsive to Anglo-French conflict and to a need to position Ireland favourably in the clash between the only two countries that really mattered. In this, she and Edgeworth share a significant common ground, exploiting the same opportunities afforded by Ireland's lack of a strictly defined public sphere, and negotiating the same gendered obstacles to the articulation of a voice at once both Irish and female. Morgan, however, made a virtue out of marginality, and unlike Edgeworth she addressed her audience in her prefaces and in autobiographical asides in her writing in order to suggest her position as embattled and perilous, remarking for instance that 'to be a woman was to be without defence, and to be a patriot was to be a criminal'.[25]

In her adoption of this speaking position, Morgan was heavily influenced by Germaine de Staël, who described the woman writer in a post-revolutionary culture in the following, apparently despairing, terms:

> '*Isn't she is an extraordinary woman?*' Every thing is comprised in these words; she is left to the strength of her own mind, to struggle with her afflictions; the interest usually inspired by women, the power which is the safeguard of men, all fail her at once; she drags on her isolated existence like the Pariahs of India, amongst all those distinct classes into none of which she can ever be admitted, and who consider her as fit only to live by herself, as an object of curiosity, perhaps of envy, although, in fact, deserving only the utmost pity.[26]

Staël's portrayal of the woman writer as pariah is predicated on her analysis of the collapse of aristocratic power and the rise of the bourgeoisie and, in spite of its emphasis on isolation and marginalisation, it is a strategic response designed to retain a position from which to speak and write. The problems associated with this strategy in the context of post-Union Ireland will be discussed in chapter 2, but its attractions are obvious. Following the decisive defeat of aristocratic power, sovereignty is proclaimed to reside in 'the people', constituted as male and middle-class. The woman writer's claim to represent thus comes under severe stress and scrutiny, hence Staël's creation of the 'Pariah', the female figure who belongs to no class, who is extraordinary but (arguably) ultimately unthreatening.

Edgeworth's writing career took shape in the same post-Revolutionary environment as those of Staël and Morgan, but was characterised by the retention of a pre-Revolutionary Enlightenment outlook focused on questioning the values accorded to 'public' and 'private' experience. As noted above, the idea that the eighteenth century was characterised by the rigid division of public and private, as completely separate and gendered spheres, has been subject to increasing questioning and critique. Evidence is accumulating which indicates that educated and intellectual women contributed to a reconsideration of the meanings of public and private. It was certainly difficult for women to assume 'public' identities, but what they proposed was that certain forms of privacy could be of social worth and value equal to public identity and activity, and that men as well as women could assume these private but none-theless crucial and valuable roles.[27] This is no mere side issue when it comes to reinterpreting Edgeworth's role as an Irish writer, because for Edgeworth the ideal of a space neither fully private nor fully public, neither exclusively male nor exclusively female, was located in the estate, a space in which men and women could exercise socially useful roles and communicate freely with one another. One of the central arguments of this book, therefore, is that Edgeworth's repeated endorsement of the estate as an ideal community needs to be interpreted less in terms of her ethnic and class position as a member of an Anglo-Irish landowning family, and more in terms of her resistance, as an educated and intellectually powerful woman, to the prospect of confinement to a narrow and suffocating role in an exclusively domestic sphere. As I argue in chapter 4, moreover, the construction of the estate as an ideal space is certainly not confined to Ireland: it is a key feature of *Patronage* (1814) and involves pointed criticism of British institutions, for which Edgeworth was condemned by reviewers.

Nevertheless, 'explaining' the role of the landlord-led estate in Edgeworth's fiction in terms of her gender rather than her class politics might not seem to shift the parameters of the discussion a great deal – in fact, it runs the risk of confirming the tendency within some branches of Irish studies to see the interests of women and the interests of the nation as fundamentally at odds. Thus it is important to stress that this perspective makes a difference to our reception of Edgeworth's writing in both aesthetic and ideological terms, and that it facilitates new and challenging interpretations not only of her work but also of conceptions of the nation. If we recognise that there is a distinct exper-ience that arises from the position of women within the Enlightenment in Ireland, we shall gain a new perspective not only on Edgeworth's writing, but also on some of the key issues in Irish culture in this period. In the remainder of this introduction I shall focus briefly on two such issues, namely French culture and influence and the relationship of Edgeworth's texts, as elite forms, with popular and traditional cultural forms. The two topics seem at first glance to be opposed: the influence of France and French culture is often regarded as both characteristic of elites and as identified with Enlightenment culture, whereas traditional and popular cultural forms have historically represented a challenge to Enlightenment ways of thought. At certain moments in Edgeworth's writing, however, they converge in unexpected ways.

THE ELITE AND THE POPULAR; OR, FRENCH BOOKS AND FOLKTALES

The study of Ireland's connections and interactions with France, particularly in this period, is a topic that continues to attract increasing interest from scholars.[28] This new research is helping to diversify the picture of France beyond being simply the source of radical political inspiration, viewed either enthusiastically or with horror, depending on political persuasion. The image of France in this period is in fact far from uniform and is often contradictory, given that pre- and post-revolutionary outlines were awkwardly superimposed on top of one another, and that francophilia was not synonymous with radical political sympathies. France could rhetorically assume the image of the home of Enlightenment, the cultural centre of Europe, a decadent regime run by and for an effeminate elite, a beacon of hope for equality and justice, or a tyrannical regime bent on cultural destruction and aggressive subordination of its European neighbours. The complexity of references to France is suggested by the fact that in Staël's *De la littérature*, quoted above, enthusiasm for the basic principles of the Revolution is combined with an unmistakeable regret for the unique position of educated and talented women in the social and intellectual life of the *ancien régime*. Enlightenment is thus positioned very ambiguously in terms of post-Revolutionary British culture – associated by some with the excesses of Revolutionary France, it also had lines of affiliation to the corrupt society of the *ancien régime*, a society which conservatives, moderates and radicals united in agreeing was peculiarly French and most definitely unBritish. As this book argues, Edgeworth's references to France, of which there are a great many, cannot be categorised as being in the service of a simple-minded counter-revolutionary agenda. Her first engagement with France as a writer came in 1782, when she undertook the translation of a work by the French woman writer and educationalist, Mme de Genlis, which suggests a depth to her engagement with the position of French women intellectuals in particular. Edgeworth in fact, as I argue in chapter 1, deploys references to France and the position of French women in the interests of a reconfiguration of private and public, thus subverting the domestic ideology on which counter-revolutionary Britain relied. *Letters for Literary Ladies* and other texts of and about the 1790s also reveal Edgeworth to be mindful of the exclusions practised upon French women in the aftermath of Revolution and thus of the limitations of Enlightenment itself.

Whatever lessons Edgeworth drew from France to reflect on the position of women in society, most critics argue that her writing consistently works to suppress the relations between Ireland and France, regarding them as subversive. The *locus classicus* for this interpretation is Colambre's rather hysterical anxiety, in *The Absentee*, that Grace Nugent's mother may have been 'a St Omar', thus implying that her sexual reputation was not above reproach. The name St Omar creates a link between female sexual impropriety, Irish Catholicism and France, because of the location of a college in which Irish Catholic clergy were educated in the French town of St Omer. There is another dimension to 'French influence' in *The Absentee*, however, as the novel can be read as a response not only to *The Wild Irish Girl* but, as I suggest in chapter 4, to Staël's novel of 1807, *Corinne; or, Italy*. In *Corinne*, the polarisation of male and female, England and Italy, results in the banishment of the woman from the national community. Corinne is actually half-English, but her inability to conform to the strictly domestic role of English women means that she must lose her identity and become an exile. Thus the 'suppression' of subversion critics detect in the blurring of national identity that characterises *The Absentee* actually works to retain a type of Irish femininity, albeit not the essentialised identity of romantic ideology. Other Edgeworth texts including *Ennui, Madame de Fleury* and *Emilie de Coulanges*, discussed in chapter 3, reveal a project to map progressive versions of the French Revolution onto Irish conditions. The challenges of this project are suggested by the identity crisis of *Ennui*'s hero and by the incorporation into the plot of elements of Irish folklore and popular culture. In *Ennui*, French revolutionary ideology meets Irish culture and history with startling results. The fusion of these elements, moreover, is facilitated by the collapse of the patrilineal system and the emergence of 'Mr Delamere', whose name, that of his wife, suggests that his identity is derived from his mother.

Ormond, which is the subject of chapter 5, also features a male protagonist whose identity is shaped by women and by Frenchness. This is achieved in a more naturalistic manner than in the earlier *Ennui*, a fact to which I shall return at the end of this introduction. Several critics have remarked on the extent to which *Ormond* includes an uncharacteristically sympathetic portrayal of elements of Irish traditional culture, but what has not been noted is that this is combined with a remarkable representation of Ormond's education as an ideal gentleman of the eighteenth century, whose ambition to acquire polite manners, good conversation, dancing skills and fluency in French is motivated specifically by his desire to attract and please women. Ormond's French education makes him *more* Irish, however, not less. It is in Paris that he is identified as 'le bel Irlandois' and it is in Paris that he meets his old friend Moriarty Carroll, a meeting which prompts him to return to Ireland. As I argue in chapter 5, the meeting between Ormond and Moriarty in Paris amounts to a fusion between the elite cultural dimensions of French influence in Ireland, and the subversive political dimensions. These apparently widely separated fields are thus brought into unity in the novel, and are interpreted progressively. Edgeworth's ability in this novel to fuse Irishness and Frenchness, the elite and the popular, suggests that the relationship of her work to popular and traditional cultural forms is not as straightforward as has previously been suggested.

The characteristic Enlightenment attitude towards local and indigenous cultures and forms of knowledge is virtually impossible to reconcile with modern sensibilities, and is one of the chief targets for postmodern and post-colonial critiques of Enlightenment. The description of Edgeworth as an Enlightenment writer has thus traditionally implied that her attitude towards popular and traditional culture in Ireland was patronising and that her ideas of progress implied the gradual obliteration of these aspects of Irish culture, as the country advanced towards a very English version of Enlightenment, characterised by cleanliness, efficiency and orderliness. In as much as Edgeworth's work represents on one level a treasury of knowledge and insight into innumerable aspects of lower-class Irish life, notably but not exclusively characteristics of speech and language, she is acknowledged as a collector and cataloguer. But in spite of her interest in documenting popular practices and in recording vernacular speech, it has been asserted that she fundamentally misunderstood and undervalued native and non-elite forms.[29] This is true in so far as she clearly did not regard traditional forms as possessing spiritual or transcendent value, or as expressing the soul of a people – in this much, the categorisation of Edgeworth as non-romantic, and arguably anti-romantic, is not disputed here. What I *do* argue is that her work does more than record popular and traditional culture; it is engaged with that culture and shaped by it, although to different ends and in different ways from those of Morgan and indeed the later nineteenth-century Celtic Revivalists.

It is surely curious that critics can assert that Edgeworth's work can 'record' aspects of traditional culture, but remain utterly aloof from them, almost as if a tape could record, but also remain blank. This position is reflective of the view of Edgeworth's texts as 'containers' – they are viewed as objects whose aesthetic and formal qualities are secondary to the moral messages and social documents they contain. They are also, to use Mitzi Myers's phrase, viewed as 'disciplinary apparatus'.[30] This argument has been made on numerous occasions with reference to the relationship between the narrative voice and the editorial voice in *Castle Rackrent*, for instance, the latter apparently safely and smugly positioned in authority over the superstitious, ignorant and comically unself-reflective narrator. The question that has always puzzled critics is, why did Edgeworth create this unique, highly localised and quite anarchic voice if her primary motivation was to 'contain' energies and perspectives of this kind? Why would the Enlightenment author exclude herself from the sphere of the universal? Aside from *Castle Rackrent*, which is effectively the translation of folk culture into an elite form, one could also refer to the allusion to change-ling beliefs in *Ennui* and to Carolan's song 'Gracey Nugent' in *The Absentee*, to indicate the importance of traditional and popular culture to Edgeworth's characters and plots. One could multiply examples, but what is important to stress is that the novels do not simply 'contain' these elements – they are shaped by them. In support of this proposal, I argue in chapter 5 that there is a crucial intertextual relationship between *Ormond* and Cosgrave's *Irish Rogues and Raparees*, probably the most popular printed text in eighteenth-century Ireland. Both *Ennui* and *Ormond* suggest that Edgeworth was influenced by popular conceptions of what Niall Ó Ciosáin has called 'the ideology of status'[31] and that her writing cannot be labelled neatly as 'elite' in opposition to popular and traditional cultural forms. In fact, if folktale, superstition and gossip represent the other to Enlightenment's official knowledges, Edgeworth's work at times shows a remarkable affiliation with this unofficial knowledge, a proposal advanced by Myers in relation to *Irish Bulls* which she claims as a sort of 'proto-post-modern' text, in that it anticipates the postmodernist collapse of the 'once hegemonic, logico-deductive models of reason and knowledge' and their replacement by 'little anecdotes and local knowledges'.[32]

All of this is of course radically at odds with the Romantic approach to traditional culture, which amounts to an appropriation and a feminisation of folklore and traditional culture generally, so that it can be accessed by the poet and transformed into art; William Wordsworth's 'Solitary Reaper' represents an apt example of this process. In Ireland in this period, the process is diverted by Edgeworth and Morgan in two very different ways. In the case of *The Wild Irish Girl*, the feminisation and romanticisation of traditional culture enabled the creation of a feminine speaking position. This resulted, however, in the identification of the writer with her own textual creation, and the determination to dismiss Morgan which was evident from the outset of her career may well relate to the identification of the woman writer with the feminised text. Edgeworth's incorporation of popular and traditional forms, by contrast, does not rely on their identification with the feminine; the response from within Irish studies to Edgeworth's apparent refusal to identify herself with a marginality gendered as feminine has been to regard her as complicit in the process of marginalisation itself. As my own arguments make clear, I regard Edgeworth's texts as actively engaged with popular and traditional culture, but I would also suggest that the interpretation of her texts as expressive of Enlightenment contempt for traditional culture may be fuelled by a fundamental discomfort with the woman writer as author of her text. The 'popular' is configured as a disruptive energy that the text seeks to contain, hence the critical language highlighted by Myers, suggesting control and rigidity: stifle, discipline, reform, school. The fact that Edgeworth's texts frequently high-light and foreground popular and traditional culture is explained through language that suggests mental instability as the implied consequence or flipside of psychological repression. This is particularly evident in Tom Dunne's use of terms such as 'fear', 'ambivalence' and 'insecurity'.[33] This critical tendency reaches a climax in the use of the word 'illusion' to describe Edgeworth's Irish fiction. Seamus Deane claims that her tales 'produce the illusion of having performed an analysis of the Irish situation',[34] while Kevin Whelan says that she 'generates a moral and political illusion'.[35] It is a short step from illusion to delusion, although one might think that Edgeworth is a very unlikely madwoman in the Irish attic. As this book sets out to show, in particular in chapters 3 and 5, Edgeworth's texts are much more than simply containers of Irish popular and traditional culture. Furthermore, this attitude towards her work is in my view indicative of unacknowledged assumptions about female authorship.

The last chapter of this book concerns itself with *Helen* (1834), Edgeworth's last novel, published after a 17-year hiatus in her writing career. *Helen* does not feature anywhere in discussions of Edgeworth as an Irish novelist, although her comments on the lack of Irish characters in the novel and the 'impossibility of drawing Ireland as she is now in a book of fiction' are constantly quoted as a statement on the decisive shifts in Irish culture and politics that followed Catholic emancipation. Aside from having no Irish characters, *Helen* also differs considerably in style from Edgeworth's earlier fiction, and some critics have argued strongly that it is Edgeworth's most aesthetically achieved work. In contrast to the plot- and message-driven tales of her earlier career, the drama of *Helen* is rooted in the three very naturalistically drawn central characters. This contrast enables us to reflect on the ideological underpinnings of 'realistic characters'. *Helen*'s believable characters are not entirely unprecedented – this is a change that can be observed in the much earlier *Ormond*, which has also been praised for being more character-focused. As I argue in chapter 5, the greater depth of character in *Ormond* is accompanied and arguably facilitated by a diminished emphasis on the individual's social function, which implies a qualification of Edgeworth's previous insistence on the necessary connection between private and public. The focus in *Helen* on drama generated exclusively through character reflects the pessimism and marked conservatism of the text, which features a young woman physically ripping apart and burning books in order to prevent the ruin of her moral reputation. *Helen* does have a great deal to say about how Edgeworth saw the position of the woman writer in Ireland in the transformed conditions of the 1830s, although in order to discover what those meanings are it is necessary to read and interpret the text, rather than comment on it as an absence, as has been the case until now. The late appearance of this novel, and its contrast with the work of Edgeworth's earlier career make it in itself a thought-provoking comment on her achievements, so I shall reserve further comment for the conclusion of this book.

Edgeworth has benefited from the work of some excellent critics – notably Marilyn Butler, Mitzi Myers and W. J. Mc Cormack. The appearance of a scholarly edition of her novels and selected works has also provided the basis for reassessment and rereading of her work. For many years, only *Castle Rackrent* and *The Absentee* were in print, but *Belinda* is now available in paperback, and the recent paperback critical edition of *Harrington*, a previously obscure text, is a welcome event.[36] It remains the case, nonetheless, that the position of Edgeworth within Irish studies has changed very little. Sharon Murphy's recent *Maria Edgeworth and Romance* introduces a number of new and thought-provoking perspectives to discussions of Edgeworth, particularly a valuable emphasis on form and issues specific to women's use of fictional forms. Murphy reiterates, however, the terms of critics such as Dunne, Deane and Whelan and their condemnation of Edgeworth's writing as the production of an illusion when she describes Edgeworth's use of romance structures in her Irish tales as 'betray[ing] her perception that the vision of Ireland she is producing in her writing is *literally* a fiction.'[37] Critical commentary on Edgeworth in fact remains split on what are effectively national lines. As Claire Connolly has pointed out, debates on the private and the public in the context of eighteen-century Britain, to which I have already referred, 'have the potential to revitalise the study of Ireland's first professional woman writer', but this potential is as yet unrealised, because work such as Guest's, for instance, 'stops short of considering the Irish side of her *oeuvre*'.[38] The apparent difficulty of producing a feminist reading of the full range of Edgeworth's work with an emphasis on her contribution to Irish literary culture is attributable to the fact that, as critics such as Gerardine Meaney, Moynagh Sullivan and Colin Graham have argued, the exclusion of women is part of the logic whereby Irish studies constitutes itself as a subject. In Graham's words, 'gender [. . .] becomes subaltern to dominant nationalism, being forced [. . .] into "affiliation" in order to press its claims.'[39] This book therefore positions itself within the project of Irish feminist criticism, which has made readers and critics aware of the gendered exclusions at work in Irish studies. It aims to contribute to a redrawing of the map of Irish culture, not simply to fill in the margins.

CHAPTER ONE

Enlightenment, Gender and the Nation

-+>-<+-

Although gender has yet to be written into the central narrative of Ireland in the 1790s, assumptions about gender play crucial roles in descriptions and analyses of Irish culture in this period. The dominant accounts in both history and literary history converge to erase women from the landscape in the 1790s, suggesting, in different ways, that although Irish men may well have emerged into history in this period, Irish women would have to wait for another historical moment. For both historians and literary critics, the relationship between the private and the public spheres proves critical in determining what it means to be a recognisable Irish subject. Ian McBride notes, for instance, that the Volunteer movement 'drew a large proportion of the adult male population into the public sphere for the first time'.[1] Joep Leerssen writes that 'Catholic Ireland in penal days was hermetically sealed off from a public forum', but that with the transformation of this situation in the nineteenth century, Catholic Ireland 'burst into print culture and appropriat[ed] the media and the public voice to cement what Benedict Anderson sees as the prime effect of print media: nation-making'.[2] Historians, as I noted in the introduction, persist both in insisting on presence in the public sphere as the pre-condition for 'visibility' and in declaring that women were consigned by the ideology of separate spheres to a 'hermetically sealed' (to borrow Leerssen's phrase) private or domestic sphere. The effect of all this is to make women in Ireland in this period invisible to history. In the literary sphere, however, Irish women in this period are clearly visible, indeed they *become* visible at precisely this moment, as writers. In certain critical accounts, however, they are nonetheless made to vanish through an association of the domestic with Englishness. Seamus Deane's analysis of the ideological translation of the female-authored, English domestic fiction of the post-revolutionary period and his argument as to its use, in Edgeworth's case specifically, as a means to contain the threat of Irishness, effectively makes Edgeworth's gender analogous to Englishness. In this construction, there is truly no such thing as an Irish woman – the space which she might occupy has been erased.

Deane's association of the domestic with a counter-revolutionary Englishness, focused amongst other things on the control of subversion in Ireland, assumes firstly the total abandonment of Enlightenment in the aftermath of the French Revolution, and secondly, an inability on the part of women writers, whether in Britain or Ireland, actively to shape the meanings of the domestic and the national. The work of historians and critics of eighteenth-century Britain suggests, however, that a simple binary opposition between public and private fails to address the complex shifts and negotiations that characterise the relationship between these supposedly distinct areas of experience. The assumption that public and private spheres in the eighteenth century were conceived as utterly distinct and gendered spaces, thus preventing women from playing any role in relation to the nation as manifested in the public sphere, is in fact no longer a sustainable proposition. For instance, in her study of women writers in eighteenth-century Britain, Harriet Guest draws on the work of historians such as Amanda Vickery, Kathleen Wilson, Hannah Barker and Elaine Chalus, to argue 'against the thesis that middle-class women were increasingly confined to domesticity by the demands of propriety', and she asserts that in the period 'domesticity is always a contested proposition'.[3]

This chapter will present readings of Edgeworth's work from the 1790s and the first decade of the nineteenth century to argue that, in common with other women writers of the period, she envisaged a presence for women in the public sphere, but in terms other than those proposed by political radicals such as the United Irishmen, whose principles and rhetoric were, like those of their radical contemporaries in Britain, frequently anti-feminist. Edgeworth's work represents a face of Enlightenment which has so far been excluded from considerations of the Enlightenment in an Irish context. Whereas the United Irish movement was exclusively male and contained a plebeian element (although its leadership was almost entirely middle class, with a sprinkling of aristocracy), Edgeworth's Enlightenment position is both feminine and elite. Too often, the elite aspects of Edgeworth's position have been emphasised with no reference to her marginalisation on grounds of gender. An analysis of her texts from the 1790s and 1800s, however, in which she engages very explicitly with the problematic of Enlightenment thought from a feminine point of view, makes both terms visible and suggests how she sought to bring them into dialogue with one another. The need for such an approach is suggested by Mary Jean Corbett's claim that Edgeworth's fiction 'adhere[s] to a Burkean paradigm',[4] with specific relation to her supposed endorsement of patriarchal norms of gender and family. Writing on *Castle Rackrent*, Corbett declares that '[t]he lack of female subordination' among the Rackrent wives 'is another sign of how far short Irish affairs fall of the Burkean model Edgeworth implicitly supports'.[5] Corbett makes no reference, however, to the gender debates of the

1790s and Edgeworth's contribution to them. The idea that Edgeworth sought to promote female subordination within a rigidly conceived patriarchal family is a claim that simply cannot be sustained when her writing on women in the context of the debates of the 1790s is reintroduced into the discussion.

Corbett's remarks do at least have the merit of reminding us of the necessity of relating the discourses of gender and the nation. By focusing on Edgeworth's supposed affiliation with Burke, however, Corbett ignores the vital role played by Enlightenment in Edgeworth's thinking. The intersection between Enlightenment, gender and nation has been acknowledged as a key cultural and political crux, and has been the subject of a number of important books from both historians and literary critics working in the British context in recent years. The resource offered by these works is enormously enriching for a study of Edgeworth, but it also presents challenges and complications because of the disputed extent to which the public role of women in eighteenth-century Britain was entwined with what has variously been described as 'patriotism' and 'nationalism'. Of particular interest is the challenge to the equation of Englishness, femininity and domesticity that forms the basis of Seamus Deane's analysis of how Edgeworth's Irish fictions work to 'anglicise' through a process of feminisation and domestication. The range of views on this question can be represented by a brief consideration of the arguments in some recent work by both historians and critics, including Linda Colley, Harriet Guest and Angela Keane. Linda Colley's enormously influential *Britons* (1992) is explicitly concerned not just with the formation of the British nation (made up, for Colley, of England, Wales and Scotland but not, significantly, Ireland) but also with the formation of a British national identity. For Colley, Protestantism is the cornerstone of this identity, although Francophobia, always lively but driven to new heights during the revolutionary and Napoleonic wars, is a significant additional element. At the time of its publication, one of the most novel and interesting aspects of Colley's book was her focus on the role of women in the emerging nation state and her emphasis on their active involvement in the new forms and manifestations of patriotism developed during the revolutionary and Napoleonic Wars. 'This was the period', she claims, 'in which women first had to come to terms with the demands and meanings of Britishness'.[6] Although Colley argues that patriotic activity was one way in which women could emerge from the kitchen and the hearth without incurring disapproval, these petitions, parades and charitable works were undertaken in the name of 'the pure-minded Women of Britain'[7] and thus tended to strengthen the ideological strictures on women's behaviour and, crucially, the characterisation of improper conduct as 'peculiarly French'.[8] A certain version of femininity is therefore thoroughly implicated in Colley's account of the post-revolutionary construction of a Britishness which was designed to repudiate any contaminating French influences. The outlines of Colley's argument can also be found in the work of literary critics writing at the same period. Gary Kelly, for instance, has argued that the economic and cultural triumph of the middle class in post-revolutionary Britain was accompanied by

> a certain figure of 'woman' [. . .] constructed to represent a professional middle-class discourse of subjectivity as opposed to communal or courtly sociability, 'nature' rather than decadent 'civilisation', 'national' culture, identity, and destiny rather than local, temporary, narrow interests of rank or region.[9]

Guest's *Small Change*, referred to above, relies much more heavily on the work of the historian Kathleen Wilson than on Colley's book, and her thesis on the public presence of women writers in some respects challenges the picture that Colley presents of women being permitted access to public spaces only on the grounds of an enthusiastic identification with 'the nation'. Guest, quoting Wilson, writes that 'though national and patriotic discourses were overtly and sometimes stridently masculinist and "depended upon a marginalisation or subordination of the feminine in their notions of national character", women were nevertheless perceived as political subjects in some contexts.'[10] Guest's use of the word 'patriotic' is of course highly significant, suggesting a form of Enlightenment national identity prior to the less intellectually palatable romantic nationalism of the nineteenth century. If Colley rewrites the eighteenth century to make it sound very like the nineteenth, Guest seems reluctant to acknowledge that the transition from one century to the other has any significance at all. She is certainly justified in her observation that the period she is concerned with, 'from the middle of the eighteenth century to the early nineteenth century, is too often carved up in literary criticism between Romanticists and eighteenth-century specialists', a division that masks the very real continuities among women writers, from, for instance, Catharine Macaulay to Mary Wollstonecraft.[11] Guest's approach could, however, be criticised on the grounds that it ignores the extent to which the 'overtly and sometimes stridently masculinist' character of national and patriotic discourses intensified as the French revolution generated a powerful counter-revolutionary response. Another way to articulate Colley's and Guest's positions would be in terms of Enlightenment: Colley's is, to a certain extent, an eighteenth century without Enlightenment, the implication perhaps being that Enlightenment was too elite and rarefied an affair to penetrate the popular consciousness which is so central to her discussion. Guest, on the other hand, appears to equate Enlightenment and nation, thus excluding from her discussion the fact that, as Seamus Deane has argued, following the French Revolution

Enlightenment was perceived by many people in Britain as fundamentally 'unBritish'.[12] Deane's argument shares common ground with Colley's and his position is similar to hers in terms of how he sketches the relationship between women and the post-revolutionary British nation. In sharp contrast to the positions of both Colley and Guest, however, Angela Keane's discussion of the relationship of women writers to the concept of the nation in the 1790s reveals that, for women writers specifically, Enlightenment and nation were very far from being synonymous, and that, for Helen Maria Williams, Charlotte Smith, Mary Wollstonecraft and Ann Radcliffe

> it is the discourse of the public sphere, not of the nation, which allows them to imagine themselves as participating citizens. It is the discourse of nationality not rationality that turns them into exiles, by naturalising a patriarchal social contract and putting it beyond rational enquiry.[13]

Keane differentiates sharply between the earlier and later eighteenth centuries, arguing that earlier models of citizenship, based on the works of the Scottish Enlightenment, were 'at least rhetorically, available to women'.[14] It is worth quoting Keane's description of the chief characteristics of the Scottish Enlightenment, as it contains terms to which I shall return later in my discussion of Edgeworth:

> The Scottish Enlightenment imagined a republic in which conversation, friendship, but most importantly, exchange became public virtues. The citizen of this republic – the commercial humanist – could take up a pen, read a newspaper, or make a purchase to fulfil his or her public duty and participate in national life. These Scottish writers and their nervous philosophical enquiries made conceptually possible a balance between subjective will and the greater good, sentiment and sociability, individual desire and consensus in the mobile, historical environment of commercial society. They made a public virtue out of private interest.[15]

For Keane, the 1790s brings to an end the enabling identification of women with the English nation, and she emphasises the extent to which writers such as Helen Maria Williams and Charlotte Smith sought to uphold an ideal of cosmopolitanism in the early nineteenth century and were rewarded with exclusion from a national canon of literature which took shape under the sign of romanticism. For these writers, according to Keane,

> it is the discourse of the public sphere, not of the nation, which allows them to imagine themselves as participating citizens. It is the discourse of nationality

not rationality that turns them into exiles, by naturalising a patriarchal social contract and putting it beyond rational enquiry.[16]

As this chapter will go on to illustrate, Maria Edgeworth repeatedly and explicitly argued the case for the value of Enlightenment ideals of citizenship and of the public as those which are most accessible to women. The potential for her to be regarded as 'unBritish' as a result raises a profound dilemma, given her commitment to Ireland. Whereas Deane and others have concluded that this pressure results in Edgeworth's adoption of a specifically English femininity positioned in the role of enlightened instructress with relation to an 'unruly' Irish masculinity,[17] I argue in this chapter that Edgeworth makes use of references to France, to fashion and to aristocracy to develop a unique Enlightenment perspective that accommodates women but does not conform to the demands of post-revolutionary British nationalism.

The works that are discussed in the following pages, *Letters for Literary Ladies*, 'Angelina', 'Forester' and *Belinda*, all focus on the controversial relationship between women and Enlightenment, a debate which had taken on a highly politicised and national dimension in this period. They are also all, not entirely coincidentally, works which refer to Thomas Day, a close friend of Maria's father, Richard Lovell Edgeworth, who was remarkable for his early passionate commitment to the ideas of Rousseau and who used his influence over R. L. Edgeworth to prevent Maria Edgeworth from becoming a published author in 1782. Even after Day's death Edgeworth fought to overcome his disapproving shadow, to the extent that Marilyn Butler has described the relationship between Day's work and Edgeworth's as 'personal, emotional, and conflicted'.[18] Thomas Day had an extreme and hostile attitude towards France, towards mainstream society, and towards 'fashionable' women. According to R. L. Edgeworth, Day 'had as large a portion of national prejudice in favour of the people of England, and against the French, as any man of sense could have'.[19] His concept of an ideal woman notably did not extend to an appreciation of an educated intelligence:

> Mr Day had an unconquerable horror of the empire of fashion over the minds of women; simplicity, perfect innocence, and attachment to himself, were at that time the only qualifications which he desired in a wife.[20]

The influence of Day on Edgeworth's early writing career is usually referred to in relation to *Belinda*, a text to which I shall return. As both Marilyn Butler and Mitzi Myers have suggested, however, the effect of his opposition to female education and to women authors, given its direct impact on Edgeworth's early career, needs further emphasis. Edgeworth's apparent need, psychologically and imaginatively, to overcome Day's objections to women writers in general and to her own literary ambitions specifically, may be one of the reasons why, in her early works, we can see a strategic defence of the very things he abhorred. In contrast to Day's ideal of Rousseauvian retreat from the world characterised by a fantasy of gender relations in which men act as the sole educators of and ultimate authority figures with respect to women, Edgeworth envisages the recuperation of this Rousseauvian retirement in order to make it a space that men and women can inhabit equally. Given that it was the publication of Edgeworth's translation of *Adelaide and Theodore*, a work by the French writer and educationalist Mme de Genlis to which Day objected so forcefully in 1782, it is worth considering briefly the influence that Genlis had on Edgeworth in this regard.

Within an anglophone context, the response of women writers to Rousseau has tended to be dominated by Mary Wollstonecraft's *A Vindication of the Rights of Woman*, which features an extended critique of the ideas expressed in Book 5 of Rousseau's *Emile; or, on Education* (1762). Relatively little attention is given to that fact that French women writers also engaged in vigorous critiques of Rousseau, which were all the more pertinent and direct, since Rousseau's ideal woman, Sophie, was intended as an alternative to the metropolitan culture of the Parisian *salonnières*, the female leaders of intellectual life and culture.[21] Genlis's *Adelaide and Theodore* (1782) was an extremely popular and successful work on education, and was one of the most explicit in its criticism of Rousseau.[22] According to Marilyn Butler, the theme and situation of *Adelaide and Theodore* matched the Edgeworths' own perception of their role and function as landlords in remote Ireland; she suggests that it corresponds 'perfectly [. . .] with their own taste for experimental education in a domestic environment' and that 'both *Letters of Julia and Caroline* [. . .] and *Leonora* (1805) resemble it in form as well as in content'.[23] Edgeworth's interest in and 'borrowing' from Genlis does indeed suggest that she sympathised with Genlis's project of recuperating Rousseau's ideal of retirement and making it a space that women could inhabit. But Edgeworth, to a much greater extent than her French mentor, appeared to desire the domestication of Enlightenment in this retired feminine space: in other words, to reform the Enlightenment salon and to make it acceptable in post-revolutionary culture. She attempted to divorce the value of rational enquiry from the damaging associations it had acquired, largely via Rousseau, with urban effeminacy and corruption, and at the same time she attempted to recast Rousseau's idealised world of retirement in a feminine mould.

Genlis's *Adelaide and Theodore* takes the form of an exchange of letters between two women, one a lady who has decided to live in retirement in the country in order to devote herself to her children's education, the other a sophisticated friend in the French capital. The work is a blend of storytelling and treatise, and encompasses not only the delineation of an educational programme for both boys and girls, but also a running commentary on the proper employment of women as mothers and educators. The Baroness D'Almane, the ideal mother/educator, explains to her friend, the Viscountess Limours, that in order to pursue the educational plan that she and her husband had in mind, it was essential to remove their children 'far from the pomp and magnificence of the metropolis'.[24] She also points out to her disgruntled friend that leaving Paris is no great sacrifice, as she is 'indifferent to the last degree to those trifling matters, which employ so many people in the world; I find myself interested in things only which are useful'.[25] The Baroness D'Almane, as this last quote indicates, has a great deal in common with the virtuous mothers who appear regularly in Edgeworth's fiction.

It is indeed easy to imagine the Edgeworths, secluded in their restricted social circle in Longford, seeing themselves as Irish counterparts of Genlis and her fictional creation, the Baroness D'Almane. Both parties share extremely similar ideas on the value of a retired, largely domestic lifestyle. The Baroness D'Almane argues that fashionable society precludes the possibility of serious reading and conversation, whereas the tranquillity of retirement makes intellectual engagement and improvement possible. She also points out the superior delights of pleasing those whose judgement we respect and for whom we have a genuine attachment; the Baroness cannot conceive it 'possible to have any desire to please those we do not love', thereby explaining her preference for small domestic gatherings over 'grand entertainments, dress, and cards'.[26] In a very similar vein, Caroline, the virtuous domesticated matron of Edgeworth's 'Letters of Julia and Caroline', points out to her friend Julia that whereas 'you will be content with indiscriminate admiration – nothing will content me but what is *select*'.[27] The durability of this conviction will register with readers of Edgeworth's later fiction, as it constitutes an underlying theme in almost all her novels, including *Ennui*, *The Absentee* and *Patronage*.

Where Edgeworth and Genlis differ significantly, however, is in their investment in the Enlightenment. Genlis proudly termed *Adelaide and Theodore* an 'antiphilosophical' work,[28] and was in general hostile to the *philosophes* and what she termed their 'false philosophy':[29] she was critical of their dismissal of religion and echoed the popular denunciation of Voltaire and d'Alembert for lack of patriotism.[30] Dena Goodman has suggested that the portrayal of the salons as mere scenes of fashionable frivolity implies a more generalised hostility to the Enlightenment project itself,[31] an argument that seems to be borne out in Genlis's case. In spite of her overt critique of Rousseau's educational theories, she implicitly endorsed his view that Enlightenment thought was the product of a corrupt, urban, feminised milieu. Even before the outbreak of revolution Genlis was at pains to dissociate herself from the *salonnières* of *ancien régime* France, women including Marie-Thérèse Geoffrin, Julie de Lespinasse, Marie Du Deffand and Germaine de Staël's mother, Suzanne Necker, who sponsored the project of Enlightenment by hosting its leading figures and providing a social space within which ideas could take on life. Genlis records, for instance, a visit to Suzanne Necker's salon, at which the young Germaine Necker was habitually present; Genlis was intensely critical of Necker for exposing her daughter to the destructive influences of the guests.[32] Edgeworth's *Letters for Literary Ladies*, by contrast, is not only openly supportive of key Enlightenment principles, it also expresses a complex empathy with the women of the *ancien régime* (Genlis herself among them), whose influence, in the post-revolutionary period, was regarded as part of the corruption of that earlier era.

Letters for Literary Ladies is Edgeworth's earliest and in some ways her most systematic discussion of women and Enlightenment. It has for a long time been dismissed as relatively insignificant, but more recently Mona Narain has argued that in the *Letters* Edgeworth 'circumvents dominant, patriarchal literary authority and actively interrogates aspects of it, an act that allows her to find an authorial voice'.[33] Similarly, Harriet Guest has recently located it among 'accounts of domesticity' which 'represent women as able to fulfil public roles'.[34] Deploying the concept of domesticity in order to argue for women's presence in the public sphere is a strategy which, amongst other things, challenges the counter-revolutionary construction of England as a nation characterised by the strictly and separately gendered nature of public and private spheres, in contrast to the corrupt confusion of sex and politics held to typify *ancien régime* France. In *Literary Ladies* Edgeworth signals her commitment to Enlightenment, but to a form of Enlightenment which is aware of the grounding of ideas in specific times and places, rather than as disembodied and transcendental ideals. She makes reference to Voltaire, and what one might term a 'high' Enlightenment, but this is combined with the ideas of the Scottish Enlightenment, with which Edgeworth was very familiar and which Angela Keane, as cited above, has aligned with a model of citizenship based on 'commercial humanism'. In this way Edgeworth attempts to preserve the opportunities afforded by the discourse of rationality in preference to that of nationality. The difficulties involved in this project should not be underestimated. The revolution controversy had made it almost impossible not to deploy nationality as a strategy, whatever side one happened to be on: Burke's *Reflections on the Revolution in France* (1790) may well have played a significant role in defining Englishness in opposition to the violent abstractions of revolutionary France, but, as one critic has noted, Mary Wollstonecraft's response to Burke in her *Vindication of the Rights of Men* (1791) 'reflected a rational and patriotic author fighting against a hysterical Francophile'.[35] In spite of this, *Letters for Literary Ladies* argues for the benefits of a rational and enlightened femininity without suggesting that such a phenomenon is exclusive to or characteristic of any one national culture.

The three short texts which make up *Letters for Literary Ladies* ('An Essay on the Noble Science of Self-Justification', 'Letters of Julia and Caroline' and 'Letter to a Gentleman on the Birth of a Daughter, with an Answer') all argue that women have a right to education on the basis of equality in terms of a shared, human capacity for reason. 'Letter to a Gentleman' is the most substantial of the three and directly addresses the arguments for and against the education of women. 'Letters of Julia and Caroline' unfolds the unhappy consequences that Edgeworth predicts for women who are encouraged to develop their sensibility at the expense of their reason, as the idealised Caroline attempts to steer her friend in the direction of reason and virtue. 'An Essay on the Noble Science of Self-Justification' (inserted, according to Edgeworth, at the insistence of the publisher in order to increase the length of the text) differs from its companion pieces in that it proposes to advise women on how to circumvent 'male' logic and rationality, thus acting as a satire on the ways in which women have been encouraged to dispense with reasoned argument. 'Letters of Julia and Caroline' and the 'Essay' were written in 1787, while 'Letter to a Gentleman' was probably written in 1793, and the text eventually published in 1795.[36] A second edition was published in 1798, in which substantial changes were made in the 'Answer' to 'Letter to a Gentleman', as it 'was thought to weaken the case it was intended to support'. Edgeworth assured her readers that the 'letter has been written over again; no pains have been spared to improve it, and to assert more strongly the female right to literature'.[37] Comparing 'Letters of Julia and Caroline', a pre-revolutionary text, with the original 'Letter to a Gentleman' and its subsequent revision in 1798 gives an interesting insight into the impact of the revolution on the discourse of Enlightenment rationality and on the ways in which Edgeworth overcame, or sought to overcome, the resulting suspicion of Enlightenment.

In Seamus Deane's words, Burke's *Reflections on the Revolution in France*, the text which enshrined oppositions between Frenchness and Englishness, created post-revolutionary France as 'a foreign country [. . .] a new territory, the territory of theory'.[38] It is thus striking that we find in 'Letters of Julia and Caroline' words and phrases that derive from this foreign country. According to this text, it seems, the only problem with theory is that one might not have enough of it: Caroline attempts to convince her friend Julia that failure to reason and analyse successfully arises 'from the *insufficiency*, not the *fallacy*, of theory' (43); she urges Julia to 'analyse' her 'notions of happiness' and explain her 'system' (39); Edgeworth also proposes that 'philosophy' is not an agent of moral and social disintegration, but rather the indispensable basis for sound thought and conduct. Caroline points out to Julia, who has modelled herself on the feminine character outlined by Rousseau, that general principles cannot be absolutely dispensed with, and that no one acts by 'instinct' alone:

> If general observation and experience have taught you, that slight accomplishments and a trivial character succeed more certainly in obtaining this end [of pleasing], than higher worth and sense, you act from principle in rejecting the one and aiming at the other. You have discovered, or think you have discovered, the secret causes which produce the desired effect, and you employ them. Do not call this *instinct* or *nature*; this also, though you scorn it, is *philosophy*. (43)

Edgeworth also asserts that philosophy is not incompatible with attention to the actual, when Caroline states that her answer to Julia is 'the answer of fact against eloquence, philosophy against enthusiasm' (46). Edgeworth's alignment of philosophy with fact, in opposition to eloquence and enthusiasm, suggests that she emphatically rejects the construction of Englishness that we find in Burke's *Reflections*. Her ability, in 'Letters of Julia and Caroline', to combine 'philosophy' and 'fact', and her experience, in Genlis's writing, of a French model that combines femininity and aristocracy with rationality and utility suggests that even in a post-revolutionary context her writing will not fall easily into the available categories of radical and reactionary, each defined by national as well as political sympathies. But this basic position is subject to a certain stress in 'Letter to a Gentleman', the one text of the three in *Letters for Literary Ladies* that was written after the Revolution, and also after the publication of two key texts, Burke's *Reflections* and Mary Wollstonecraft's *Vindication of the Rights of Woman*. The 'Letter' and the 'Answer', incorporating the revisions of 1798, represent a response to the altered political and intellectual climate of the post-revolutionary era. One can on the one hand observe an awareness of the conservatism that was gathering strength and confidence, and on the other a determined counter-claim, that the increasing involvement of women in intellectual life will continue to contribute to the improvement and progress of society in general. 'Letter from a Gentleman' also departs somewhat from the strict rationalism of 'Letters of Julia and Caroline' by introducing the concept of 'fashion' as a feature of psychological and social life. Edgeworth's perhaps surprising deployment of this idea can be further traced in the fictions she produced in subsequent years, and is, I argue, central to her vision of how women could maintain the possibility of active involvement in society.

The revolutionary context is announced on the first page of 'Letter to a Gentleman', in which the letter-writer sketches the disagreement between himself and his friend as follows:

You are a champion for the rights of woman, and insist upon the equality of the sexes: but since the days of chivalry are past, and since modern gallantry permits men to speak, at least to one another, in less sublime language of the fair; I may confess to you that I see neither from experience nor analogy much reason to believe that, in the human species alone, there are no marks of inferiority in the female. (1)

By incorporating phrases (already it seems) indelibly associated with Mary Wollstonecraft and Edmund Burke respectively, Edgeworth here acknowledges that the debate on women and education has, by the 1790s, been placed in the realm of the revolution controversy. The ideas of the letter-writer are clearly modelled on those of Burke. In the following quotation, for instance, he refers dismissively to the prevailing rationalist position, and opposes it to a reliance on 'sentiment' and 'custom':

Morality should, we are told, be founded upon demonstration, not upon sentiment; and we should not require human beings to submit to any laws or customs, without convincing their understandings of the universal utility of these political conventions. (5)

One can compare this to Burke's defence of prejudice, implicitly opposed to reason, as the basis for action:

Prejudice is of ready application in the emergency; it previously engages the mind in a steady course of wisdom and virtue, and does not leave the man hesitating in the moment of decision, sceptical, puzzled, and unresolved. Prejudice renders a man's virtue his habit; and not a series of unconnected acts. Through just prejudice, his duty becomes a part of his nature.[39]

As recent commentators have noted and explored, Burke's counter-revolutionary rhetoric relies on an image of the English nation constituted as a family, with a consequent ideological insistence on women's confinement to a purely domestic realm.[40] In 'Letter to a Gentleman', Edgeworth articulates very clearly what the implications are for women of Burke's rejection of Enlightenment and his mystification of the nation. Like Burke, the 'Friend' declares that he is 'by no means disposed to indulge in the fashionable ridicule of prejudice' (5), as prejudice rather than rational thought is proposed as the only sure guarantor of female virtue:

Allow me, then, to warn you of the danger of talking in loud strains to the sex, of the noble contempt of prejudice. You would look with horror at one who should go to sap the foundations of the building; beware then how you venture to tear away the ivy which clings to the walls, and braces the loose stones together. (5)

In addition to his deliberately provocative rehabilitation of the word 'prejudice' Burke also emphasises the almost transcendental value of 'custom'. Again, Edgeworth takes this concept and reveals its impact on women: whereas, the letter-writer claims, men have the advantage of 'every assistance that foreign or domestic ingenuity can invent, to encourage literary studies', women are excluded from 'academies, colleges, public libraries, private associations of literary men', 'if not by law, at least by *custom*, which cannot easily be conquered' (2, my emphasis).

Contrary to the claims of Mary Jean Corbett, the *Letters* are, therefore, alert to the implications for women and their interests of Burke's anti-revolutionary arguments. In addition, Edgeworth conflates this voice with that of a more Rousseauvian account of the corrupting effects of female leadership, specifically in relation to France:

> Trace the history of female nature, from the court of Augustus to the court of Louis XIV, and tell me whether you can hesitate to acknowledge that the influence, the liberty, and the *power* of women have been constant concomitants of the moral and political decline of empires; – I say the concomitants: where the events are thus invariably connected I might be justified in saying that they were *causes* – you would call them *effects*; but we need not dispute about the momentary precedence of evils, which are found to be inseparable companions: – they may be alternately cause and effect, – the reality of the connexion is established [. . .]. (4)

In addition to these politicised objections the Gentleman proposes a number of more prosaic obstacles, questioning for instance what 'utility' can result from the cultivation of women's intellects and suggesting that although they may show talent for entertaining or ornamental literature, they are unlikely ever to excel in the 'useful arts' or 'exact sciences' (3). He also suggests that it is for women's own good that they are to be prevented from pursuing literature, as they would be unable to withstand literary spite and gossip, and would be rendered unmarriageable. He concludes by appealing simply to the status quo:

> You will, in a few years, have educated your daughter; and if the world be not educated exactly at the right time to judge of her perfections, to admire and love them, you will have wasted your labour, and you will have sacrificed your daughter's happiness. (13–14)

The original 1795 'Answer' to this complex composite argument is shorter and plainer in style than the revised version of 1798, but what strikes one most about it is the extent to which it admits and thereby appears to validate the conservative and reactionary fears of the first letter-writer. The opening paragraph is perhaps the weakest of the whole text:

> If I were not naturally of a sanguine temper, your letter, my dear friend, would fill my mind with so many melancholy fears for the fate of literary women, that I should be tempted to educate my daughter in the secure 'bliss of ignorance'.
>
> I am sensible that we have no right to try new experiments and fanciful theories at the expence [*sic*] of our fellow-creatures, especially those who are helpless, and immediately under our protection. Who can estimate the anguish which a parent must feel from the ruin of his child, when joined to the idea that it may have been caused by an imprudent education: but reason should never be blinded by sentiment, when it is her proper office to guide and enlighten.[41]

In contrast to the affirmative use of 'system', 'theory' and 'philosophy' in 'Letters of Julia and Caroline', the terms 'experiment' and 'theory' here include in their field of meaning the negative connotations which they had acquired in counter-revolutionary discourse. The enlightened father also 'agree[s]' with his conservative friend

> in thinking, that the strength of mind, which makes people govern themselves by reason, is not always connected with abilities in their cultivated state. I deplore the instances I have seen of this truth; but I do not despair: I am, on the contrary, excited to examine into the causes of this phaenomenon [*sic*] in the human mind: nor, because I see some evil, would I sacrifice the good on a motive of bare suspicion.[42]

The anguish of a parent over the ruin of a child ('ruin' here specifically implying a daughter) and the deplorable instances of cultivated people acting in an irrational manner suggest the excess and catastrophe which act as signifiers for revolution. The 1795 'Answer' addresses the fears about female misconduct explicitly, once again admitting that

> It is too true that women, who have been but half instructed, who have seen only superficially the relations of moral and political ideas, and who have obtained but an imperfect knowledge of the human heart, have conducted themselves so as to disgrace their talents and their sex: these are conspicuous and melancholy examples [. . .].[43]

Admissions and equivocations of the sort that we find in the 1795 Answer suggest that Edgeworth had become acutely aware of the fact that female character had become a way in which to read or interpret the causes and effects of revolution. They also indicate that she was at first unable to construct an argument that separated women's right to intellectual freedom from styles of female behaviour that were perceived as threatening and destructive. The writer on whom Edgeworth first modelled herself, Genlis, who was widely regarded as a boudoir politician by virtue of her relationship with her employer, the Duke of Orleans, vainly attempted to clear herself of the charge by making an absolute distinction between the woman of letters, represented through her writing, and the socially prominent and visible 'female politician'. She asserted a fundamental incompatibility in these positions:

> Nobody will believe, that a woman, who has spent her whole life in the cultivation of the arts and sciences, who never solicited a favour at court, nor ever was seen at the house of a minister; who was considered in a manner untameable; one that shut herself up in a cloister when but thirty years of age, that she might complete the education of her daughters, and initiate, in the rudiments of science, some who were yet in their cradles; having renounced, at once, the court and society, hath spent 13 years in teaching, and in the publication of two and twenty volumes; I say, no one will believe that such a woman has been a political intriguer.[44]

Edgeworth's project, which began in *Letters for Literary Ladies* and remained a constant theme throughout her writing, was to construct the intellectual woman so that, as Genlis asserted, 'nobody would believe' that there was any link between her and the spectral woman of intrigue, whom conservatives and radicals alike credited with the collapse of *ancien régime* France. In the 1798 Answer, in spite of the oppressive weight of counter-revolutionary discourse, of which she was evidently aware, she succeeds in making a case for continued freedoms for women, and argues that this will be beneficial rather than destructive to society.

The 1798 Answer reveals a profound commitment to the optimistic and progressive thought of the Enlightenment, balancing the ideas of thinkers from both the Scottish and the French schools. Edgeworth, for instance, on at least two occasions makes reference to Dugald Stewart's *Elements of the Philosophy of the Human Mind* (1792), a work grounded in and representative of the Scottish Enlightenment. She links the progress and improvement in women's education to progress generally, and suggests that the advances made in the education of women have contributed to, or at the very least been accompanied by, the more general and widespread diffusion of knowledge in society, irrespective of gender:

Formerly the fair sex was kept in Turkish ignorance; every means of acquiring knowledge was discountenanced by fashion, and impracticable even to those who despised fashion; – our books of science were full of unintelligible jargon, and mystery veiled pompous ignorance from public contempt: but now writers must offer their discoveries to the public in distinct terms, which every body may understand; technical language no longer supplies the place of knowledge, and the art of teaching has been carried to such perfection, that a degree of knowledge may now with ease be acquired in the course of a few years, which formerly it was the business of a life to attain. All this is much in favour of female literature. (20)

This passage rests on the conviction that women were crucial to the processes of civilisation in general. In France, the association of women with the civilising process was particularly strong, and had normally been considered an object of national pride. The 'stadial history' developed by the Scottish Enlightenment was less focused than that of the French on the centrality of women to the civilising process, but it nonetheless placed great emphasis on the relative status of women as an indication of the stage of development achieved by any given society or culture.[45] By contrast, the Rousseauvian critique of effeminacy and corruption arose from the basic argument that civilisation itself was a corrupting influence that drove men further and further from virtue and the 'state of nature'. It was patently obvious to women, whatever their political or social views, that Rousseau's theory of 'natural man' was incompatible with improvement in the conditions of women's lives and that his claims as to the corruption involved in civilisation were a broadside attack on the role of women in society. Wollstonecraft, for example, described these theories as 'plausible, but unsound': declaring that women must seize the opportunity presented by the doctrine of 'improvable reason' in order to escape the crippling limitations prescribed for them in law and custom.[46] The reliance on reason, however, was quite evidently insufficient. The limitations of tradition were soon to be replaced by exclusions that derived from the demands of bourgeois revolution:

in the rhetoric of the Revolution, the entire struggle for the achievement of legitimacy, for the creation of a new legitimate public embodiment by the Revolutionary governing class, was predicated not on an inclusion of the female, but on its exclusion.[47]

The fact that Edgeworth's arguments for the inclusion of women in this hostile post-revolutionary climate rest less on the strict principle of rationality than they do on the continued application of the ideas of the Scottish

Enlightenment is evident in her modified citation of Bernard Mandeville's *The Fable of the Bees* (1705). Mandeville's articulation of what could be termed the 'commercial ethos', the idea that social emulation and material consumption were to be encouraged as socially beneficial, initially provoked outrage. This moral condemnation did not last, however, and 'by the late eighteenth century the value of a heightened propensity to consume was widely accepted – it was the lynchpin of *The Wealth of Nations*. The "doctrine of beneficial luxury" had taken over from the doctrine of the "utility of poverty."'[48] Edgeworth rewrites Mandeville's famous phrase, 'Private vices are public benefits' as follows:

> Private *virtues* are public benefits: if each bee were content in his cell, there could be no grumbling hive; and if each cell were complete, the whole fabric must be perfect. (37)

This aligns her with Smith and other figures in the Scottish Enlightenment, whose ideas were characterised by a balance of the social and the psychological, the abstract and the material, and who succeeded in formulating the concept of 'enlightened self-interest', arguing that individual desires and social imperatives could be brought into harmony. But Edgeworth also uses this 'commercial humanism' explicitly to challenge the increasing insistence on a gendered division between public and private. The harmonious connection between self and society which was central to the Scottish Enlightenment is put to work by Edgeworth in order to prevent the domestic sphere being defined in terms of its lack of public meaning. She proposes a metonymic model for understanding society, in which the private is understood as the mirror image of the public, rather than its opposite. Edgeworth clearly foresees the consequences of a 'separate spheres' ideology and argues that it is for the good of society that women should be educated, so that men 'will not be driven to clubs for companions; they will invite the men of wit and science of their acquaintance to their own houses, instead of appointing some place of meeting from which ladies are to be excluded' (36–7).

Given the post-revolutionary context of this text, it is significant that Edgeworth challenges the reactionary strategy of setting Englishwomen in opposition to their French counterparts, and suggests that the customs and manners of the English could be improved upon by adopting some of the characteristics of French social life:

> The countenance expressive of sober sense and modest reserve continues to be the taste of the English, who wisely prefer the pleasures of domestic life. – Domestic life should, however, be enlivened and embellished with all the wit and vivacity and politeness for which French women were once admired [. . .]. (36)

The 'Answer' of 1798 can therefore be described as a concerted attempt to resist the banishment of women to a private sphere that is defined in opposition to the public sphere. In doing so, it relies to a considerable extent on the principles of Scottish thinkers such as Adam Smith, Dugald Stewart and John Millar – a fact which should cause no surprise given Edgeworth's intellectual influences. What may come as a surprise is that the text contains far more disruptive ideas, which reject the 'safe' acceptance of women's place within the overall scheme of human progress. This disruption is channelled through the subversive use of the idea of fashion.

In this text, the release of women from the prison of 'Turkish ignorance' (see above, p. 33) is represented not as being the result of the triumph of enlightened insight, but as a by-product of changing fashions in public and social life. The Gentleman insists that his friend must 'admit the expediency of attending to that *fashionable* demand for literature and the arts, which has arisen in society' (20, my emphasis). Progress is represented as arising from socially formed tastes and desires:

> The same objects excite different emotions in different situations; and to judge what will astonish or delight any given set of people some years hence, we must consider not merely what is the fashion of to-day, but whither the current of opinion runs, and what is likely to be the fashion of hereafter. (19)

The observation that 'the same objects excite different emotions in different situations' is clearly very far removed from the position associated with Rousseau, who strove to convince people of the superiority of 'natural man', whose tastes would be pure and uncorrupted, in contrast to those of a being shaped by and responsive to social demands. But fashion is also at odds with reason, considered in its most abstract form: there is clearly no rational basis for preferring one type of fabric or hairstyle over another. And yet this is the word that Edgeworth chooses to use to describe changes in the 'current of opinion' – thus suggesting that Enlightenment itself is partly a product of fashion.

The location of Enlightenment within a culture of fashion and by extension femininity was, as we have seen, the source in part of Rousseau's hostility to the *philosophes*, whose work took place within the female-sponsored space of the *salon*. In 'Letter to a Gentleman' Edgeworth suggests that although women may lead fashions and gain influence through them, women are also peculiarly vulnerable to the social and cultural changes dictated by 'fashion', broadly understood. Paraphrasing Voltaire's *Philosophical Dictionary*,[49] Edgeworth reflects on the varying standards and judgements to which women are subjected:

The changes that are made in the opinion of our [the male] sex as to female beauty, according to the different situations in which women are placed, and the different qualities on which we fix the idea of their excellence, are curious and striking. Ask a northern Indian, says a traveller who has lately visited them, ask a northern Indian what is beauty, and he will answer, a broad flat face, small eyes, high cheek bones, three or four broad black lines across each cheek, a low forehead, a large broad chin, a clumsy hook nose, &c. These beauties are greatly heightened, or at least rendered more valuable, when the possessor is capable of dressing all kinds of skins, converting them into the different parts of their clothing, and able to carry eight or ten stone in summer, or haul a much greater weight in winter. (36)

Observations on the apparently inferior position accorded to women in 'primitive' societies were a staple of the kind of stadial history practised by Scottish Enlightenment historians and referred to above. The emphasis on the desirability, in such a society, of a woman's ability to haul and carry large loads implied that in these societies women were regarded on the same level as live-stock; the apparently inescapable conclusion was that women of eighteenth-century Europe should rejoice in the position that they had attained in that civilised and enlightened age. Edgeworth subverts this complacency very thoroughly, however, when she implicitly compares the subordinate position of women among the 'Northern Indians', widely regarded as anomalous survivals of an earlier, more primitive age, with the position of women in another society which had more recently become a casualty of history, *ancien régime* France:

If, some years ago, you had asked a Frenchman what he meant by beauty, he would have talked to you of *l'air piquant, l'air spirituel, l'air noble, l'air comme il faut*, and he would have referred ultimately to that *je ne sçais quoi*, for which Parisian belles were formerly celebrated. (36)

'The same objects excite different emotions in different situations': women are 'the same objects', but according to the situations in which they are 'placed' they can be admired, reviled or ridiculed. Edgeworth's equation of native American women and 'Parisian belles' of former times on the basis of their shared subjection to 'fashions' in male taste and opinion is all the more sub-versive because it conflicts with eighteenth-century economic and social theory, in which fashion was held to be a phenomenon peculiar to advanced commercial societies. It was a commonplace to observe that in 'traditional' societies such as China, India and Japan, which lacked any great social mobility and therefore, a basis for social emulation, styles of dress changed very little over time. The absence of fashion in such societies was referred to as marking one of the key differences between 'western' and 'eastern' women: Mouradj d'Osson wrote for instance in 1741 that 'Fashions which tyrannize European women hardly disturb the fair sex in the East: hair styles, cut of clothing and type of fabric are almost always the same.'[50]

Edgeworth thus on the one hand makes use of the progressive Enlightenment arguments of stadial history, but on the other extends the application of those ideas in such a way as ultimately to subvert them. She effectively equates the North American 'savage' with the ultra-sophisticated Parisian man-about-town, thus destabilising the cherished presumption of superior civilisation on which Enlightenment so problematically rests. Her citation of Voltaire is ambiguous in this context. The great *philosophe* could be imagined as superior to these variations in taste and judgment, commenting on them on a metadiscursive level. However, her use of an Enlightenment text to comment on the abrupt and disorienting changes in France since 1789 functions, I would argue, to bring Enlightenment into uncomfortable proximity to the instability of the revolution, thus disrupting its claims to transcend the temporary conditions of time and place on which its adherents commented so confidently.

The meanings that accrue to 'fashion' in 'Letter to a Gentleman' are thus complex and challenging. Initially, fashion features relatively neutrally, as an aspect and agent of progress, and as a means to register the fact that human beings adapt and respond to changes in their social environment, a usage that reflects the 'commercial humanism' of the Scottish Enlightenment. Subsequently, however, it appears that Edgeworth regards this process as one in which women are reduced to passive objects; lacking agency they are 'placed' in various situations and judged accordingly. Ultimately, however, Edgeworth succeeds in using fashion as a critique of *male* Enlightenment; the 'objects' (women) have remained the same – it is the male who has been subject to fashion, dissolving the distinction between 'savage' and 'civilised' in the process. *Letters for Literary Ladies* thus reveals Edgeworth to be at one and the same time reliant on key principles of both the French and Scottish Enlightenments (theory, philosophy, reason, progress and the general good) and also capable of subverting these principles in order to reveal their patriarchal and ethnocentric origins. Edgeworth's fictional texts of this period, *Belinda*, 'Angelina' and 'Forester', provide further confirmation of her conviction that both genders should participate in shared forms of public life, whilst also maintaining a subversive critique of the patriarchal biases of Enlightenment philosophy.

Belinda has been lauded by Mitzi Myers as 'at once the best and most misread (or underread) woman's fiction of the revolutionary decade'.[51] The novel has often been read as a contribution to the post-revolutionary construction of the 'domestic woman', a figure defined in opposition to both the worldly women of the *ancien régime* and revolutionary enthusiasts such as Mary Wollstonecraft and Helen Maria Williams. This kind of reading is certainly easy to produce, but any reading inevitably falls short of its object, as this is a novel which presents 'a chaotic variety of characters and events that prohibits political fixity'.[52] The reading offered here thus does not attempt to replace others, but to draw attention to aspects of the novel which have not figured significantly in previous accounts.

'Abroad and At Home' was the title that Edgeworth had originally conceived for her 'moral tale'; a title that would have been in many respects more suitable, as it foregrounds the allusive and at times allegorical nature of the plot, and avoids the implication that Belinda's 'entrance into the world' is the moral, psychological and dramatic core of the work. Belinda's relative insipidity compared with the novel's riskier and more entertaining characters was immediately noted by early reviewers, who complained that

> The character of the heroine herself creates so little interest, that she appears to have usurped the superior right of Lady Delacour to give the title of the work: for it is to the character and agency of the latter, in our opinion, that the tale owes its principal attractions.[53]

As with many of Edgeworth's novels, however, there are so many characters in *Belinda* that it is hardly a matter of privileging either Belinda or Lady Delacour. The novel has the quality of a kaleidoscope, in which flashing images of belles, beaux, rakes, fops, servants, conjurers, colonials and émigrés pass before our eyes in sometimes bewildering sequence. The original sketch for the tale focused on the contrasting figures of Belinda and Lady Delacour, but the finished novel includes (amongst other characters) two additional female figures, Harriet Freke and Virginia St Pierre, a young girl with whom Clarence Hervey, Belinda's would-be lover, becomes entangled. Harriet Freke is an outrageous and destructive friend of Lady Delacour's, whose impatience with the limits prescribed for women is such that she habitually dresses as a man, and 'braves' public disapproval through speech and behaviour that is stigmatised as unfeminine. Whereas the creation of a character such as Mrs Freke has been successfully interpreted as a means of allowing for the reformation of Lady Delacour, by displacing on to her those aspects of Lady Delacour's resistance to domesticity that could not be reformed, the insertion of the complex and unlikely subplot involving Virginia appears harder to justify.

Both Harriet Freke and Virginia, however, represent Edgeworth's determination to situate her tale within the context of political and philosophical controversy. In an early article on this topic, Colin and Jo Atkinson identify the thickness of allusion to texts and ideas which belong to the revolution controversy, specifically as it related to women's character and conduct.[54] The chapter in which Harriet Freke attempts to win Belinda to her clique is entitled 'The Rights of Woman', and in it Harriet challenges Mr Percival with a range of radical arguments which advocate a form of gender equality, and dismisses the felt need for distinct codes of feminine behaviour and 'delicacy'. Aside from the obvious reference to Wollstonecraft, there are several identifiable allusions to Mary Hays's *The Memoirs of Emma Courtney*, which relays the story of a woman who decides to break with feminine delicacy by actively pursuing the man she desires. The function of this character, and this scene, has been the focus of much of the debate on the novel. It may have been a device to reassure readers that the views expressed, however liberal, were not revolutionary. Other critics focus on the deviance and threat that Harriet represents in the novel as a whole – by goading Lady Delacour to undertake a duel she is the cause of the injury to her breast, thus representing subversion of the ideal of domesticity that the novel seeks to promote. Susan C. Greenfield's very suggestive discussion draws attention to the persistent undercurrent of homoeroticism in the relationship between Lady Delacour and Harriet, and suggests that the desire to promote the ideal of the domestic woman, which appears to drive and motivate the plot, is undercut by the difficulty with which this apparently 'natural' role is enforced: 'if Harriet has to be painfully maimed to become a woman, how essential can her femaleness be?'[55] The unease with the idea of 'natural' identities and roles is a theme to which I shall return. Elizabeth Kowaleski-Wallace suggests that the prominence of such a deviant figure can be related to Edgeworth's 'patriarchal complicity' – her identification with her father as a means to achieve a literary voice. Kowaleski-Wallace argues that Harriet Freke represents the unalterable deviance of femininity, which remains despite Edgeworth's promotion of a reformed and rationally oriented female character. Referring to Harriet's (literal) 'downfall', injured in a 'mantrap' whilst engaged in another of her escapades, Kowaleski-Wallace concludes that the device is 'arguably excessive, [but that] it nonetheless serves [Edgeworth's] polemic, for the novel insists that such "freakishness" must always yield to the principle of rationality'.[56] As we have seen in *Letters for Literary Ladies*, however, the scope of rationality is limited by the unlikely influence of fashion. *Belinda*, similarly, displays a complex awareness of the 'fashionable' as a condition of women's existence.

At an early stage in Belinda's negotiation of the complex and dangerous world of fashionable society, she is made privy to the intimate details of her hostess's private life. The cautionary tale that Lady Delacour relates to Belinda, revealing the emptiness of her married life and her personal unhappiness, suggests that consumption and the pursuit of fashion can result in the annihilation of the self, as when Lady Delacour discovers that her power to command money has disappeared and her 'signature was no longer worth a farthing'.[57] Her signature, the sign of the self, is worth nothing to her because it can no longer be exchanged for money, and clearly has no other value. The crucial importance of consumption is evident everywhere in *Belinda*. The novel presents us with a dazzling picture of a society which habitually assesses the value of people, objects and events in terms of their novelty or fashion-ability. Marriot is devoted to the horribly noisy but terribly fashionable macaw, Lady Delacour spends fifty guineas on a flowering aloe which possesses no attractive qualities other than its extreme rarity, thus guaranteeing the success of her gala, and Belinda herself is reduced to the role of commodity, 'as well advertised as Packwood's razor strops' (25).[58] The role of fashion in driving commerce and the circulation of money is highlighted: Marriot, Lady Delacour observes, has spent four guineas on her macaw, and other items of expenditure are frequently referred to and itemised; Belinda's birth-night dress is elliptically referred to as 'fifty guineas' worth of elegance and fashion' (72). The character of Lady Delacour and her miserably dissipated life would seem to suggest that fashion is destructive, associated with the rejection of woman's role in the creation of a private space in the home for herself, her husband and her children, and leading to the annihilation of the authentic self. However, it must be borne in mind that the changes made to the novel include not only the rehabilitation of Lady Delacour but also the inclusion of the subplot con-cerning Virginia St Pierre, created by Clarence Hervey in order to be utterly free of the influence of fashion. The fact that Clarence's plan to create a 'natural' woman, free of fashionable artifice, comes to him after reading Rousseau makes it clear that the Virginia subplot functions as a critique of Rousseau. But it is also made clear in the text that Clarence Hervey's experi-ment is a reactive product of the very fashion that he deplores: in *Belinda*, nature is never an alternative to culture, however corrupt and damaging that culture may be.

Thomas Day's entrenched opposition to female authorship (see p. 23 above) was the original source for 'Letter from a Gentleman' and his influence also looms large in *Belinda*, which borrows the Virginia subplot from an episode in Day's life.[59] The story is related in several sources, but, in summary, Day was so influenced by Rousseau's pronouncements on femininity, in particular his hostility to the worldly, sophisticated feminine type he associated with Parisian salons, that he determined to create a woman modelled as closely as possible on Rousseau's Sophie, so that he could be sure of a suitable wife. His method was to adopt two young orphans and then to educate them himself, to ensure that they would be 'uncontaminated' by 'fashionable' notions of femininity. Edgeworth's fictional reworking of Day's actions can be regarded as an act of creative self-assertion – weaving into her fictions elements of the man whose objections to the idea of women writing and publishing had been so passionate that Richard Lovell Edgeworth tacitly delayed his daughter's publishing debut until after Day's death.

In his *Memoirs*, R. L. Edgeworth describes Day's eccentric scheme as 'a design more romantic than any which we find in novels'.[60] He also comments on Day's apparently illogical decision to take the two girls to France – 'something strange', given that (as quoted above) he 'had as large a portion of national prejudice in favor of the people of England, and against the French, as any man of sense could have'.[61] However, this apparently strange decision had 'a considerable advantage':

> From their total ignorance of the French language, an ignorance, which he took no pains to remove, his pupils were not exposed to any impertinent inter-ference; and as that knowledge of the world, from which he wished to preserve them, was at one entrance quite shut out, he had their minds entirely open to such ideas and sentiments, and such only, as he desired to implant. Mr. Day had an unconquerable horror of the empire of fashion over the minds of women; simplicity, perfect innocence, and attachment to himself, were at that time the only qualifications which he desired in a wife. He was not perhaps sufficiently aware, that ignorance is not necessary to preserve innocence: for this reason he was not anxious to cultivate the understandings of his pupils.[62]

When Edgeworth comes to the fictional reworking of Day's experiment, she relocates it within an explicitly post-revolutionary context:

> He [Clarence Hervey] had been in France, just before the revolution, when luxury and dissipation were at their height in Paris, and when a universal spirit of licentious gallantry prevailed. Some circumstances, in which he was per-sonally interested, disgusted him strongly with the Parisian belles; he felt, that women, who were full of vanity, affectation and artifice, whose tastes were perverted, and whose feelings were depraved, were equally incapable of con-ferring, or enjoying real happiness. Whilst this conviction was full in his mind, he read the works of Rousseau [. . .]. He was charmed with the picture of Sophia, when contrasted with the characters of the women of the world, with whom he had been disgusted. (362)

Edgeworth thus maps Day's hatred of the 'empire of fashion' onto a (post-)revolutionary context.

Virginia's story is a somewhat uneasy blend of comedy, satire, and essay-istic reflection, tinged with darker elements of violence and tragedy. In the

Memoirs of Richard Lovell Edgeworth, Maria Edgeworth, in an 'Editor's note', explains Day's aversion to French manners in terms of his youth, commenting that letters written from France 'when he was scarcely twenty'

> may, perhaps, amuse the reader. His expressions of contempt and horror of French society must not be taken literally or seriously. Mr. Day did not understand French sufficiently at this time, to judge of foreign conversation. His exaggerated opinion of Rousseau was recanted [. . .] after he attained to years of discretion.[63]

This implicitly excuses the extremity of his ideas, and the same tone is initially in evidence in the description of Clarence Hervey's plan, particularly the unexpected difficulties he encounters when searching for a suitable female upon which to bestow his ideal of education:

> He was some time delayed, by the difficulty of finding a proper object for his purpose: it was easy to meet with beauty in distress, and ignorance in poverty; but it was difficult to find simplicity without vulgarity, ingenuity without cunning, or even ignorance without prejudice [. . .]. (362)

However, unlike her account of Thomas Day, written in the context of her father's *Memoirs*, when both men were dead, the fictionalisation of the events in *Belinda* allows Edgeworth to explore the effects of this absurd plan on the unfortunate 'object', Virginia. Her subject status is made immediately apparent when Clarence's first action, having rescued her from destitution following the death of her grandmother, is to change her name – 'the name of Rachel he could not endure' (369) – and to call her instead after the heroine of Bernadin St Pierre's novel, *Paul et Virginie*. This echoes Day's naming of one of his wards: he 'called her Sabrina from the river Severn, and Sidney from his favourite, Algernon Sidney'.[64] As Caroline Gonda has noted, this naming is reflective of the extent to which Virginia's naturalness is simply a projection of Clarence's (sophisticated) desires: 'Virginia's artlessness is as much a fictional construction as her name'.[65] Virginia's simplicity and innocence have been created in response to Clarence's demands for a woman free of conventional characteristics: 'I should be glad that my wife were ignorant of what *every body knows*. Nothing is so tiresome to the man of taste and abilities as *what every body knows*' (373). He performs an emblematic experiment, in which he asks her to choose which she would prefer, a moss rose bud, or a pair of diamond earrings. Her dismissal of the valuable jewels, in favour of the rose which reminds her of her grandmother's cottage, 'charms' Clarence, who has the advantage of knowing the conventional value placed on the earrings. This form of ignorance, which underlines the innumerable ways in which society accords entirely arbitrary and conventional value to objects and people, suggests not just Rousseau's 'natural man', but also the image of the 'noble savage'.

Virginia's isolation acquires even more pronounced overtones of an imaginary space outside civilisation when her retreat is invaded by Phillip Baddley and Mr Rochfort, who have made their way to Windsor to spy on what they are convinced is Clarence Hervey's mistress. Virginia reacts in horror, in a scene whose language evokes a hostile incursion into virgin territory:

> Virginia was astonished, terrified, and disgusted, by their appearance; they seemed to her a species of animals, for which she had no name, and of which she had no prototype in her imagination. That they were men she saw; but they were clearly not *Clarence Herveys*; they bore still less resemblance to the courteous knights of chivalry. Their language was so different from any of the books she had read, and any of the conversation she had heard, that they were scarcely intelligible. (384)

The implied association between Virginia and the 'virgin land' of Britain's former American colonies has not escaped critics.[66] What has not been noted, however, is Edgeworth's suggestion that the very idea of such a 'virgin territory' is a construct imposed from without, which disempowers its object. The space invaded by Baddley and Rochfort is, after all, no wild frontier, but a walled garden within civilised society. Clarence, as a man of 'taste and abilities', delights in Virginia's ignorance of '*what every body knows*'; thus her charm is a function of his own philosophical construction of virtue and vice, as he has determined the meanings of 'natural' and 'artificial'.

Edgeworth depicts not only the tyranny involved in this system, but also resistance to that assumption. Virginia is distressed by fantasies of resistance to the patriarchal authority which controls and contains her – and which has in fact created her as its object. Deprived of the ability to know and to name her own feelings, and thus unable to articulate her sense that her feelings towards Clarence are of respect and gratitude rather than 'love', Virginia's fears and her resentment of the powerless position in which she has been placed find expression through the unconscious, in her dreams. Her own desires are expressed through the figure of a nameless man, whose picture she has seen, who appears in her dreams as a hero of romance, the genre with which she is most familiar. Her relentlessly obtuse companion, Mrs Ormond, refuses to acknowledge the disruptive potential of these dreams. Faintly aware that she has feelings and desires which exceed the careful planning of her secluded education, Virginia persists in her questioning: 'I wonder how I come to dream of such things' (384). Her unconscious fantasies soon assume a more violent character, when she dreams of a medieval tournament, in which her hero, in white plumes, is locked in fierce combat with an anonymous opponent:

> I wished him to be victorious. And he was victorious. And he unhorsed his adversary, and stood over him with his drawn sword; and then I saw that the knight in the black plumes was Mr Hervey, and I ran to save him, but I could not. I saw him weltering in his blood, and I heard him say, 'Perfidious, *ungrateful* Virginia! you are the cause of my death!' (388)

Even within the educational laboratory which Hervey thinks he has constructed, there is the potential for disruption and the uncontrollable. Virginia's conscious desires are only to please Hervey and do what is considered appropriate, and yet she threatens to be the cause of Hervey's misery. Through a misguided sense of what is expected of her, Virginia agrees to marry her guardian, unaware that by this time he has fallen in love with Belinda, as he has recognised that she is his equal, while Virginia, as a result of the system which has been imposed on her, remains his 'inferior', capable only of being either 'his pupil, or his plaything' (379).

Virginia's 'naturalness' is closely associated, in fact more or less synonymous, with sexual ignorance. Her 'innocence', symbolised by her spontaneous offer when she first sees Hervey of one of the roses she has gathered, is the result of her grandmother's insistence that she should never lay eyes on a man:

> In this cottage she has lived with me, away from all the world. You are the first man she ever spoke to; the first man who was ever within these doors. She is innocence itself! (366)

In the same way that the meaning of feminine 'virtue' was limited to sexual chastity and propriety, 'naturalness', in Virginia's case, is limited to her behaviour towards men. By choosing the roses instead of the diamonds, and by offering Clarence the flowers she has gathered, Virginia shows that she has no knowledge of the fact that beauty can be traded like a commodity, and that its value can be increased by manipulation in the form of flirting. In her grandmother's mind, the preservation of Virginia's innocence depends equally on her protection from men and on the restriction of her access to the written word. She associates literacy with sexual temptation and disgrace, blaming her daughter's seduction in part on her enthusiasm for scribbling love-letters. Consequently, Virginia is not taught to write. Even if she had acquired that skill, Clarence's decision to change her name means that Rachel/Virginia cannot, at this point, write her 'own name'. The writing of one's name is a potent symbol of selfhood and autonomy, and whereas the pursuit of fashion threatens to deprive Lady

Delacour of the meaning of her name, Clarence Hervey's fanatical desire to nullify the influence of fashion means that Virginia has *never* 'owned' her own name. Clarence claims that he, as a man of taste and abilities, delights in his prospective wife's ignorance because it distinguishes her from the usual, the conventional; this claim effectively places Virginia on the same level as Lady Delacour's flowering aloe – she is the object which proves him to be a highly discerning consumer. Clarence has already proved his mastery of the highly artificial behaviours which govern fashionable society when he boasts that he could manage a hoop as well as any woman in England, and demonstrates this skill in the assumed guise of the 'countess de Pomenars', a wealthy émigrée. His mastery of this role is disturbed only when he lurches forward ungracefully to hand Belinda a comb she has dropped. Clarence's feelings for Belinda thus have the potential to disturb the assumed mask of fashion; the Virginia project, on the other hand, in spite of his philosophical posturings, is just another reflection of fashionable thought, about which he must learn to discriminate. In *Belinda*, women are threatened with the loss of the self both through the irrational pursuit of fashion and through the subordination of femininity on which the radical philosophies of the eighteenth century rest. Whatever the dangerous seductions of fashion, *Belinda* suggests that Edgeworth rejects the allure of 'Nature'. This rejection is also made explicit in 'Forester', one of her *Moral Tales*, published in the same year as *Belinda*.

In 'Forester', Edgeworth explores the desire of the eponymous hero to escape from what he regards as unacceptable compromises with social convention. Forester's ideals are Rousseauvian: he longs to leave behind the world of polite dinner-table conversation and dancing and to engage instead in 'honest toil', which he imagines will be far more ennobling. Following a humiliating experience at a ball, he runs away from his guardian's home to seek employment with a gardener, where he hopes to find his path to virtue less compromised and complicated. In the *Moral Tales*, 'Forester' is paired with 'Angelina; or, l'amie inconnue' (described by R. L. Edgeworth as a 'female Forester'), and both have similarities to Elizabeth Hamilton's *Memoirs of Modern Philosophers*.[67] Both Edgeworth and Hamilton take a comic look at the excesses to which 'modern philosophy' may lead, but Edgeworth's work is more liberal than Hamilton's – a fact signalled not least by the age of the protagonists in both cases. *Moral Tales* were designed for an adolescent or young adult readership, and both Forester's and Angelina's disgust with the shallowness of the life that they see around them is thus represented as part of a stage in the psychological and social adjustment of the individual to the world. This could be regarded as a patronising dismissal of social critique in terms of understandable but temporary adolescent rebellion, but this device allows Edgeworth to situate extreme social critique in terms of 'normal' behaviour, and thus to give a very sympathetic portrayal of beliefs which were often represented in the period as seditious and dangerous. The attraction of her two protagonists to modern philosophy facilitates the incorporation of the theme into her work, as well as defusing it through association with youthful enthusiasm. In the case of Angelina, the heroine's desire to seek out her 'unknown friend' (a sentimental author who styles herself 'Araminta') is explained by her disgust with the shallow life led by her guardian, Lady Diana Chillingworth. The extremes of sentimental thinking will, it is implied, continue to be attractive unless meaningful alternatives are proposed, as they are in this case in the figure of Lady Frances Somerset. Forester, meanwhile, begins to question his rejection of the comfortable and privileged life into which he has been born when he realises that it is not synonymous with selfish pleasures and idleness. The implication in both cases is that extreme responses to social injustice are only to be expected if a more attractive model of social leadership is not provided.

Both protagonists have to deal with the reality of class when they embark on their philosophic journeys of discovery. Forester discovers to his chagrin that the gardener and his family have virtually no conversation, and that he is left alone to muse on the parallels (or lack of them) between his life as a gardener and the pastoral idyll of Virgil's *Eclogues*. Angelina is taken aback when she realises that she is no longer paid the respect to which she has become accustomed, and that she is expected to make do with rather rustic standards of comfort in Araminta's cottage. Like *Belinda*, these tales are to an extent a reasoned defence of aristocracy and wealth. In all of Edgeworth's fiction, aristocratic dissipation and vice are regarded very severely, but the potential for social change is nonetheless located to a considerable extent in those privileged with enough wealth to pursue education and culture. There is, moreover, a strong association in these fictions between the possibilities afforded by a privileged lifestyle and the agency of women. Forester's impulsive decision to leave his inherited wealth and privilege in order to pursue a virtuous life of honest labour is, for example, precipitated by his humiliation in female company. At a ball which he has only reluctantly attended, he retrieves a flower dropped by his guardian's daughter, Flora Campbell, but when he attempts to hand it to her, she and the other young girls are horror-struck by his filthy hands and fingernails. Unable to cope with their ridicule and the shame he feels, he decides that he has had enough of the 'artificiality' of polite society. Forester's disdain for society often takes the shape of disdain for femininity and associated behaviours. He has utter contempt for dancing and dancing masters (invariably French), and he is disgusted when his friend Henry Campbell tackles the mismanagement of a local charity school by ingratiating himself with the school's temperamental patroness. Forester himself, preferring the direct approach, confronts the school's manageress directly – which results only in the punishment of the child on whose behalf he had intervened. As he gradually comes to realise that wealth is not invariably productive of vice, Forester also begins to be less suspicious of aspects of femininity which he had previously despised. As he contemplates reintroducing himself to the Campbell family, he pays for dancing lessons and buys a new suit of clothes, with the unspoken hope that his new, more polished exterior and manners will appeal to Flora Campbell. Forester thus learns to respect the implicitly feminised social forms which he had previously dismissed as useless and artificial, and also learns that simplicity is not necessarily a virtue.

The persistence of fashionable femininity, rather than a strictly rational domestic femininity, is suggested in *Belinda* by the irrepressible Lady Delacour's stage-managing of the story's conclusion – "'shall I finish the novel for you?'" she asks; "'nobody can do it better'" she is assured (477). This ending is in sharp contrast to the ending originally planned for the novel, in which Lady Delacour's headlong pursuit of dissipated pleasures culminated in her death. The reformation which Lady Delacour undergoes has been highlighted as perhaps the most significant of the changes made between the outline sketch and the finished novel; most critics have, however, focused on the introduction of Harriet Freke as a kind of scapegoat onto whom the irredeemable aspects of Lady Delacour's character were transferred. The reformation of this aristocratic female character should, however, also be considered as a decision to retain her (reformed) influence within the fictional world of the text.[68] Lady Delacour has, in this final scene, lost none of her wit, which she does not allow to be cramped by the appearance of a severe morality. In this final scene, in fact, Lady Delacour stresses the continued importance of appearance: "'What signifies being happy, unless we appear so?'" (478).

Edgeworth's response to the challenges of the French revolution, in particular its impact on women such as herself, is distinguished by the retention of a materialist conception of Enlightenment which is sceptical of pure reason, in part because of her awareness of the ways in which women's roles and characters were subject to change based on differing cultural and social demands. A reading of *Letters for Literary Ladies* and *Belinda*, as well as 'Forester' and 'Angelina', reveals a concern in her work that extremes of both radicalism and conservatism could result in the prescription of severely limited roles for women. Lady Delacour, intelligent, educated and fashionable, possesses the 'wit and vivacity and politeness for which French women were once admired' and which Edgeworth proposed in 'Letter to a Gentleman' should be a part of English domestic life. Edgeworth's writing in the 1790s and in the very early 1800s thus reveals an argument in favour of the kind of fashionable, feminised society that was widely regarded as specifically and dangerously French in the post-revolutionary period.

'French influence' has emerged as one of the key points of debate and interpretation in discussions of 1790s Ireland but, as with the responses to Enlightenment I noted at the beginning of this chapter, the meanings of that influence have been dominated by, if not exclusively limited to, debates on the extent to which revolutionary principles were diffused throughout the population. As we can see, French influence is crucial to Edgeworth's conception of women's claim to agency in society. That influence is, however, a compound of Enlightenment principles and a critique of those principles conveyed through the figure of the woman of fashion. The reaction against the French-identified woman of fashion produced the image of the 'natural woman', revealed here as a fantasy shaped by male desires and thus in herself – or itself – a product of 'fashion'. Fashion thus emerges not as Enlightenment's other, but as a critique of Enlightenment and a means of limiting its appropriation and subordination of women.

To mention fashion in even remote contiguity to 1790s Ireland is to risk appearing absurd – dangerously recalling Marie Antoinette's apocryphal comment that the masses crying out for bread should eat cake. The attribution of this remark to Marie Antoinette is in itself a powerful reminder that femininity is effortlessly conflated with the recklessly trivial concerns of the elite and is positioned in opposition to the needs of 'the people'. In practice, however, it is not always easy to distinguish the trivial from the substantial, and fashion could play a role in disseminating apparently much weightier ideas. Consider, for instance, William Drennan's first impression of Lord Edward Fitzgerald, following a passionate outburst from Fitzgerald in the Dublin parliament in 1793:

> A warm debate in the House last night from which the audience was excluded on Lord Edward Fitzgerald, the husband of Pamela Egalité, saying that the majority of that House and the Lieutenant were the worst subjects the King had. Our society [the Society of United Irishmen] was belaboured. Hobart read part of our address I hear, but as the gallery was driven out I cannot yet know the circumstances. [. . .] It is said he [Fitzgerald] refused to ask pardon. The House was in a flame – and it is not known today whether he is to do it this evening or not. His brother the Duke and the opposition will it is likely prevail on him. Tandy says he is an honest hearted fine fellow and not easily moved, greatly irritated as he must be by having been deprived of his commission. It is not unlikely that he and his elegant wife will lead the fashion of politics in a short time, if he stays here.[69]

Drennan identifies Fitzgerald initially by association with his *wife*, who was the adopted daughter of Edgeworth's first literary model, Mme de Genlis, and who was moreover widely assumed to be the natural daughter of the French Duke of Orleans, known as Philippe Egalité by virtue of his republican sympathies.[70] Fitzgerald's political influence and his role in disseminating and popularising radical ideas are, according to Drennan, enhanced by his association with a woman who had a form of public identity and who displayed social sophistication and fashionability. 'French influence' figured as radical political ideas and 'French influence' figured as a type of feminine fashionability are not, therefore, as antithetical as they might first appear, suggesting that the public sphere to which political radicals such as the United Irishmen addressed themselves was not as purely masculine as it has been claimed to be. Drennan and his like-minded male colleagues may have an exclusive, gender-determined right to make public statements in the House (Fitzgerald denounces, Hobart reads an address) but the further dissemination of these ideas relies on other forms of communication which explicitly involve women, particularly elegant and fashionable women like Pamela Fitzgerald. All of the texts discussed in this chapter reveal Edgeworth's awareness that to demonise this type of femininity was to abandon the ideal of a sphere of influence in which women and men could both participate and thereby contribute to the shaping of their society.

My aim in this chapter has been to show how a new reading of the texts that Edgeworth produced in and around the revolutionary decade opens up a space for the possibility of an Irish feminine identity other than one predicated on the prior entry of Irish men into the public sphere. In the following chapter I consider the texts of the Union and the immediate post-Union period, in the context of the blow that the Union dealt to dreams of an autonomous Irish public sphere.

CHAPTER TWO

Women, Writing and the Irish Public Sphere After the Union

Irish identity in *Castle Rackrent* and *An Essay on Irish Bulls*

➤➤⤙⤙

In his poem 'Glendalloch', an exemplary piece of literary romantic nationalism, the former Volunteer and founder member of the United Irishmen, William Drennan, interprets the Act of Union as the death of the Irish nation:

> Where shall her sad remains be laid?
> Where invocate her solemn shade?
>
> HERE be the mausoléum plac'd,
> In this vast vault, this silent waste; –
> Yon mould'ring pillar, 'midst the gloom,
> Finger of Time! shall point her tomb;
> While silence of the ev'ning hour
> Hangs o'er Glendalloch's ruin'd tower.[1]

Drennan's authorship of this poem provides a perfect illustration of Joep Leerssen's proposal that the Act of Union can be located as a decisive break between the 'Enlightenment patriotism' of the eighteenth century and the romantic nationalism of the nineteenth. In his words, the 'abolition of the Dublin parliament signals the end of the ideology known as Patriotism'.[2] One of the things that got lost along with that ideology was a particular ideal of Irish masculinity, as a brief look at Drennan's writings indicates. A marked feature of his writing is the extent to which it is intended to produce the kind of masculine public sphere that was seen as the hallmark of political liberty, an effect which is particularly evident in the work for which Drennan is best known, *Letters of Orellana* (also known as *Letters of an Irish Helot*). The *Letters* were written at the highpoint of Drennan's involvement with the Volunteers, whose campaigning contributed directly to the restoration of legislative independence to the Irish parliament. Volunteer patriotism was modelled on that of classical republicanism: 'preparing to defend his country, the volunteer could see himself as an eighteenth-century equivalent of the citizens of ancient Greece and Rome'.[3] In *Letters of Orellana*, Drennan castigates the Volunteers, who he feels lack the resolve to secure the reforms they have demanded. He does so using language and imagery which make political maturity inseparable from adult masculinity. According to Drennan, the national spirit of Ireland, as embodied in the actions of the Volunteers, 'became a strolling player, went to "enact Brutus in the capitol", totally *forgot her part*, threw off her warlike attire, and sunk down again – a wretched woman.'[4] The claims of Irish Protestants to descend from Saxon heroes such as Alfred are dismissed as 'the fairy tale of infancy',[5] while the achievement of national self-determination is equated with the progress from youth to 'manhood'.[6] The habitual curiosity of the Irish, perpetually asking the question '*What news? What news?*' is castigated as indicative of a character 'made up of a boy's curiosity, a girl's timidity and a dotard's garrulity. If you be MEN, to whom I address myself, MAKE NEWS.'[7] Political reform is here inseparable from an ideal of adult masculinity, as it is in perhaps the most important piece of political rhetoric of the 1790s, Wolfe Tone's *Argument on Behalf of the Catholics of Ireland*, in which Tone dismisses anti-Catholic prejudice as unworthy of politically mature Irish*men*:

> Let us, for God's sake, shake off the old woman, the tales of our nurses, the terrors of our grandams, from our hearts; let us put away childish fears, look our situation in the face like men.[8]

The United Irishmen may have been revolutionary and radical, as distinct from the reformist Volunteers, but both were animated by the ideal of a national public sphere characterised as explicitly and strenuously masculine. The death of the Irish nation so bleakly described in Drennan's poem thus involves the disappearance of that masculine public sphere.

In this chapter I want to read *Castle Rackrent* and *An Essay on Irish Bulls* in terms of their representation of the public sphere and as reflections on the principles of Enlightenment as they pertain to Ireland immediately after the 1798 rebellion and the Union. Can it be merely coincidental that at the precise moment in which the short-lived Irish public sphere was closed off for Irish men, an Irish woman entered the literary public sphere by publishing two texts which broke new ground in the discursive construction of Irishness? To date, the enormous success and impact of the generic 'Irish novel' in the post-Union period has been considered in isolation from the gender of its most famous authors, Edgeworth and her contemporary Lady Morgan. Given the intensity with which the image of autonomous masculinity coloured the rhetorical constructions of a politically independent Ireland, it is hardly far fetched to consider the idea that women writers would have responded in distinctive ways to the collapse of this dream. This is not to say, however, that there is a single 'female' response; the reverse is in fact the case. As I intend to show, Morgan's representation of Ireland in *The Wild Irish Girl* (1806) takes a very particular view of the role of the woman writer in the ambiguous public sphere of the post-Union period. Strongly influenced by Germaine de Staël, Morgan turns a marginal position into one which favours the articulation of a female voice, thus creating an identification between Ireland and femininity which proved tremendously influential. The difference between Edgeworth and Morgan, therefore, can be considered in terms of their different attitudes towards the Irish public sphere and the woman writer's relation to that sphere after the Union.

The Wild Irish Girl (1806) has been identified as the defining text of the post-Union period: according to Joep Leerssen it 'occupies a pivotal position, and marks a turning point in the literary representation of Ireland'.[9] *The Wild Irish Girl* deployed the trope of the 'national marriage' as a means to address the paradoxical situation of Ireland within the union – a means to account for the persistence of Irish 'difference' in the context of political assimilation. Staël's *De la littérature considérée dans ses rapports avec les institutions sociales* ('Literature considered in relation to social institutions') is a key source text for *The Wild Irish Girl*, and Morgan's representation of Anglo-Irish union takes on a very particular complexion when read in the light of Staël's text. In spite of the fact that Morgan's admiration for Staël has long been acknowledged, the precise extent of her indebtedness has never been fully explored.[10] One of the things that made *De la littérature* so available for Morgan's representation of Ireland was that it is, amongst other things, a reflection on the principle of union. In this pioneering treatise of literary sociology, Staël rewrote the narrative of European history by describing the invasion of the Roman Empire by the barbarians of the North as, in the words of the *Edinburgh Review*, an 'amalgamation of the two races' that 'produce[d] a mighty improvement on both'.[11] Staël's preoccupation with the concept of union reflects the fact that the union between Britain and Ireland was far from being unique in Europe. The historian James Livesey suggests that the Act of Union of 1800 should be regarded 'not as the second of two moments in the creation of the United Kingdom but as one of a plethora of European territorial dismemberments and integrations performed between 1770 and 1815.'[12] Thomas Bartlett similarly observes that the 'notion of union was very much in vogue' at the end of the eighteenth century.[13]

In addition to her interest in the concept of union, Staël shared with her Irish contemporaries a recent experience of violence and civil upheaval. By

1800, the year in which *De la littérature* was published, France had experienced a decade of almost unimaginable violence and conflict. The execution of the royal family, the Terror, civil war and revolutionary war had all contributed to the violence and bloodshed. Staël insisted nonetheless that events that appeared violent and destructive could produce lasting social benefit. Her primary conviction was perfectibility: 'in studying history, it appears to me that one acquires the conviction that all the principal events tend towards the same end, universal civilisation'.[14] The insistence on perfectibility has been identified as the cornerstone of her text, but rather like Darwin, whose breakthrough was not evolution but the principle of natural selection, Staël's intellectual break-through was the proposition that *union* was the mechanism by which this progress occurred, thus enabling the interpretation of conflict as progress. The fall of the Roman Empire and the invasion of Europe by Northern tribes according to Staël, therefore, was an absolutely necessary precondition for the development of European civilisation. The *Edinburgh Review* referred to this theory as a 'bold and ingenious speculation', rightly identifying it as the text's most important and most original idea.[15] The invasion of the Northern bar-barians, Staël claimed, initiated the civilisation of those peoples, a process which ultimately contributed to the perfection of European civilisation, while the energy of the barbarians reinvigorated the inhabitants of the Empire.

Staël's text was of course as much political as it was historical, and the potential for contemporary analogies with the 'barbarians' and 'Romans' of her historical narrative are fully exploited. On the one hand, the Third Estate can be seen as the 'Goths and Vandals', overturning the refined civilisation of the French *ancien régime*. On the other hand the 'North' and the 'South' of medieval Europe are also identifiable as present-day England and France, at war following the French Revolution.[16] What is perhaps unexpected is that these two apparently quite different analogies frequently collapse into one another. Although, in Burkean rhetoric especially, the French Revolution figured as the very antithesis of British identity, insofar as the revolution is bourgeois Staël sees its effects as akin to a partial 'anglicisation' of French culture. Staël presents this as the most desirable (if not necessarily the most likely) outcome of revolution. Like her father Jacques Necker, Staël was an anglophile, and in her posthumously published *Considerations on the French Revolution* she criticised the French for attempting to innovate when framing a new constitution, claiming that 'the English constitution offered the only example of the solution' of combining a constitutional monarchy with repre-sentative government, and arguing that 'a mania of vanity' induced the French to reject the English example.[17] She consistently upheld the British constitution as a model, and argued that a moderate constitutional monarchy would have been the best possible outcome of the revolution. The centrality of England to

Staël's thinking is reflected in the fact that her comments on Northern culture in *De la littérature* are almost wholly focused on England: she makes some brief references to Scandinavia and includes one chapter on Germany, against which there are four chapters specifically devoted to English literature and culture, including an entire chapter on Shakespeare, whose virtues and flaws she examines as representative of 'the spirit of Northern literature'.[18] According to Staël, the hallmark of Northern culture is secure enjoyment of political liberty. She claims that Northern literature is of a piece with a population which will not tolerate servitude and subjection: 'the poetry of the North accords much more than that of the South with the spirit of a free people'.[19] She also claims that the position of women in this society was (or is, given that present-day England is implied) vastly superior to that in 'Southern' societies: 'Northern people [. . .] have always had a respect for women unknown among Southern people; in the North they enjoyed independence, whilst elsewhere they were condemned to servitude.'[20] Staël's theory of progress through union and her championing of the British model are radically undermined within her own text, however, firstly by her ambivalence as to the role played by women in the transformed social order; and secondly by the portrayal of Britain as charac-terised by insularity and a stubborn refusal to accommodate 'foreign' influences.

Staël's comments on the role of women in pre-revolutionary France follow a standard line, portraying women as powerful social arbiters, and conceding to critics of that past era that 'they had, undoubtedly, too much influence on [political] affairs in the former regime'.[21] This concession could operate stra-tegically, in order to establish the basis for 'improvements' in the new, post-revolutionary era, in which the refined and ultra-civilised society of the *ancien régime* is united with the more manly and energetic influences of a bourgeoisie modelled on English lines. But Staël abandons her cherished concept in this instance. She in fact dismisses the idea that French women could achieve respect and admiration by uniting their talent for wit and elegance with the domestic virtues of their English counterparts:

> If the French could endow their wives with all the virtues of English women, their reserve, their taste for solitude, they would do well to prefer such qualities to all the gifts of a brilliant mind. However, what they would obtain from their wives would be a lack of reading, a lack of knowledge, and conversation devoid of an interesting idea, a felicitous expression, or elegant language.[22]

The reduced state which Staël envisages for women in the new social order is, moreover, not simply the result of shortcomings within the French nation. As Staël's *Considerations on the French Revolution* makes clear, she was in any case less than convinced that English society offered anything other than very restricted roles for women, remarking that Englishwomen were notably timid and retiring in conversation, and that they appeared by contrast with French-women to be dull and uninformed.[23] Her ambivalence as to the 'improvements' of a politically advanced society is further indicated, in *Considerations on the French Revolution*, in her assertion that the invisibility of Englishwomen in social life is inextricably bound up with the institutions of political liberty she admires so much: 'in a free country, men preserving their natural dignity, females feel themselves subordinate'.[24] In Staël's account, English society is in fact characterised by a public/private divide which she links directly to the much wider participation by men in politics and government which the English representative system allows.

Staël's core concept, union as the mechanism of progress, thus fails to offer any hope of improvement when it come to the status of women in society. It is also cast in grave doubt when Staël suggests that England itself is characterised by a stubborn resistance to absorbing ideas and influences from foreign cultures and societies. England is thus peculiarly resistant to the Staëlian project of progress through union. She refers to the English being 'separated from the continent' and says that they 'have never involved themselves in the history and practices of neighbouring peoples'.[25] Claiming that the spread of literature and information by means of print contributed to a cosmopolitan European culture, Staël makes the following statement about the persistence of English insularity:

> The discovery of printing has necessarily diminished the condescension of authors towards the tastes of their own people; they think more of the opinion of Europe; and however important it is that plays that are to be performed should be successful when they are produced, now that their fame can reach other countries, writers increasingly avoid allusions, jokes and characters which can only please the people of their own country. The English, however, will be the last to conform to these conventions of taste, for their liberty is founded more on national pride than on philosophical ideas. They reject every-thing which comes to them from foreigners, both in literature and in politics.[26]

The attractions of *De la littérature* for someone in Morgan's position are presumably obvious, and no less obvious are the troubling questions that it poses. On the face of it, Staël appears to be offering a model of union as an effect of conflict, but ultimately as a means to resolve conflict and promote progress: this enables a progressive interpretation of the recent union between Britain and Ireland. However, at certain key points, the text actually describes the failure of union. Staël also adopts an unrelentingly bleak tone when it comes to her consideration of what is in fact her own position – that of a woman writer. In the chapter 'Of Literary Women' Staël describes the woman writer in extraordinary terms as a 'pariah, forced to drag out her existence', and shunned, either hated or ridiculed. *De la littérature* could in fact be regarded as a fantastically elaborate construction of Staël's position as a woman writer struggling for recognition in a society in which intellectual women had been vilified as corrupting and destructive. This was, moreover, a position which united opinion right across the political spectrum, from French revolutionaries to British reactionaries. In spite of the stated optimism of its agenda, there-fore, *De la littérature* constructs the place of the woman writer as one of extreme marginality in the post-revolutionary context.

De la littérature is, as I said at the outset, essential for an understanding of Morgan's work. As well as adopting Staël's theory of North and South as mutually defining opposites and applying it to England and Ireland in *The Wild Irish Girl*, Morgan also adopted Staël's image of the woman writer as irredeemably marginal, and in fact played more and more on this idea in her later works. The extent to which Morgan positioned her works as 'other' to England can perhaps be appreciated by considering Staël's description of the 'typical' English novel. According to Staël, it is as a result of the peculiarly private nature of women's lives in England that English writers have excelled in a certain branch of literature: 'novels that do not treat of the fabulous, that are not allegorical, that make no historical allusions, but are founded on the construction of character and the events of private life'.[27] This description is of course based on a highly selective account of the eighteenth-century English novel, but it is nonetheless true that historical allusion and allegory are not part of the central tradition of the English novel, and are crucial to the design and agenda of *The Wild Irish Girl*. (Edgeworth's tales and novels are of course similarly remote from Staël's description.) It was precisely through the use of allegory, which enabled her to write novels which dealt on one level with senti-ment and feeling and on the other with politics and history, that Morgan made her innovative and influential contribution to the English-language novel. Staël adds to her remarks on the English novel that 'love has been the subject of these kinds of novel' and that 'the existence of women, in England, is the principal cause for the inexhaustible fertility of English writers in this genre'.[28] *The Wild Irish Girl* openly adopts and deploys the gendered constructs of national culture proposed in *De la littérature*, but instead of conforming to the purely domestic milieu which Staël insists is the special provenance of English fiction, Morgan uses romantic love to shape and express ideas about national and political formations, creating what Claire Connolly calls 'a knot of erotic and political energy'.[29] The conjunction of the political and the erotic is often read in terms of radical potential, but I suggest that Morgan's adoption of Staël's paradigm is not in any way radical and results in a very limited and limiting construction of Ireland, partly because Morgan maps onto Staël's binary oppositions a sectarian politics, effectively constructing Ireland as monolithically Catholic.

The fact that *The Wild Irish Girl* portrays Ireland as 'other' to England is well established: for Joep Leerssen it encapsulates the idea of the 'auto-exotic', or 'self-as-other'.[30] This otherness is expressed in a variety of ways – through the depiction of a sublime landscape and references to the genre of gothic fiction, for instance, and of course in the person of the 'wild Irish girl' herself, Glorvina, who exercises such a powerful fascination over the English hero, Mortimer. But the specifically erotic quality of this otherness, as far as Glorvina is concerned, is released through references to French novels, chief amongst them Rousseau's *La Nouvelle Héloïse*, signalling the fact that both France and Ireland occupy, in Morgan's view, the same position in relation to England. Mortimer makes a gift to Glorvina of several novels, 'all precisely such books as Glorvina had *not*, yet *should* read, that she may know herself, and the latent sensibility of her soul'.[31] With the exception of Goethe's *Werther*, all are French novels, which prompts Mortimer to remark:

> Let our English novels carry away the prize of morality from the romantic fictions of every other country; but you will find they rarely seize on the imagination through the medium of the heart. (139)

Mortimer then begins to observe the 'sentimental sorcery' of Rousseau at work in the behaviour of Glorvina, who, he conjectures, 'begin[s] to feel she has an heart' (143). On one level, this might seem to suggest an equivalence between Ireland and France, both 'exotic' from the normative English point of view, both invested with erotic potential. It is hard to ignore the fact, however, that, as 'other', Glorvina is very clearly shaped in terms of the hero's desires. The radical implications of female desire are thus effectively neutralised: Glorvina only feels she 'has a heart' in response to the ideas suggested to her by Mortimer's favourite books.

The political implications of this construction in the specific context of the Act of Union are made apparent in the way in which Morgan proposes her own, locally adjusted, version of the Staëlian 'North' and 'South'. Although these terms can clearly be mapped onto England and Ireland respectively, Morgan also insists on an internal division between the north and the south of Ireland itself, a distinction which is elaborated by the priest Father John when Mortimer accompanies him on a journey to the north of Ireland:

> Here [. . .] the bright beams which illumine the gay images of Milesian fancy are extinguished; the convivial pleasures, dear to the Milesian heart, scared

at the prudential maxims of calculating interest, take flight to the warmer regions of the south; and the endearing socialities of the soul, lost and neglected amidst the cold concerns of the counting-house and *the bleach green*, droop and expire in the deficiency of that nutritive warmth on which their tender existence depends. (192)

Mortimer's guide freely admits that this region is 'the palladium of Irish industry and Irish trade', and presents a crass contrast with the 'Southern provinces', in which the 'wretched native [. . .] either famishes in the midst of a helpless family, or begs his way to England' (192). In spite of this he concludes that, although a visitor might admire and respect the 'Northerns of this island', 'on the heart they make little claims, and from its affections they receive but little tribute' (192, 193). The reason for this striking contrast is, according to Father John, that in the north of Ireland, Scottish character has been has been 'engrafted' upon the 'true' Irish character (168). This episode therefore uses Staël's paradigm not to suggest internal differences within Ireland, but in fact to exclude Presbyterian Ulster from the text's construction of Irishness.

It is evident that in writing *The Wild Irish Girl* Morgan was keen to present Irish Catholics in as favourable a light as possible, for obvious reasons: emancipation had not, as anticipated, followed the Union and it appeared that deep-rooted anti-Catholic prejudice, at both elite and popular levels in Britain and Ireland, was a serious obstacle.[32] The text therefore features references to the 'picturesqueness' of Catholic ritual, to the lack of bigotry Mortimer encounters, to the benevolent, essentially conservative leadership of Catholic clerics, and so on. None of this explains, however, why the descendants of Scottish settlers, overwhelmingly Presbyterian and settled in Ulster, *have* to be excluded, marked as 'not belonging'. The leading role played by Ulster Presbyterians in the United Irish movement may have played a part in Morgan's anxiety to expatriate them; although according to Ian McBride, the collapse of radicalism in the Presbyterian community was very rapid indeed following the disastrous events of 1798.[33] The dualistic structure itself, however, borrowed from Staël, demands the representation of Ireland as culturally and ethnically monolithic. Ireland cannot be represented as displaying internal contrasts (or even conflicts) because all contrasts must be drawn between Ireland and its partner in union. What is more, the same essentialism applies to the other partner in this union: it is specifically constructed as England, rather than Britain, by the exclusion of Scotland.

This exclusion is achieved in an interesting case of linguistic slippage which occurs during a discussion of James Macpherson's Ossian poems.[34] The response to Macpherson's work in Ireland differed significantly from that in Britain. The view of Macpherson as a fraud was very generally held in Ireland, but for reasons other than those of British sceptics. Whereas in England the high antiquity claimed for the poems aroused scepticism, in Ireland the argument focused on the origin of the tales, which Macpherson naturally claimed were native to the Scottish Highlands. The denunciation of Macpherson's claims to 'authenticity' was inevitable from an Irish point of view. Unlike the situation in Scotland, Irish scholars and enthusiasts did not, therefore, engage in debates about the extent to which the translations might have been stylistically and morally cleaned up, focusing instead on his 'theft' of Irish material. The discussion of Macpherson in *The Wild Irish Girl* functions superficially as one of the very many proofs of Irish culture and civility: given the huge popularity of the Ossian poems, Morgan, like many others in Ireland, was keen to prove that the material was Irish in origin. Glorvina's father, the 'Prince of Inismore', gives vent to feelings of wounded patriotism in relation to Macpherson's 'theft', and Father John provides evidence of Ossian's Irishness based on scholarly antiquarianism. The really significant moment, however, occurs when Glorvina succeeds in mediating between the cultural claims of the Irish and the need to assimilate to English modes. She describes the eighteenth-century overlay in Macpherson as part of the necessary progress of poetry, a progress symbolised as the shift from speech to writing:

> Long before I could read, I learned on the bosom of my nurse, and in my father's arms, to recite the songs of our national bards, and almost since I could read, the Ossian of Macpherson has been the object of my enthusiastic admiration. (111)

Glorvina goes so far as to 'acknowledge the superior merit of Mr Macpherson's poems, as compositions, over those wild effusions of our Irish bards whence he compiled them' (111), and concludes by saying that 'when my heart is coldly void, when my spirits are sunk and drooping, I fly to my English Ossian, and then my sufferings are soothed' (112). Glorvina's reference to Macpherson's text as the 'English Ossian' differentiates it linguistically from the Irish-language originals which she first experienced, but also conveniently obliterates Macpherson's Scottishness. Together with the marginalisation of the 'Scottish colony' in the north of Ireland, this provides a very clear picture of what, in Morgan's representation, had been united in the recent Act of Union. Morgan effectively bolsters metropolitan cultural hegemony by making it clear that Ireland's interests lie in being assimilated and reconciled to England. The construction of this political relationship through the metaphor of erotic love contributes to its exclusive nature: in both erotic and political relationships, it seems, three is most definitely a crowd.[35]

The Wild Irish Girl, as the originator of the national tale genre, could not have been written without *De la littérature*. Staël's comparative method and her construction of France and England as mutually self-defining opposites form the conceptual and structural basis of Morgan's national tale. It is vital to acknowledge that Staël's post-revolutionary view of culture is coloured by doubts and anxieties as to the role of the woman writer, and that her thesis is underpinned by a view of England as a place in which men can function as free agents in a public sphere and women, in consequence, have a particularly restricted sphere of action. *The Wild Irish Girl*'s eroticisation and sentimental-isation of politics are one way in which an Irish woman writer could, in these circumstances, insert her voice into the public sphere. This attention to the specifically gendered quality of Morgan's work conflicts with Leerssen's description of her characteristic strategy, the 'auto-exoticist reflex', as 'the main literary repercussion of the collapse of Patriotism in Ireland'. Leerssen goes on: 'To put it crudely: Ireland, if it cannot be a nation in its own right and is reduced to a province, is increasingly described in the discourse of marginality and in terms of its being different or picturesque.'[36]

As we have seen, however, the adoption of a marginalised position was also suggested to Morgan by her literary exemplar, Germaine de Staël, and Morgan seems to have actively embraced the marginal position involved in a feminised intervention in matters of public concern. In other words, the construction of a marginalised, auto-exoticised Ireland arises out of the intersection between the options open to Morgan as a woman writer in the context of the Union and the attendant collapse of a (masculinised) Patriot ideology. Leerssen has little to say about Maria Edgeworth, whom he regards as having very little in common with Morgan, but when he does attempt to account for the dif-ferences between the two writers he, like many others, focuses on class – 'the difference [. . .] between their respective family backgrounds'.[37] The following analysis of *Castle Rackrent* and *An Essay on Irish Bulls* will propose that the 'differences' stem in part from the very different approach that Edgeworth adopts towards the problem of articulating a voice in the Irish public sphere after the Union. The different routes of access to and intervention in the public sphere imagined in these texts create a very different picture of Irishness after the Union: it is characterised not in terms of romantic otherness, but as a function of the instability in the public sphere and an alternating reliance on and questioning of Enlightenment promises about self and society.

One way in which to describe the controversial relationship between the narrative voice and the voice of the editorial commentary in *Castle Rackrent* is in terms of how it approaches the status of a text in the public sphere of print: the Preface explicitly articulates doubts and questions about what kind of utterances can claim a place in this sphere and defends its offer of a highly unconventional voice. *Castle Rackrent*, as has often been pointed out, is some-thing of an exception in Edgeworth's career. Its exceptionality is further described by some critics in terms of its superiority to her later fiction, in that it is claimed as a near-miraculous display of creativity uniquely untainted by didacticism.[38] According to this view, the textual apparatus was an after-thought, an (unsuccessful) attempt to control the subversive meanings of the narrative. This interpretation has been challenged more recently, by Robert Tracy for instance, who suggests that such readings of *Castle Rackrent* have caricatured the relationship between the narrative and its editorial apparatus, and who argues that the text is 'much more sophisticated and complex than it once seemed' and that 'to return to this text in the light of recent feminist and postcolonial critical writings is to recognise its explicit and implicit subtleties'.[39] Marilyn Butler has also cautioned against reading the editorial commentary as a 'straightforward' assertion of authorial control, and suggests instead that 'read as a philosophical tale, [*Castle Rackrent*] becomes virtually parodic, an absurd example of intellectuals (the antiquaries of the Glossary) slumming among the children of nature'.[40]

Some recent feminist criticism has, however, focused once again on the supposed disjunction between Thady's narrative and the voice of the editor, reviving the tradition of regarding the former as the creation of Maria Edgeworth, for once in her life escaping the control of her father, and the latter as the product of Richard Lovell Edgeworth's belated intervention.[41] This implies that the narrative and the editorial commentary are gendered, as feminine and masculine respectively. The supposed gendering of the different voices in the text takes on further layers of meaning when considered in relation to the public and private spheres. Ann Owens Weekes broke new ground in discussions of *Castle Rackrent* by emphasising the importance of the 'domestic plot', which had hitherto been virtually ignored, and it will be clear that my own reading of the text is informed by it. She points out that Edgeworth developed Thady's voice initially as a way of amusing her aunt Ruxton and cousin Sophy:

> The genesis of this text is important not simply as a historical note but because it accounts to a large extent for *Castle Rackrent*'s excellencies. Writing 'for amusement only' and thus freed from the restraints she felt when publishing or going public, Edgeworth explored with her intimate confidantes the contra-dictions in the landlord–tenant relationships and the uncertainties and potential dangers in the marriage contract.[42]

This argument positions Edgeworth very close to Thady, describing the voice of his narrative as arising out of the closeness between Edgeworth and her female relatives, and therefore aligning the narrative with privacy and femininity. Weekes points out that the Preface, with its comments on the significance of private life, 'points to the important patterns that Edgeworth inscribed in the text', but she also describes the Preface primarily as an act of 'deflection' and 'distancing'.[43] She thus points to a much more interesting reading of the relation between editorial voice and narrative voice, but fails to pursue it. As I want to argue, in as much as the Preface claims the 'public' value of the private narrative that it presents to the reading public, *Castle Rackrent* claims the existence of some relationship between these two supposedly separate spheres. The text thus has vital implications for what place Edgeworth imagined for her writing in the Irish 'public sphere' at this key moment.

The well-known account of the composition of *Castle Rackrent*, as given by Maria Edgeworth in 1834, is often used to support the claim that Thady's narrative, considered in isolation from the rest of the text, is the unpremeditated product of a moment of creative inspiration. Edgeworth describes herself almost as a medium: '[Thady] seemed to stand beside me and dictate, and I wrote as fast as my pen could go'.[44] Marilyn Butler describes this account in terms of 'modesty' and remarks that it 'has run like a contagion through the critical literature on *Castle Rackrent*'.[45] Brian Hollingworth is similarly sceptical of the view that *Castle Rackrent* is 'a piece of unsophisticated vernacular reportage which chanced to be published in 1800'.[46] Hollingworth reminds us of what should be a self-evident fact, that 'to publish an Irish story in January 1800 was a political act'.[47] The haste with which the editorial apparatus was added and then sent for publication, he claims, is indicative of the Edgeworths' desire to situate the text alongside pamphlets and other pieces on Ireland and Irish politics in advance of the Act of Union. W. J. Mc Cormack implicitly endorses the view of *Castle Rackrent* as a contribution to what he calls the 'pamphlet war' by including it in his own listing of pamphlets published on the Union question between 1797 and 1800.[48] It is, however, clear that *Castle Rackrent* represents a very singular contribution to this debate, firstly because it appears to insist on private rather then public discourses as sources of truth, and secondly because, in spite of statements which appear to endorse the Union, its ultimate effect according to many commentators is to undermine the very notion of union between the 'Ireland' represented in Thady's narrative and the 'England' addressed by the editorial voice. Daniel Hack has suggested that 'the text chiastically rearranges Richard Edgeworth's ambivalence, so that whereas he believed in Union but voted against it, the text votes in favour of Union but makes it inconceivable'.[49] The danger here, I suggest, is the familiar lapse into the binary opposition between editorial and narrative voices, the one 'voting in favour of union', the other 'making it inconceivable'. The fact is that the voice of the editorial apparatus is far from being consistent. In the Notes and Glossary, the voice is sometimes that of a folklore collector; sometimes it is that of the enlightened commentator, assuring his English audience that

Ireland is no longer as backward as the narrative makes it seem; and sometimes, such as in the note on the use of wigs in Ireland, it gravely asserts 'facts' that are even more comic than those voiced by Thady. This makes it all the more puzzling that, in the last paragraph of the preface and in the conclusion of the tale itself, in which the editorial voice takes over abruptly from Thady's narrative, such a specific agenda with respect to the Act of Union is apparently claimed for the narrative. If we accept Hollingworth's suggestion that the haste which characterised the publication of *Castle Rackrent* reflected the desire of the Edgeworths to contribute to the Union debates, we might ask ourselves why the Edgeworths were so anxious to publish a text of such indeterminate meaning at such a sensitive political time.

The key issues here, I suggest, are exactly those of indeterminacy and sensitivity. The editorial comment which concludes Thady's narrative presents a famous and rather disturbing image of union in its question: 'Did the Warwickshire militia, who were chiefly artisans, teach the Irish to drink beer, or did they learn from the Irish to drink whiskey?' This makes clear something that is never explicitly mentioned, and that is that the Act of Union referred to in *Castle Rackrent* was proposed just two years after the violence of the United Irishmen's rising, and the state violence that followed it. The extent to which the Union was conditioned by the events of 1798 is a matter of some debate among historians, but the view expressed by Patrick Geoghegan, that 'the Irish Act of Union was made out of the embers of the 1798 rebellion', is widely held.[50] Furthermore, Claire Connolly has observed that the military suppression of the rebellion was carried on simultaneously with the government campaign in favour of union, thus making the 'conjunction between parliamentary and military powers' highly visible – not least as they were embodied in the person of Lord Cornwallis, 'acting uniquely as both lord lieutenant and commander in chief of the army'.[51] Union was therefore a concept proposed in an atmosphere of suspicion, violence, fear and threat. The expression of opinions on the Union was an endeavour fraught with controversy, and the Edgeworth family had already had their own share of controversy during the rising, when they faced threats from rebels and 'orange' mobs alike. Even in the early 1790s, with increasing agitation for reform of the newly 'independent' Irish parliament, the emergence of the term 'Protestant Ascendancy' as a response to the demands of Catholics for some representation in the legislature indicated the increasingly divisive nature of Irish public life. Following the rising, Richard Musgrave's notorious *Memoirs of the Different Rebellions in Ireland* (1801) used the compendium of 'Catholic' atrocities to argue that Catholics must always be excluded from the legislature, and amongst the many cases for Union was its supposed necessity as a means to safeguard the Protestant Anglo-Irish from their treacherous and violent countrymen. The variety and intensity of views on the Union resulted in a huge amount of pamphleteering and comment: Mc Cormack's list of pamphlets on the union published between 1797 and 1800 runs to over 300.[52]

It is, I suggest, in response to this climate, in which public debate was widespread but was hardly ever 'reasoned', that Edgeworth (and, one assumes, her father in so far as he assisted in the publication) chose in *Castle Rackrent* to represent Ireland as a place which is articulable *not* by means of the enlightened discourse of the male public sphere, but through a highly personal and local voice. Claire Connolly proposes that R. L. Edgeworth's decision to vote against the Union, and to leave the House just before the Bill was passed, represents 'a loss of faith in the powers of persuasion and indeed public discussion altogether'.[53] It is in this context, that of a loss of faith in the possibilities of the public sphere, that we should locate *Castle Rackrent*. The text creates a unique fictional voice, emphasising its unauthoritative and 'anecdotal' nature, but placing it unambiguously in relation to the Act of Union (however ambiguous the conclusions may be, the relationship is clearly signalled). Whereas William Drennan urged his audience of (male) Volunteers to 'make news' rather than to demean their masculinity by indulging in an immature excess of loquacity, the 'editor' of *Castle Rackrent* asserts that the value of Thady's narration lies in the fact that it is delivered 'with all the minute prolixity of detail of a gossip in a country town'.[54]

As Weekes has observed, the preface argues for private, domestic narratives as a source of 'truth' with greater claims to our attention than the apparently authoritative discourse of history. History is associated with the public, and with a corresponding degree of falsehood:

> The heroes of history are so decked out by the fine fancy of the professed historian; they talk in such measured prose, and act from such sublime or such diabolical motives, that few have sufficient taste, wickedness or heroism, to sympathise in their fate. [. . .] We cannot judge either of the feelings or of the characters of men with perfect accuracy, from their actions or their appearance in public; it is from their careless conversations, their half-finished sentences, that we may hope with the greatest probability of success to discover their real characters. (5)

The editor does at first glance appear to invite readers to share with him sense of moral and intellectual superiority over the narrator. The only reason he is to be trusted, apparently, is because his 'vulgar errors' will be immediately obvious to readers. This apparent complacency is, however, subverted by the editor's subsequent observation that 'we never bow to the authority of him who has no great name to sanction his absurdities' (6). The preface is thus much more challenging to the idea of truth than some have supposed. Here, Edgeworth slyly suggests that readers really prefer to have their thinking done for them. By claiming that the public are disposed to accept 'great names' as authorities she undermines one of the fundamental principles of the 'Republic of Letters', in which ideal, rational subjects are imagined to be able to discriminate between texts and utterances on the basis of reason.[55] Implicitly, Edgeworth also suggests that the attribution of authority to a speaker or writer is culturally and socially determined rather than arising as a result of the operations of enlightened reason. The voice of the Preface, therefore, far from positioning itself in unambiguous superiority to Thady's narrative, suggests some of the ways in which questions of gender and class operate either to include or exclude texts and speakers from the realm of public discourse. Rather than make clear and unambiguous distinctions between reliable and unreliable speakers, as some critics have asserted, *Castle Rackrent* takes huge, and successful, risks by bringing readers face to face with the difficulty of establishing a reliable point of view.

Instead of viewing *Castle Rackrent* as a burst of exuberant creativity, unsuccessfully tethered to a respectable intellectual agenda, there is therefore room to consider it as a text that sets out to play with, if not exactly to undermine, the idea of all writing as shaped by agendas, whether ideological or aesthetic. The preface begins, as noted above, by disputing the claims of history to objectivity or 'truth'. Historians, it is suggested, sacrifice truth to the need to represent men as heroes or villains. Literature, too, is compromised by its own concerns, in this case aesthetic concerns: 'those who are used to literary manufacture know how much is often sacrificed to the rounding of a period, or the pointing of an antithesis' (6). This philosophical concern with the relative nature of truth and the extent to which truth is determined by ideological convictions is, moreover, not solely the preserve of the educated editorial voice: Thady's narrative builds towards the collapse and exposure of the ideological system on which it is based, a crisis which provokes the narrator into reflective self-examination.

Thady's stated purpose is to tell his story 'out of friendship for the family', and the reader of course derives much pleasure from seeing this purpose subverted, whether intentionally or unintentionally. The 'family' that Thady apparently sets out to praise is defined very narrowly by him: his loyalties – unsurprisingly – flow in the same direction as the right of inheritance. Thady's constantly reiterated use of the word 'family' to describe what is in fact a system of property ownership and transfer prompts us to consider other meanings of the word, which are notable by their absence in the text. Feminist readings of *Castle Rackrent* have highlighted its subversive relationship to what one critic has called 'patrilineal orthodoxies', and it has been noted that with the exception of Sir Patrick, none of the Rackrent men produces heirs, and that their marriages are spectacularly unsuccessful.[56] The apparently unstructured quality of the narrative, which features frequent digressions and interjections, conceals the fact that Thady's attitude to and relationship with each of the wives is dwelt on at some length, and his presence at the scenes of their departure becomes a significant motif. The departure of Sir Murtagh's wife, originally of the Skinflint family, suggests some of the peculiar tensions of the relationship:

> She had a fine jointure settled upon her, and took herself away to the great joy of the tenantry. I never said anything one way or the other, whilst she was part of the family, but got up to see her go at three o'clock in the morning. 'It's a fine morning, honest Thady', says she; 'good bye to ye', and into the carriage she stept, without a word more good or bad, or even half a crown; but I made my bow, and stood to see her safe out of sight for the sake of the family. (14)

Thady's sense that the 'honour of the family' requires a formal acknowledgement of this kind also betrays the recognition that he, as a servant, is the only person who thinks to offer this courtesy. The scene is in fact highly stylised. The redundant woman and the servant are, in this representation, equals.

The next Lady Rackrent, Sir Kit's wife, experiences marital cruelty of a kind normally associated with Gothic fiction. Her crime is not to make her personal wealth available to fund her husband's reckless, spendthrift lifestyle. Thady represents her imprisonment by Sir Kit as an understandable reaction to intolerable provocation. Following Sir Kit's death and her release, however, he clearly considers the possibility of forming an alliance with her:

> Had she meant to make any stay in Ireland, I stood a great chance of being a great favourite with her; for when she found I understood the weathercock, she was always finding some pretence to be talking to me, and asking me which way the wind blew, and was it likely, did I think, to continue fair for England. But when I saw she had made up her mind to spend the rest of her days upon her own income and jewels in England, I considered her quite as a foreigner, and not at all any longer as part of the family. (23)

Sir Condy's wife, Isabella, is portrayed in much greater detail than the Rackrent wives of previous generations: she is, for instance, the only wife whose first name is given to us. Isabella is comically depicted as a sentimental heroine who has lost her way and ended up in a narrative that fails to answer any of her expectations. She attempts to insulate herself from the chaos around her and the realisation of the mistake she has made in marrying Sir Condy by reading *The Sorrows of Werther*. *Werther* is, as we have seen, symbolically deployed in *The Wild Irish Girl*, where Glorvina is made available for the union of English and Irish through her reading of the novel. Here it suggests that Isabella has married Condy with particular expectations that are both 'modern' and highly unrealistic. Unlike the previous marriages, in which the financial motives for marriage are overwhelmingly and, in Sir Kit's case, brutally apparent, the marriage of Condy and Isabella is an awkward mix of financial and emotional considerations. The portrayal of the marriage focuses, for the first time, on the couple's incompatibility and unhappiness in a relatively realistic domestic framework. Isabella, for instance, complains of Condy's drinking because it disrupts the kind of marital companionship she is hoping for. Condy expresses an ineffectual desire to make his wife happy and allows her personal freedom and choice, by letting her entertain and produce private theatricals at Castle Rackrent. It is significant that unlike Sir Murtagh's wife Isabella exercises her freedom not by thrifty and lucrative housekeeping practices, but by spending and consuming.

Isabella's departure from Castle Rackrent differs from that of her predecessors, in that she leaves Condy and returns to her family, the Moneygawls, when it becomes apparent that the estate is utterly bankrupt. Having surreptitiously witnessed the scene in which Isabella announces her decision to leave, and then literally witnessed the memorandum in which Condy attempts to ensure some financial provision for his wife, Thady, once again, describes the departure of the lady of the house and displays sensitivity as to the conditions under which she leaves:

> The next morning my lady and Mrs Jane set out for Mount Juliet's town in the jaunting car; many wondered at my lady's choosing to go away, considering all things, upon the jaunting car, as if it was only a party of pleasure; but they did not know, till I told them, that the coach was all broke in the journey down, and no other vehicle but the car to be had; besides, my lady's friends were to send their coach to meet her at the cross roads; so it was all done very proper. (41)

In spite of Thady's assurances that everything was 'done very proper', it becomes apparent that the departure of this Lady Rackrent marks a phase in the fortunes of the family which his world-view cannot accommodate. Thady's assertions of loyalty and friendship are at this point seriously undermined by the fact that his son Jason has established a stranglehold on Condy's fortune and estate. Critics have argued for Thady's complicity in Jason's schemes, thus portraying him as a cynical manipulator who uses his 'loyalty' as a mask to conceal his self-interest.[57] Thady is certainly self-interested: he openly regards the family as a legitimate source of income and advantage, and does not actually hide this as he does not think that it is wrong. His moral certainty does not last, however. The collapse of Condy's marriage and Judy McQuirk's contemptuous response to Thady's suggestion that she might be the next Lady Rackrent – 'what signifies it to be my lady Rackrent, and no castle?' (51–2) – leaves Thady with the uncomfortable realisation that he no longer knows where his interest lies. Judy laughs at his folly in 'following the fortunes of them that have none left' (52) and his sister Sheelagh then agrees that he is an 'unnatural' father not to applaud Judy's desire to marry his son, Jason. Thady reflects on the sudden complexity of a situation of which he had been master:

> Well, I was never so put to it in my life: between these womens [*sic*], and my son and my master, and all I felt and thought just now, I could not, upon my conscience, tell which was the wrong from the right. (52)

Thady's use of the words 'wrong' and 'right' should be considered very carefully. It is evident that for Thady moral and material considerations are closely connected. What he experiences here, for the first time, is a sense of disjunction between his notion of what is morally right – his loyalty to Sir Condy – and what is materially advantageous – Judy's shrewd assessment of Jason's wealth and power. Far from indicting Thady as barbarous or infantile, his perplexity as to the relationship between virtue and self-interest places his narrative in the context of contemporary philosophical and political debate. Classical notions of virtue centred on the ideal of the heroic sacrifice of self-interest, and Thomas Hobbes had described self-interest as a selfish, destructive impulse that had to be kept in check by the state, but philosophers of the Scottish Enlightenment, in works such as Adam Smith's *Theory of Moral Sentiments* (1759), had proposed self-interest as a means of social progress and improvement and suggested that individual virtue was in fact characterised by its contribution to the social good. Edgeworth's affinity with this school, as discussed in the previous chapter, is evident in characters such as Angelina and Forester (heroes of two of the *Moral Tales*), who thought that living in society was incompatible with virtue and happiness. In *Castle Rackrent*, however, Edgeworth presents us with two versions of self-interest, neither of which seems to bear any relation at all to the social good. Thady's difficulty may be due in part to the fact that the subject of his narrative, the 'story of a family', is not as straightforward as it appears. Thady indicates that for the story to make any sense at all some people must be excluded, treated 'quite as foreigners'. This relates to the struggle to shape coherent meanings and to decide what is 'wrong' and what is 'right'. The tensions culminate in the scene just discussed, in which Thady for the first time finds himself unable to reconcile the two meanings of family: the claims of his son and the claims of his master are completely at odds, and one of the two must be excluded for Thady to feel that what he is doing is right.

The narrative thus acts as an extension or illustration of the scepticism expressed in the preface as to the ability of the educated and literate public to decide for themselves what is true or reliable, and what is not. Both editorial commentary and narrative betray uncertainty about fundamental principles of Enlightenment. In experiencing a crisis in his own previously complacent sense of 'wrong' and 'right', however, it could be said that Thady undergoes one of the stages in the process of Enlightenment: he no longer has confidence in what he has 'traditionally' believed. This is an interesting version of Enlightenment, to say the least. Firstly, it has come about as a result of a collapse in the material and social world, and renders him unfit to continue in the role he has played, but with no other role he can assume. It should also be noted that it is two women of the Irish lower classes who expose Thady's own confusion to him. When Judy asks 'What signifies it to be my lady Rackrent, and no castle?' she reveals that she at any rate is not a slave to inherited notions of status and deference. This is Enlightenment as an effect, rather than an ideal, an Enlightenment that is explicitly linked to social and economic modernisation, with the elements of loss and trauma that that entails. The Union that is referred to in the text as imminent will, it is implied, hasten these changes, given that the replacement of Irish gentlemen with British manufacturers is envisaged. Contrary to the common assumption that the editorial commentary is unsuccessful in its insistence that the archaic practices described in *Castle Rackrent* are features of 'former times', it appears that the Ireland depicted on the eve of Union is actually 'modernised', although the effects of such a modernisation are disorienting and destabilising. Declan Kiberd, in a very suggestive reading of *Castle Rackrent*, argues that in this text, Edgeworth 'destroy[s] the epistemological foundations – of realism and science – on which the Union was based'; but could it be instead that the text envisages the Union as the outcome of a collapse of Enlightenment 'realism and science'?[58]

An Essay on Irish Bulls exhibits a similar uncomfortable clarity with regard to Enlightenment. Mitzi Myers has in fact suggested that *Irish Bulls* anticipates the postmodernist collapse of the 'once hegemonic, logico-deductive models of reason and knowledge' and their replacement by 'little anecdotes and local knowledges'.[59] At the risk of stating the obvious, *An Essay on Irish Bulls* explores the notion of national particularity. In its ironic proposal to investigate the precise nature of the 'Irish Bull', to determine and pinpoint exactly what kind of linguistic blunders and absurdities can properly be termed 'Irish', the text exposes the way in which notions of national character and national particularity are as much the product of social, economic and political power imbalances as they are 'traditional', 'inherited' or 'essential'. The introductory chapters claim that a rigorous application of logic will be used to sweep away what is 'spurious' and to arrive at reliable definitions. These claims are, however, ironic and disingenuous: the aim of the authors seems to be to illustrate that the 'existence' of Irish bulls cannot be proven or disproven, because their existence forms part of a system of prejudice. Like *Castle Rackrent*, therefore, *Irish Bulls* confronts situations in which Enlightenment orthodoxies are challenged to the point of collapse. Whereas Edgeworth, in *Letters for Literary Ladies*, insisted on the continued usefulness of 'philosophy' and 'reason', here when key words such as 'reason' and 'custom' are deployed, they imply that English attitudes to Ireland fall well below the standard of rational behaviour which is supposed to be indicative of an advanced society:

> We need not apprehend, that to ridicule our hibernian neighbours unmercifully is unfriendly or ungenerous. Nations, it has been well observed, are never generous in their conduct towards each other. We must follow the common *custom* of nations, where we have no *law* to guide our proceedings.[60]

> We must not listen to what is called reason; we must not enter into any argument, pro or con, but silence every Irish opponent, if we can, with a laugh. (87)

The 'common custom' of nations places Ireland in the same position as France with respect to England:

> That species of monopolising pride, which inspires one nation with the belief that all the rest of the world are barbarians, and speak barbarisms, is evidently a very useful prejudice, which the English, with their usual good sense, have condescended to adopt from the Greeks and Romans. They have applied it judiciously in their treatment of France and Ireland.[61]

Edgeworth acknowledges that national identity relies on the demonisation of the 'foreign', and that Ireland and France play the same role in the negative definition of English identity in contrast to an assumed hostile other. In fact, the prejudices against the Irish are in certain respects greater than those against the French, given that 'no Irishism can ever deserve to be Anglicised, though so many Gallicisms have of late not only been naturalised in England, but even adopted by the most fashionable speakers and writers' (86).

One of the most extraordinary features of *An Essay on Irish Bulls* is the authors' insistence on placing their discussion of language and culture within a sharply realised political context, the 'heated paranoid atmosphere of the 1790s'.[62] They do not shrink from associating the apparently harmless comic stereotypes perpetuated in England with much more dangerous and divisive prejudices. In the chapter entitled 'Irish Newspapers', the authors move, seemingly at random, from trivial and comic examples to those which are drawn from the recent experience of violence which had convulsed the country. The disposition to attribute 'blame' without regard to facts is common to assumptions of stupidity and assumptions of criminality: 'By this convenient mode of reasoning, an Irishman may, at any time, be convicted of any crime, or any absurdity' (83). This observation is made with reference to the conviction of an Irish physician in a 'popish plot'. The reference to popish plots was at this precise moment replete with contemporary meaning, with a vocal faction insisting on describing the rebellion in exclusively and violently sectarian terms, simply the latest in a series of 'popish' attempts to overthrow the Protestant state.[63] The text itself indicates this connection, by moving from the seventeenth-century example to contemporary newspaper reports of violent crime and the activities of the 'united men'. Unlike Richard Musgrave, whose dogged intent was to prove the unchangingly treacherous nature of the Catholic Irish, the Edgeworths suggest on the one hand that the persistence of prejudice and stereotype is a more serious obstacle to political progress, and on the other that the hysteria occasioned by political and civil violence is an unsound basis upon which to act. Referring to the decision of the authorities in Munich to draw up a catalogue of banned books, and then, absurdly, to ban the catalogue itself, the authors ironically remark: 'But this might be done in the hurry occasioned by the just dread of revolutionary principles' (83). The rapidity with which reason gives way to unreason is reflected in the following remarks on the United Irishmen's rising:

> It has often been said, that the language of a people is a just criterion of their progress in civilization; but we must not take a specimen of their vocabulary during the immediate prevalence of any transient passion or prejudice. It is to be hoped, that all party barbarisms in language will now be disused and forgotten; for some time has elapsed since we read the following article of country intelligence in a Dublin paper: –
>
> 'General – scoured the country yesterday, but had not the good fortune to meet with a single rebel.'
>
> The author of this paragraph seems to have been a keen sportsman; he regrets the not meeting with a single rebel, as he would the not meeting with a single hare or partridge; and he justly considers the human biped as fair game, to be hunted down by all who are properly qualified and licensed by government. (85)

Further references to the rising are found throughout the text, in chapters entitled 'Practical Bulls' and 'Irish Wit and Eloquence'; in an indirect reference, the 'Hibernian Mendicant' tells of his rivalry with an English soldier who abuses the Irish as savages: this dispute, originating in verbal insults, has a fatal outcome.

As a contribution to the debate on the Union, these sharply observed and highly political comments are apparently at odds with the 'sincere wish to conciliate both countries' (153) which the authors assure us is theirs. Much of *Irish Bulls* is recognisable as belonging to the general Edgeworthian perspective on Ireland, not least the authors' declaration that they are 'more interested in the fate of the present race of its inhabitants' (152) than in the ancient kings and tribes beloved of antiquarian historians. Equally characteristic are the frequent references to Scotland as an important future partner for Ireland in the Union, rather than focusing exclusively on the relationship with the dominant English nation, as Morgan, for instance, does. It is, nonetheless, rather difficult to accept the description of *An Essay on Irish Bulls* as 'a tactical and tactful way of interpreting 1800, as an invitation to another national partner to join the British nation in which the Scots had already established the ground rules for diverse but equal membership'.[64] The image of the Union as it emerges from the pages of *Irish Bulls* is negatively coloured by the persistence of stereotype and prejudice, aspects of the Anglo-Irish relationship which have remained stubbornly intractable. Whereas *Castle Rackrent* imagines Ireland in the immediate post-Union period as traumatically enlightened as a result of social and economic modernisation, *Irish Bulls* represents the Anglo-Irish relationship, in satirical fashion, as one of the limits of Enlightenment. The conclusion of the last inset narrative, 'The Irish Incognito' is that the irrational, negatively constructed Irishness which has been produced by the long and often hostile history of interrelation between Ireland and England will just have to be worn, like a badly fitting suit.

In this story, Phelim O'Mooney lays a wager with his brother that he can travel in England 'incognito' for four days, without being detected as an Irishman more than eight times. He is supremely confident that he will succeed, because he has mastered a perfectly 'correct' English pronunciation, and 'not the smallest particle of brogue is discernible on [his] tongue' (136). His intention is also to secure a promise of marriage from a wealthy Englishwoman – who might, he feels, be prejudiced against marrying an Irishman. Assuming the name 'Sir John Bull', Phelim sets out on his travels, determined to find a bride and win the wager. The story thus uses popular fictional tropes as well as the stereotype of the 'Irish adventurer'. Perfect English accent notwithstanding, Phelim soon realises that he has to be extremely alert to escape detection. The possibility of being recognised as an Irishman arises when he orders breakfast (refusing eggs, because he 'knew it was supposed to be an Irish custom to eat eggs at breakfast'), when he looks over his bill (fearing to make a 'Hibernian miscalculation' [137]) and when he realises that the name of a Dublin hatter is pasted inside the crown of his hat. His determination not to be detected means that he takes some rather extreme measures: he sacrifices his hat, for instance, rather than admit to owning it, and sends his trunk, marked offendingly with his initials, by a slow wagon, claiming that he is conveying it for a friend.

Ireland's political status creates further opportunities for detection. Waiting for his luggage in the custom-house, Phelim looks on while a 'red-hot countryman' (137) complains loudly to the custom-house officers when an offending piece of Irish poplin is revealed in his trunk: 'he fell upon the Union, which he swore was Disunion' (138). Phelim is extremely careful to maintain an attitude of calm and indifference to this tirade, but soon afterwards is detected for the first time when he enthusiastically praises '*our* Speaker' (138) – John Foster, the last speaker of the Irish parliament. The contexts within which Irishness may manifest itself, then, other than by linguistic markers (which include the recognisably 'Irish' name, O'Mooney) are varied. Political contexts are, however, clearly important, as are external assumptions and expectations. Phelim avoids ordering eggs, because eating eggs at breakfast is *supposed* to be an Irish habit. The most persistent assumption about Irishness, according to the adventures of Phelim O'Mooney, is that of the supposed Irish tendency to produce 'bulls' or blunders. Having only been found out once in three days, Phelim is 'detected' six times in rapid succession for saying something which is greeted as a 'typically Irish' mistake. The extraordinary feature of these detections is that they are not detections at all, but assumptions and attributions of Irishness. When Phelim refers to a 'ship upon the face of the earth' (145), he is immediately mocked by a sneering porter:

> 'ship upon the face of the water, you should say, master; but I take it you be's an Irishman.'
> O'Mooney had reason to be particularly vexed at being detected by this man, who spoke a miserable jargon, and who seemed not to have a very extensive range of ideas. He was one of those half-witted geniuses, who catch at the shadow of an Irish bull. [. . .] But it was in vain for our hero to argue the point; he was detected – no matter how or by whom. (145)

Each of the subsequent detections follows this pattern: Phelim is successful in passing himself off as an Englishman, except in cases where he expresses himself freely and produces images and examples of figurative language which are mocked at by the fashionable and vulgar alike as 'Irish bulls'.

Phelim's visit to England ends in a prison cell. Accused of forgery for presenting a draft signed by Phelim O'Mooney, but in the person of John Bull,

Phelim simply refuses to speak. He has by now become convinced that if he were to speak, he would instantly be 'detected' as an Irishman. In this case, this detection would enable him to clear himself, but as this would also mean that he would lose his bet, he prefers to be (temporarily) accused of being a criminal rather than to acknowledge himself, or be detected, as an Irishman. The implication, difficult to deny, is that Irishness and criminality are not far removed from one another. The atmosphere established at the outset of the story, in which Phelim has a series of 'lucky escapes', is thus further underlined by his arrest, suggesting that Irishness is, almost literally, a fugitive identity. When the fourth day of his bet is finally over, Phelim happily indulges himself in singing loudly and talking to himself, and is able to explain his confused identity to the authorities. He returns to Ireland, joins the business concern of his sensible brother, and 'never relapsed into sir John Bull' (151).

Castle Rackrent and *An Essay on Irish Bulls* are of course typical of the post-Union Irish text in so far as they claim to represent Ireland whilst addressing themselves to Britain. This has an interesting implication, namely that while the public sphere in which Edgeworth participates as the author of these texts is certainly not the public sphere of the bourgeois nation, neither is it that ideal and universally accessible location, the 'Republic of Letters': these texts in fact mark a place between these two spaces. Both texts raise the prospect of an ideal readership free of prejudice, only to confirm that it does not exist. Prejudice in the Preface to *Castle Rackrent* is construed in relation to class and status as well as nation, while in *Irish Bulls* it has a more specifically national quality: nations, with their self-interest and 'monopolising pride', are antithetical to the exercise of enlightened judgment. 'The Irish Incognito' proposes that Irish people should embrace an Irish identity with pride, but at the same time it makes painfully clear the fact that this identity is secondary to English national identity, which determines what it means to be Irish. The version of identity proposed in the text is therefore neither contained within the rationalist environmentalism of the Enlightenment, nor within the essentialism of romantic nationalism as formulated in *The Wild Irish Girl*. As such, *Irish Bulls* can indeed be categorised as postmodern, in so far as it sees in Irish identity a construct without origins or coherence, in Phelim O'Mooney a subject without a centre. Phelim O'Mooney recalls the female figures in *Belinda*, Virginia and Lady Delacour, caught between the discourses of Nature and Fashion and unable to claim a stable identity. If Edgeworth is postmodern, however, hers is a highly critical and political postmodernism that derives from an awareness that Enlightenment is available to some, but not to all. This may, in theory, invalidate Enlightenment as a project by negating its foundations in notions of abstract universal reason, but it does not actually alter the fact that there are beneficiaries of that project.

Maria Edgeworth is notorious for never addressing her audience directly, in her own voice. Her father provided all of the prefatory notes for her work, and when she did assume the position of direct address, she did so as an impersonator, assuming the personae of two gentlemen in *Letters for Literary Ladies* and the masculine voices of the editors of *Castle Rackrent* and *Irish Bulls*. In the case of the latter two texts, the involvement of her father in the work facilitated the adoption of this voice and the masking of her own authorial gender. *Castle Rackrent* was of course first published anonymously, making Edgeworth an 'incognit(a)' of sorts. The trope of impersonation thus links the author and her character. Rather than draw parallels between the subject position of being Irish and being a woman writer, I would suggest that Edgeworth exploited the fractured and indeterminate nature of the Irish public sphere in order to construct a form of authorial identity that accommodated the contested discourses of Irishness and femininity.

This interpretation of Edgeworth's earliest post-Union texts positions them in opposition to Lady Morgan's response to Union in *The Wild Irish Girl*. Morgan's novel relies on a subject constructed as unified by means of connection with the past and extends this to the unification of the national community. In this context, Morgan and Walter Scott have more in common with each other than either of them have with Edgeworth. The reconciliation of divisive histories which was the project of the romantic national tale, as exemplified in *The Wild Irish Girl*, was taken up and amplified in Walter Scott's historical novel, beginning with the epoch-making *Waverley* (1814). There are of course differences between Morgan and Scott, chief among which is Scott's privileging of time over space – *The Wild Irish Girl* retains the structure of the Enlightenment tour as a means of exploring cultural difference whereas the journey of Scott's hero through space is accorded less explanatory power than the location of the narrative 'sixty years since'. Where Scott and Morgan converge, however, is in the reflection of national progress in the progress of the hero and heroine towards adulthood. As we have seen, Glorvina's reconciliation of Ireland to England is mirrored in her own progress from the bosom of her nurse to literate adulthood. The assimilation of Scotland into Great Britain, similarly, is mirrored in Waverley's ultimate adult rejection of the misguided enthusiasms of his youth, fed by his family's oral and unauthorised history. In both cases therefore, it hardly needs to be pointed out, the past is preserved as an aspect of the self whilst being safely contained. In Edgeworth's texts, in contrast, the disjunctions of the present are manifested in individuals who experience, as in the cases of Thady and Phelim O'Mooney, radically disorienting shocks to their sense of themselves. In these early texts, such disjunctions are threatening and are associated with a kind of scepticism and pessimism. What emerges in Edgeworth's subsequent fiction, however, is the proposal of the disoriented and disconnected self as the source of reconciliation: by constructing a subject who cannot assert continuity between past and present Edgeworth creates a position from which to imagine a different future. In contrast to the characterisation of Edgeworth as a counter-revolutionary writer, I shall argue in the following chapter that she imagines this subject as born out of revolution. In *Ennui*, therefore, as we shall see, the Earl of Glenthorn joins the gallery of Edgeworth characters who cannot be named, a feature which qualifies him to be a future leader of Ireland.

CHAPTER THREE

Revolution and Memory in 'Madame De Fleury', 'Emilie De Coulanges' and 'Ennui'

-+->-<-+-

Some time ago my dear Aunt Charlotte amongst some hints to the Chairman of
the Committee of Education, you sent me one which I have pursued – you said
that the Early Lessons for the poor should speak with detestation of the spirit of
revenge – I have just finished a little story called Forgive & Forget upon this idea.

Maria Edgeworth to Charlotte Sneyd, 1799[1]

Memory – and forgetting – play important and highly controversial roles
in Irish culture, especially in relation to the 1790s and in the accounts
and interpretations of that period. The memory of past grievances, chiefly a
conviction that those who were now tenants had been dispossessed of lands and
estates, appeared to some commentators to be ineradicable in the lower-class
Catholic population and was understandably considered dangerous by the
ruling establishment, as an ever-present source of seditious unrest which could,
and apparently did, give rise to recurrent episodes of violence and disorder.[2]
The plot of Edgeworth's 1809 novel, *Ennui*, in which the village blacksmith
discovers that he is in fact by birth the Earl of Glenthorn, and promptly takes
up residence in Glenthorn Castle, clearly alludes to this undercurrent in Irish
culture. It is, moreover, Edgeworth's only novel to incorporate the 1798 rebellion
into its plot. *Ennui* therefore represents a creative and imaginative reworking of
the elements of grievance, memory and revolutionary plots, an explosive
mixture which continues to provoke sometimes bitter controversy.

The role played in the 1798 rebellion by popular memory and consciousness
has been intensely debated and contested in the past decade. In the case of
events in Wexford, in particular, some historians have argued that the rank-
and-file participants had been 'politicised' (through newspapers, pamphlets,
membership of clubs and so on) and that their involvement was expressive of
their commitment to the radical, non-sectarian politics of the United Irish
leadership.[3] Others argue, however, that the motivation of the rebels in

Wexford was strongly marked by sectarianism, and far from being part of a new, radical moment in Irish history, the rebellion was based on atavistic loyalties and hatreds, nurtured by the kinds of folk-memory referred to above.[4] This is of course a simplified sketch of two polarised positions, but it does suggest the fault-lines of the dispute. The key question, for the purposes of this chapter, concerns the very different claims that are made as to the extent to which these memories are available for reorientation towards political radicalisation. Tom Dunne, basing his arguments on the evidence of Irish-language poetry, uses the term 'subaltern' to describe the lower-class combatants in 1798, which in his usage suggests that their mentality remains intractable from the point of view of official political ideologies.[5] Whelan, on the other hand, sees no serious obstacle to the process of politicisation, while Jim Smyth acknowledges the distance that separates the Catholic Defenders from the leadership of the United Irishmen, but describes the mentality of the Defenders in terms of a blend of the 'old and the new' – sectarian, anglo-phobic, millenarian, tapping into 'rich folkloric versions of Irish history' – but also 'revolutionary', drawing 'inspiration from the French and American experience'.[6] Joep Leerssen, however, a literary critic rather than a historian, goes further in making an explicit connection between 'unofficial' forms of memory and radical challenges to an inevitably conservative establishment:

> Harbouring grievances, wishing to 'pay back' the oppressor for past misdeeds, threatens the ideal of harmonious solidarity. Thus the conservative stance is often remarkably anti-historicist, and tends to stress the need to let bygones be bygones. One of the things that Burke hated most of all in the French revolution was precisely this tendency to settle old scores, which, Burke felt, threatened national cohesion in a historical sense as much as its class struggle threatened national cohesion in a societal sense. Since Burke's time, the refusal to 'forgive and forget' has been deplored by the paternalist elite as cramped intransigence and a mark of political immaturity.[7]

Leerssen compares the historical consciousness of 'Catholic Ireland' to that of other marginalised groups including gay men and women and ethnic minorities, using the term 'traumatised history'. In Leerssen's discussion, memory and unofficial forms of history, which he calls 'community remembering', thus have an implicitly radical edge, as they are in conflict with the desire of a paternalist elite to have people 'forgive and forget'.[8]

The focus on memory, whether claimed as radical or conservative, has tended to obscure the fact that the creation of the Society of United Irishmen was facilitated by a will to forget the past. Forgetting was an essential part of the unprecedented and short-lived union of 'Catholic, Protestant and

Dissenter' that emerged from the United Irish movement. Theobald Wolfe Tone, the United Irishmen's most important propagandist and the most unequivocal voice in favour of admitting Catholics to the full rights and benefits of citizenship, wrote at the formation of the Society in Dublin:

> In thus associating, we have thought little about our ancestors – much of our posterity. Are we for ever to walk like beasts of prey over fields which these ancestors stained with blood? In looking back, we see nothing on the one part but savage force succeeded by savage policy; on the other, an unfortunate nation scattered and peeled, meted out and trodden down! We see a mutual intolerance, and a common carnage of the first moral emotions of the heart, which leads us to esteem and place confidence in our fellow creatures. We see this, and are silent. But we gladly look forward to brighter prospects [. . .] to a peace – not the gloomy and precarious stillness of men brooding over their wrongs, but that stable tranquillity which rests on the rights of human nature, and leans on the arms by which these rights are to be maintained.[9]

The rebellion itself, which brought the bloodstained fields of the past into the present, seemed to put an end to the project of forgetting a divisive past in favour of a shared and peaceful future. The political landscape had been fundamentally altered by the rebellion, which had apparently proved that divisions could not simply be buried in oblivion and that popular memory, on both sides of the sectarian divide, was a much more powerful force than any utopian political ideology.

The typical cultural products of the post-Union era, the novels of Lady Morgan and the poetry of Thomas Moore, are therefore concerned to contain the past in the interests of peace and reconciliation, rather than to harness or exploit its radical potential. The second half of the eighteenth century had seen an awakening of interest among the Anglo-Irish in the native culture and traditions of Ireland, a development which has been associated – wrongly, in the eyes of some historians – with the growth of what is variously termed 'Protestant patriotism' or 'colonial nationalism'.[10] According to Katie Trumpener, this interest in antiquarianism, which she terms 'bardic nationalism', underwent a transformation in the 1790s, a decade which witnessed the greatest convergence between cultural nationalism and political radicalism, but which also ultimately blurred the figure of the bard as a symbol of resistance to British cultural imperialism. According to Trumpener, the events of the 1790s 'transformed the meaning of cultural nationalism. Proto-Jacobin in many respects during the last decades of the eighteenth century, cultural nationalism often appears in the 1810s and 1820s as reactive or reactionary'.[11] *The Wild Irish Girl* is reactive rather than reactionary, and its politics are liberal, but it is notable that Morgan emphasises the role of the displaced Catholic gentry and nobility in transmitting cultural traditions: claims of past grievance are thus not associated with a resentful populace, but with the ailing Prince of Inismore, and are tempered by the mediating charms of his daughter Glorvina. Mary Jean Corbett argues consequently that Morgan is committed to 'the notion that aristocratic power, properly exercised, can be a force for good', a claim which, based on a reading of *The Wild Irish Girl*, seems justified.[12] The past can be accessed and rehabilitated, therefore, if channelled through proper authorities.

In contrast to Lady Morgan, Edgeworth displayed scepticism about antiquarianism and although, as we have seen in chapter 2, she was equally as critical of British claims to a monopoly on civilisation, she was far less likely to turn to the resources of Ireland's pre-colonial past in order to make this point. In spite of the fact that texts such as *The Wild Irish Girl* indicate that there is no necessary connection between radicalism and the 'romantic' deployment of the Irish past, there is a tendency nonetheless to regard Edgeworth's 'Enlightenment' lack of interest in Ireland's past as indicative of a concern to deny what Leerssen might call its 'traumatised' history and thus to validate the status quo. As my opening quotation indicates, Edgeworth was aware of the potential of memory to fuel resentment and thus resistance to power. In the context in which she was writing, 1799, the resentment that the 'poor people' would have been feeling would have been much more immediate than the kinds of folk-memory of dispossession which are assumed to create anxiety in the landlord class. It was widely recognised that the suppression of the rebellion had been unjust, brutal and excessive, and that many innocent people had suffered. Government action had made it all too easy to interpret 1798 as yet another instance of the ruling minority's abuse of power. The plot of *Ennui*, as I have suggested, is an acknowledgment rather than a repression of the currency and potency of popular memory and consciousness. There is no doubt, however, that Edgeworth saw memory as divisive rather than progressive, but what I want to propose here is the possibility that forgetting can continue to have something of the radical and even revolutionary meanings with which it was associated in the thought of the United Irishmen and in the French Revolution. The amnesia-inducing plot of the novel represents a rejection of the determining power of memory and the past over the present and the future. My argument is that the evident desire in *Ennui* to detach individuals from their remembered pasts is motivated by an attempt to map onto Irish circumstances the positive interpretations of the revolutionary process that one finds elsewhere in Edgeworth's fiction.

The novel's central plot twist, in which Christy O'Donoghoe, the village blacksmith, takes possession of Glenthorn Castle, which subsequently becomes 'a scene of riotous waste', is, according to Tom Dunne, a straightforward reflection of the paranoia engendered by the scare stories of the 1790s, in which the entitlements of Protestant landowners were challenged by dispossessed Catholics. *Ennui*'s plot, he argues, reflects the 'insecurity and ambivalence which characterised the [Edgeworth] family's perception of its colonialist role'.[13] There is another way of reading this, however, and that is in relation to Niall Ó Ciosáin's discussion of the 'ideology of status' in popular culture in Ireland. As Ó Ciosáin points out, popular genres such as chivalric romances, criminal biography and historical writing are all concerned with the vital question of 'social hierarchy and its legitimacy'.[14] These texts consistently affirm the nobility of blood and the legitimacy of inherited status. Although such texts have been interpreted as conservative in so far as they reinforce established power relations, Ó Ciosáin points out that 'the versions of nobility contained in the texts could equally be used as ideals against which to measure and criticise the actuality'.[15] The potential for such critical and subversive applications of an ideology of nobility in Ireland are immediately self-evident. *Ennui* is thus on an ideological level reactive to popular conceptions of status, whilst on a formal level it represents an instance of the penetration of the elite by the popular, by incorporating a plot which derives from folklore and popular literature. *Ennui*, however, overlays these local, popular myths of social and political subversion and restitution with alternative readings derived from the recent history of the French revolution. In doing so, Edgeworth combines the appeal of folk memory with a radical elite perspective which seeks to find new beginnings rather than revert to old forms. The radicalism of Edgeworth's position can be appreciated by contrasting it with that of her contemporary, Walter Scott, whose fame was soon to eclipse hers. According to John P. Farrell, Scott, like Edgeworth 'look[ed] back to the crises of social and political enmity [in Scotland] and imagined them in the light of modern revolution'.[16] Scott, however, unlike Edgeworth, 'looked back to Scotland's past and imagined its decline into the bourgeois present'; his work is moreover characterised by 'a historical imagination radically disturbed by the premonition of tragedy'.[17]

Certain aspects of *Ennui*, including the main protagonist's journey to and tour through Ireland as a wide-eyed, first-time traveller, alternately amazed and appalled, have prompted critics to discuss it in the context of the national tale. As I shall suggest below, however, Glenthorn's journey to Ireland bears a closer resemblance to revolutionary emigration than it does to the earnest progress of the enlightened travel narrative; thus I propose to read its revolutionary themes in relation to two tales which explicitly narrate the French Revolution, *Madame de Fleury* and *Emilie de Coulanges*, whose central characters undergo the extraordinary upheavals of the Revolution, losing everything but gaining something new in the process. In proposing to read *Emilie de Coulanges* and *Madame de Fleury* alongside *Ennui* it is important to note that although not published in the same series of *Tales of Fashionable Life*, all three tales were written after Edgeworth's trip to France and Switzerland in 1802–3; *Ennui* has been described as 'the intellectual first fruit' of that tour.[18] A comparison of *Ennui* with these two tales, however, reveals that when considered on 'home ground' in Ireland, the concept of revolution is pressed to the limits of meaning, in contrast with the containment of revolution within a model of progress in *Madame de Fleury* and *Emilie de Coulanges*. In the two latter tales, a sharp distinction is maintained between the external – the environment in which the individual finds him or herself – and the internal space of the mind. In *Ennui*, this stable core is swept away.

Madame de Fleury represents the revolution directly, making references to such notorious revolutionary institutions as the Committee for Public Safety. The context in which the revolution is located is, however, highly unusual, if also typically Edgeworthian. The tale opens with Madame de Fleury's realisation of the numbers of children who are neglected and uncared for because their mothers are forced to work outside the home and cannot afford either childcare or school fees, and her decision to open a school for the daughters of these women. The character of Mme de Fleury herself is based on that of the real-life Mme Pastoret, whom Edgeworth met while in Paris. Mme Pastoret charmed Edgeworth for her quality of combining Parisian grace and gaiety with a commitment to intellectual pursuits and charitable work.[19] The school on which Edgeworth based her tale was established in 1801, but Edgeworth relocates the school's founding to the pre-revolutionary era. This fictional manipulation of facts thus highlights the poverty which the school attempts to redress as one of the underlying causes for the revolution. It also, most importantly, enables Edgeworth to imagine how the very different social classes represented by Madame de Fleury and her pupils would experience the revolution.

The tale does not represent the revolution as a unprecedented catastrophe, but rather as a 'change of fortune' to which well-educated individuals should be able to adjust:

> In these times, no sensible person will venture to pronounce that a change of fortune and station may not await the highest and the lowest; whether we rise or fall in the scale of society, personal qualities and knowledge will be valuable. Those who fall, cannot be destitute; and those who rise, cannot be ridiculous or contemptible, if they have been prepared for their fortune by proper education. In shipwreck, those who carry their all in their minds are the most secure.[20]

The image of revolution presented here is a curious compound of instability and stability. On the one hand, the possibility of unprecedented change is admitted: the upper classes may fall and the lower classes may rise. On the other hand, the 'scale of society' seems to remain constant, so that there is some continuity in the external environment. Most importantly, the passage represents the mind, the self, as a stable entity which may adapt to external change but provides the vital thread of continuity ensuring that the individual is 'secure'. The image of the self-contained individual, a survivor of shipwreck, recalls of course the iconic subject of the British Enlightenment, Robinson Crusoe. As Christopher Hill first pointed out, Crusoe's survival depends not only on the goods salvaged from the ship but on his 'mental furniture' (the 'all' he carries in his mind) – his habits of hard work, self-discipline and his desire firstly to acquire territory and then secure and enlarge it.[21]

Like Crusoe's shipwreck, revolution is a kind of practical testing ground for Edgeworth's faith in her own ideal of education. But whereas *Robinson Crusoe* was a fantasy with roots in the social and economic philosophies of eighteenth-century Britain, the revolution was shockingly, bloodily real. It was one thing to be interested in the *theory* of an education which produced individuals who were not totally dependent on their social role, and could adapt and adopt new roles; it is quite another to respond to revolution as an actual event in these terms. *Madame de Fleury* thus represents a particular and rather arresting kind of post-revolutionary Enlightenment, one which assimilates massacres, executions, regicide, deportations, land confiscations, the dissolution of religious orders, the creation of new armies, institutions, a new language – and calmly insists that a proper education on sound Enlightenment principles will equip the individual to negotiate these extraordinary changes.[22]

There is, moreover, a suggestion that if the classes are already aware of their mutual dependence, the transformations brought about by a revolution will ultimately result in an acceleration of social progress. In the weeks and days immediately prior to the outbreak of revolution Mme de Fleury worries for the future of her pupils: she foresees 'the temptations, the dangers, to which they must be exposed, whether they abandoned, or whether they abided by, the principles their education had instilled' (229). But this paternalistic care for the fate of her pupils is, however, soon replaced by a dependence on their affection, their generosity and their willingness to take risks on her behalf.

As in 'Letter from a Gentleman' and *Belinda*, the concept of fashion features in *Madame de Fleury* as a way in which to approach the topic of revolution and social change. The more conventionally Enlightenment assumptions of this tale, in contrast with the texts dealt with in chapter 1, are evident in so far as Edgeworth seeks to distinguish change as a positive concept from negatively construed revolutionary 'fashions'. The key function of Edgeworth's ideal education seems in fact to be to create a subject who adapts to change without, however, falling victim to ephemeral fashion. This distinction is expressed by the introduction of the characters of Manon, a working-class girl, and the abbé Tracassier, both of whom look on the revolution as an opportunity for personal gain and power. Manon is a cousin of one of Mme de Fleury's pupils, Victoire, but she advises her cousin that 'she would be much happier if she *followed the fashion*', and adds scornfully that 'nuns, and schoolmistresses, and schools, and all that sort of things [*sic*], are out of fashion now – we have abolished all that' (230). Manon herself regards the revolution as a means of acquiring simply material possessions; she begins by looting milliners' shops and bakeries and then becomes the mistress of a revolutionary apparatchik. She invites Victoire to visit her in her new home, a splendid 'hôtel' that was formerly the property of an aristocrat.

Fashions change, however, and when Manon's lover loses his influence and thereby his wealth, she is left utterly destitute, dying alone in a hospital, as Edgeworth sombrely informs us. The 'abbé' Tracassier shows a similar willingness to embrace the new revolutionary fashions. Whereas in the pre-revolutionary period he had attempted to dictate both as a literary and religious despot in Mme de Fleury's salon (he had for instance objected to Mme de Fleury that Sister Frances, the nun in charge of her school, was not sufficiently orthodox), as soon as the revolution breaks out, he abandons his religious principles and becomes a member of the Committee for Public Safety. He now pursues Mme de Fleury on the grounds that she is a *'fosterer of a swarm of bad citizens'*, who are being educated in *'detestable superstitions'* and the corrupt principles of the *ancien régime* (232). Tracassier is foiled by the efforts of Mme de Fleury's pupils, notably the resourceful Victoire, who helps her patroness to escape to England with a false passport. Meanwhile, the son of the steward to the Fleury estate, Basile, achieves influence with a general in the French army for whom he performs loyal and admirable service as a secretary, map-maker and military surveyor. The general's military success is founded on Basile's expertise, and he therefore generously offers to use his current popularity with the Directory to request a favour for his loyal secretary. Basile requests permission for the Fleurys to return to France and resume ownership of all their property. In the ensuing row, Tracassier finds himself siding with the wrong party: 'From being the rulers of France, they [Tracassier and his adherents] in a few hours became banished men, or, in the phrase of the times, *des déportés*' (254).

The return of M and Mme de Fleury to their château, to the delight of their loyal tenants and followers, suggests the reinstatement of pre-revolutionary relationships, but there are important qualifications to this 'restoration'. The scene has switched from deprived and urban Paris, where the tale opened, to the French countryside, and a festival: 'never was *fête du village* or *fête du Seigneur* more joyful than this' (254). This is the second festival to feature in the tale, the first being one held at Mme de Fleury's school to celebrate the achievements of her star pupil, Victoire. According to the editors of the tale, this alludes to a genre of countryside festival, the 'rosière' or rose festival, in which aristocratic women dispensed charity to the rural poor; the editors suggest that 'problems arose from telling such a story after the Revolution'.[23] Shifts in the relationship between the people and their rulers can be tracked in the changes to festivals and other aspects of popular culture over time. A feature of nations based on ideas of popular sovereignty is the replacement of local and regional customs, often sponsored by local gentry and nobility, with national holidays and rituals. The *rosière*, accordingly, in the revolutionary period, was transformed, and featured a young girl selected to symbolise Liberty. But the celebration of a festival of the estate of M and Mme de Fleury at the tale's conclusion suggests a desire to re-establish older forms of social leadership, retaining elements of deference and patronage, in spite of the changes of the revolutionary period.

The social convulsions of the revolution have, however, altered the relationship between the classes by providing a vivid illustration of their mutual interdependence:

> The proofs of integrity, attachment, and gratitude, which she received in these days of peril, from those whom she had obliged in her prosperity, touched her generous heart so much, that she has often since declared she could not regret having been reduced to distress. (239)

The revolution has also created a new middle class. Although Victoire marries her fiancé Basile in a ceremony presided over by Mme de Fleury, the pair owe their future not to her, but to the new institutions of a radically changed France. Through his experiences in the revolutionary army, Basile has become a well-connected professional, rather than succeeding his father as steward on the estate, as would surely have happened in the absence of revolution. Although as the tale closes we are invited to imagine a golden era of peace and harmony on the Fleury estate, it seems clear that Basile's and Victoire's future lies elsewhere, and not within the restricted social forms available in the structure of a landlord-led rural economy. Mitzi Myers has noted that *Madame de Fleury* is 'dense with covert allusions to Ireland's perilous situation [. . .] and its answers are home truths'.[24] One way of looking at the tale would be as a redescription of Irish social instability in terms of the French Revolution, a version in which Irish tenants are *best* imagined as French plebeians. Edgeworth's suggestion that revolution can bring about mutually beneficial effects on the classes brings to mind Staël's claim that the invasion of the 'barbarian' *sans-culottes* would ultimately improve the state of French civilisation. The narrative of the revolution in *Madame de Fleury* is essentially optimistic, charting a social, cultural and economic reformation of France. In his transformation from steward's son, presumably expected to inherit his father's position, to independent middle-class professional, Basile for instance could be regarded as a rose-tinted version of Jason Quirk.

Whereas *Madame de Fleury* narrates the revolution as a means towards the alteration of the class structure within France itself, *Emilie de Coulanges* provides a cross-cultural perspective, exploring the impact of the revolution on relationships between Britain and France. It declares its optimistic faith in progress in its opening paragraph when the young French émigrée, Emilie, comforts herself with the idea that 'things, which are always changing, and which cannot change for the worse, must soon infallibly change for the better'.[25] Here the suggestion is that the revolution, and in particular the associated phenomenon of emigration, will ultimately contribute to the growth of mutual understanding and respect between Britain and France. Positive portrayals of French émigrés are a recurrent feature of Edgeworth's fiction: examples include Madame de Rosier, 'the good French governess', and minor characters in *Angelina* and *Forester*. These and the characters in *Emilie de Coulanges* are clearly designed to act as correctives to crude anti-French stereotypes. Seamus Deane has, however, argued that proclaiming a welcome to refugees from revolutionary France was another way of expressing hostility to the revolution and was of a piece with the demonisation of French character, particularly in the case of the warm response received by exiled French clergy: 'the fleeing French clergy were no longer papists; they were Christian fugitives from an atheistic and revolutionary France – old enemies become new friends'. According to Deane, 'the contrast between the émigrés and the revolutionaries (already established by Burke) became part of the contrast between the old and the new France'.[26] Edgeworth was not alone, however, in proposing a progressive and liberal interpretation of revolutionary emigration. Both Charlotte Smith and Frances Burney, for instance, addressed the phenomenon of the Emigration by challenging the prevailing post-revolutionary tendency to condemn the French character. In the same year in which she married the penniless French émigré Alexandre D'Arblay, Burney, addressing specifically the 'Ladies of Great Britain and Ireland', remarked that 'we are too apt to consider ourselves rather as a distinct race of beings, than as merely the emulous inhabitants of two rival nations'.[27] Charlotte Smith, for her part, was acutely conscious that émigrés could potentially be used as tools in counter-revolutionary rhetoric, and her poem *The Emigrants* (1793), on the subject of the exiled French clergy, opens with a dedication to William Cowper in which she laments the use that has been made of revolutionary atrocities by reactionaries in Britain. She expresses the hope that, ultimately, 'this painful exile may finally lead to the extirpation of that reciprocal hatred so unworthy of great and enlightened nations'.[28] Both Smith and Burney acknowledge that the foundations on which the ideas of English and French national character have been built are deeply divisive, but their hope is that the phenomenon of the Emigration will contribute to the dismantling of those structures.

Emilie de Coulanges indicates that Edgeworth, in common with her liberal-minded contemporaries, saw the Emigration as, potentially at least, an enactment of the theory that apparently destructive circumstances could be conducive to progress. The Emigration, which forced thousands of French to seek refuge in what was technically a hostile state, was interpreted, by Chateaubriand for instance, as the source for a new cosmopolitan consciousness, a view which is not entirely without foundation: 'given the scale of the Emigration, it can hardly be disputed that those scattered to the four winds did, to varying degrees, discover new truths regarding the countries that offered them asylum'.[29] Emilie's thoughts on arrival in England articulate this apparently paradoxical situation:

> The English are such good people! – Cold, indeed, at first – that's their misfortune: but then the English coldness is of manner, not of heart. Time immemorial, they have been famous for making the best friends in the world; and even to us, who are their natural enemies, they are generous in our distress. (261)

Edgeworth dramatises her theme though the drawing-room enactment of national hostility in the figures of Emilie's mother, Mme de Coulanges, and her English hostess, Mrs Somers. The tale can be read as a comedy of manners; it has been described as 'an original psychological study of the problematics of charity and indeed of friendship in a competitive consumerist society', but the manners, the misunderstandings and the final resolution are all distinctly national.[30] The personality clashes between Mme de Coulanges and Mrs Somers are clearly intended to be read in the context of Anglo-French rivalry and antagonism, and to suggest that the revolution offers the possibility to reconfigure these relationships. In fact, *Emilie de Coulanges* can be regarded as plotting the idealised union between the North (England) and the South (France) that Germaine de Staël proposed in *De la littérature*.

The blissfully oblivious Mme de Coulanges frequently enrages her hostess by her insistence on the superiority of all things French:

> sometimes the English and French music were compared – sometimes the English and French painters; and every time the theatre was mentioned, Mad. de Coulanges pronounced an eulogium on her favourite French actors, and triumphed over the comparison between the elegance of the French, and the *grossièreté* of the English taste for comedy. (281)

Mme de Coulanges denounces Shakespeare as a 'bloody-minded barbarian', to which Mrs Somers responds by dismissing this image as 'Voltaire's Shakespeare' (282) – a reference to Voltaire's *Letters on England*. Mrs Somers refers her guest to Elizabeth Montagu's *Essay on Shakespeare*, and claims that English literature is superior to French by virtue of its unique humour (281–2). Mme de Coulanges displays what could be described as old-fashioned assumptions of French cultural superiority, while Mrs Somers displays that 'typically English' lack of interest in the cultural productions of other nations which was noted by Staël. Mme de Coulanges and Mrs Somers persist in characterising their respective nations by means of the oppositions of great canonical authors, and each struggles to assert the superiority of her own national author. This, it is implied, is an outmoded and sterile contest. While the older generation appear to be trapped in antagonistic patterns, Emilie reads Englishness as a set of values and customs that pertain directly to contemporary living and are, moreover, useful to her. 'Englishness' in *Emilie de Coulanges* is not represented by Shakespeare, but by a code of middle-class virtues, which, it is suggested, can be applied to post-revolutionary France. Whereas Mme de Coulanges is not only acutely aware of differences in manners and customs, but also assumes complacently that whatever is different in England is also deficient, Emilie calls England a 'charming country', and reflects that she and mother might never have known it, 'but for this terrible revolution' (261). She also privately acknowledges that the revolution has spared her the inevitable 'marriage de convenance' which was the lot of girls of her class. Emilie balances the losses she and her family have suffered as a result of the revolution against the new freedom and independence she experiences: when she and her mother leave Mrs Somers's house (relations having broken down completely), Emilie displays her new-found resourcefulness, earning money for their keep by copying music manuscripts and assuring her mother that she 'should infinitely prefer living by labour to becoming dependent' (268). In *Emilie de Coulanges*, revolutionary emigration is represented as a process of modernisation, in which members of the French aristocracy and gentry can be transformed into a professionalised middle class, a process that completes and also redeems the revolution. *Emilie de Coulanges* imagines the consequences of revolutionary emigration in terms of a progressive union along the lines of that proposed in *De la littérature*. In the manner of the national tale, therefore, this tale ends with a marriage that unites two nationalities when Emilie marries an Englishman – Mrs Somers's son, as it turns out, who helped Emilie and her mother to escape from captivity in Paris, but whose identity was unknown to her. The couple are set to return to Paris, thus completing the process of social and national reformation in France. Mme de Coulanges is initially less than delighted that her daughter is to marry an unpolished Englishman, but she is mollified by the suggestion that a dormant title in the Somers family might be revived to give the union some additional glamour. Thus not only does the experience of emigration to England direct the French gentry and upper classes towards the necessity of social responsibility, they are in fact 'restored' through their alliance with an English family.

Seamus Deane's suggestion that the welcome extended to French émigrés acted as a way of differentiating between 'old' France, which is supposedly to be preferred to 'new' revolutionary France, is thus certainly not borne out in the case of *Emilie de Coulanges*. The effect of the emigration here is a 'union' which contributes to the modernisation of France, although certainly not along revolutionary or jacobinical lines – the revolution, however, is central to the process whereby this modernisation occurs. The improvements associated with these changes are particularly important for women: Emilie's release from the prospect of a merely formal marriage of convenience is a direct consequence of their enforced emigration. The implication that archaic French practices are simply to be replaced by modern and improved English practices is, however, undermined by the fact that Emilie's freedom to chose her husband is actively opposed by Mrs Somers, who reacts with fury when Emilie refuses to marry her son, sight unseen. The very improbability of this episode, and its significance in prompting the émigrés to leave Mrs Somers's house, suggest that Edgeworth was at pains *not* to portray an undifferentiated Englishness as inevitably superior to French mores. Edgeworth's citation of a French authority as an intervention in the bitter, ostensibly literary, debate between Mme de Coulanges and Mrs Somers cuts across the sterile lines of opposition which their dispute has created. The 'pretensions of the English to the exclusive possession of humour' are 'attacked, with much ability' by Jean Baptiste Suard (281). This attack is cited at length, and in French. Like Mme Pastoret, whom Edgeworth so much admired and who was the model for Mme de Fleury, Suard and his wife were among those with whom the Edgeworths socialised whilst in Paris. Suard at the time was editor of a journal, *Le Publiciste*, and had been in former times a member of the *philosophe salon* hosted by Mme Geoffrin.[31] Suard's dismissal of the idea that 'humour' is an exclusively English gift displays an impressively cosmopolitan breadth of reference, referring to a wealth of authors including Aristophanes, Lucien, and Plautus, as examples of classical comic authors; Ariosto and Cervantes as examples of Italian and Spanish 'humour' respectively, and Rabelais and Molière, amongst others, as representative of French humour. One of the effects of Suard's comments is to suggest that national claims as to the 'exclusive' possession of any gift or quality may well be primarily indicative of ignorance of other cultures. If the French upper classes need a lesson in how to survive in the modern world, the English also need to learn the limitations of insularity. Through its inclusion of Suard's comments, *Emilie de Coulanges* itself acts as a means of such cosmopolitan education.

Emilie de Coulanges, therefore, in so far as it is concerned with the resolution of national cultural differences and enacts this resolution by means of a marriage, clearly bears some relationship to the national tale, while at the same time departing from its conventions in significant ways. Edgeworth upsets the apple-cart of the genre by presenting the narrative from the perspective of the 'foreign female' who is normally identified with the culture that is to be described. Above all, the destination in *Emilie de Coulanges* is not the exotic periphery, but the supposedly normative centre, whose claims to normativity are unsettled by being viewed through foreign eyes.

Both *Madame de Fleury* and *Emilie de Coulanges* read the French revolution as a catalyst for positive change. Although clearly unsupportive of the extremes of jacobinism, *Madame de Fleury* envisages the creation of an educated middle class as a lasting outcome of revolutionary upheaval; *Emilie de Coulanges*, meanwhile, using the phenomenon of revolutionary emigration, imagines the revolution as a route towards greater cross-cultural understanding. This optimism is, however, subject to a great deal of stress when Edgeworth attempts to read Ireland through the same revolutionary paradigm. *Ennui* is thick with references to the French revolution, and it is also of all Edgeworth's Irish texts the one which provides the most direct reference to the United Irishmen's rebellion, incorporating it within the plot. As we have seen, that rebellion has been read as signalling the re-emergence of socially divisive memories and the final defeat of radical attempts to overcome them. The socially progressive outcomes of revolution cannot therefore be realised in an Irish context unless the stable subject which is so much a feature of Edgeworth's other revolutionary tales is itself toppled.

The hero of *Ennui*, the Earl of Glenthorn, master of large estates in both England and Ireland, narrates his own history, describing himself as having been 'bred up in luxurious indolence'.[32] To drive the point home, he leads the reader through a headlong account of aristocratic vices, accompanied by references which introduce the spectre of the French *ancien régime* in all its excess. Lord Glenthorn's 'set' know no other occupation, it appears, than consumption. Having spent vast sums on carriages and jewels, Glenthorn then tries to escape his boredom by gambling, but soon tires of this and finds himself reduced to the most literal form of consumption: food. He becomes a 'connoisseur':

> After what I have beheld, to say nothing of what I have achieved, I can believe anything that is related of the capacity of the human stomach. I can credit even the account of the dinner which Madame de Bavière affirms she saw eaten by Lewis the Fourteenth. (169)

Glenthorn goes so far as to remark that 'epicurism was scarcely more prevalent during the decline of the Roman empire than it is at this day amongst some of the wealthy and noble youths of Britain' (169). It need hardly be pointed out that references to the fall of the Roman empire and the notorious self-indulgence of Louis XIV align Glenthorn with a tradition of aristocratic degeneracy which was already diagnosed as being among the causes for the collapse of empires and monarchies. Later, in Ireland, Glenthorn muses that '*ennui* may have had a share in creating revolutions' (249), a thesis that seems to have been proven already with respect to his life in England. Glenthorn's ceaseless search for new diversions is both symptomatic of and productive of a fall into revolutionary disorder. Edgeworth sketches the consequences of Glenthorn's actions in the image of a failed marriage followed by a household insurrection:

> ruined by indulgence, and by my indolent, reckless temper, my servants were now my masters. In a large, ill-regulated establishment, domestics become, like spoiled children, discontented, capricious, and the tyrants over those who have not the sense or steadiness to command. (180)

It is at this point, in the midst of collapse, that Glenthorn finally determines to visit his Irish properties.

Glenthorn's journey to Ireland has usually been interpreted, in general terms, according to the protocols of the national tale, although specific readings provide varying interpretations. For critics such as Tom Dunne, his journey forms a part of a tradition of 'English' commentary on Ireland which dates back to Spenser and the period of Elizabethan colonisation and conquest.[33] Katie Trumpener, by contrast, has described the journey that is an invariable component of the national tale as 'at once traveller's tale and anti-colonial tract; it sets out to describe a long-colonised country "as it really is," attacking the tradition of imperial description from Spenser to [Samuel] Johnson and constructing an alternative picture.'[34] Joep Leerssen's account of the post-union phenomenon of the 'auto-exoticisation' of Ireland also provides a potential context for *Ennui*.[35] What all of these readings have in common is their insistence or assumption that the 'traveller' whose perspective on Ireland the reader is invited to share is 'normative'. This 'normative' quality is either assumed as a function of the protagonist's Englishness, or, in Leerssen's case, a deliberate device – the focaliser is to a large extent void of distinct features, the better to reflect back an image of the otherness encountered in Ireland. Thus most of the commentary on *Ennui* fails to register the insistence with which Edgeworth portrays her 'hero', the Earl of Glenthorn, as dangerously decadent, perhaps because an acknowledgement of the emphasis on

Glenthorn's faults of character would conflict with the simplistic interpretation of the tale as a treatise on Irish flaws and the appropriate remedies. Thomas Flanagan informs us that Glenthorn decided to visit Ireland 'out of boredom with the life which he has been living' and complains that this 'is a slender reason for sending a man to a bog'.[36] Deane, although he recognises as a theme 'the benefits of educated responsibility', concludes that the tale's concern is to educate Glenthorn 'into the problems of Irish life'.[37] Tom Dunne's synopsis of the plot completely erases Edgeworth's vivid and often witty portrayal of Glenthorn's many faults, suggesting instead that the tale is designed to critique Irish character and customs: 'a languid young Anglo-Irish landlord comes to live on his Irish estate and learns how to cope with the manipulative cunning and bad habits of his Irish tenants in order to reform the estate on English lines'.[38] The description of Glenthorn as 'languid' brings a whole new meaning to understatement.

Not alone is Glenthorn, as the opening chapters of his narrative make perfectly plain, far from being neutral, normative or objective, his decision to travel to Ireland is represented as being of a piece with his psychological disorder – the need to seek new experience as a means of (temporarily) escaping ennui. Although he tells himself that he is visiting out of concern for his tenantry, in reality, as he admits, 'I was tired of England, and wanted to see something new, even if it were to be worse than what I had seen before' (182). Glenthorn's journey to Ireland is the second occasion on which he has attempted to divert himself through travel. Earlier in his life, in order to while away the time before he attained his majority, he embarked on a grand tour of Europe, and 'hurried from place to place as fast as horses and wheels, and curses and guineas' could carry him (162). It goes without saying that this type of travel did nothing to alleviate his sense of purposelessness. The difference between his earlier experience of travel and this latest decision to visit his Irish estates lies in the abject state to which he has been reduced by this point: his marriage has collapsed, and, living in isolation, surrounded by self-interested servants who have become like 'tyrants', he considers suicide as a way out of his misery. The sudden arrival of Ellinor coincides with this point of desperation, and instead of killing himself he decides to take a trip to Ireland.

Appearing out of nowhere on Glenthorn's English estate, Ellinor literally frightens the horses and causes an accident, but in doing so she prevents Glenthorn from carrying out his plan of suicide. By an ironic twist, this aversion of violent death is interpreted as if it were death: Glenthorn's fall renders him unconscious and his supposed corpse is carried to the house. By subsequently feigning death, and thus, like Condy Rackrent, managing to be present at his own 'wake', Glenthorn gains a painful insight into the self-interest which governs the behaviour of those with whom he has surrounded himself.

This is just the first of many suggestions that Glenthorn needs to be 'reborn' in order to survive. Ellinor's grief at his apparent death provokes the first instance of intense emotion registered in the text:

> The voice came from the door which was opposite me; and whilst the footman turned his back, I raised my head, and beheld the figure of the old woman, who had been the cause of my accident. She was upon her knees on the threshold – her arms crossed over her breast. I shall never forget her face, it was so expressive of despair. (172)

Still a hapless victim to the plague of ennui, Glenthorn finds as he recovers from his injuries, that Ellinor's manner of speech and fund of folk-tales provide a satisfactory distraction from the burden of his existence. Ellinor's portrayal of Ireland as an archaic and exotic country fascinates Glenthorn: she 'impressed me with the idea of the sort of feudal power I should possess in my vast territory, over tenants who were almost vassals, and amongst a numerous train of dependants' (175). There is nothing unique in the idea of the traveller to Ireland having a set of preconceptions – in *The Wild Irish Girl*, Mortimer is equipped with a familiar bundle of prejudices as he leaves England for Ireland – but the fact that Glenthorn's preconceptions revolve around a fantasy of absolute power suggest that his trip to Ireland is an attempt to avoid confronting the ways in which he has proved his own unfitness to exercise power, choosing instead a regression into a feudal fantasy. Given the regressive nature of this vision, it is somewhat ironic that Glenthorn hopes to find in Ireland 'something new'. Glenthorn's recurrent desire to see and experience new things has up to this point resulted in gross overconsumption, dissipation and unhappiness, and, it appears, his motivation in visiting Ireland is of a piece with this unhealthy tendency. The extraordinary plot that unfolds in Ireland will on the one hand finally educate Glenthorn away from the meaningless search for 'something new', and on the other confront him with situations so 'new' that they turn reality upside down. Ireland, therefore, is not 'new' in the sense of being a new flavour to consume; its effect on Glenthorn gives a more revolutionary meaning to the word 'new'.

The various episodes that make up the Irish section of the narrative effectively present quite different and sometimes incompatible views of Ireland. Marilyn Butler and Tim McLoughlin have described the action as a 'thickly detailed, mannered *staging* – which is to be deliberately non-realistic – of recent Irish history against a deliberately typed backdrop of castles, villas and over-familiar tourist traps'.[39] One of the first Irish scenes is that of Glenthorn's coach journey with Paddy, the Irish postilion, a comic episode which tends to suggest that 'Ireland' is a source of endlessly amusing characters and situations.

In contemporary reviews of the *Tales of Fashionable Life*, this scene was almost invariably excerpted as an outstanding example of Edgeworth's art – an indication that Edgeworth had calculated correctly what tickled the jaded metropolitan palate. But the Ireland of *Ennui* is both strange and familiar, exotic and humdrum. Glenthorn is greeted by his tenants with an overwhelming show of respect, deference and even affection, a display that inspires him to throw himself into a new role, that of magnanimous power. The enthusiasm of the tenants for their newly arrived lord is, however, patently no more than a piece of optimistic opportunism. When Glenthorn expresses fatigue and annoyance at the ceaseless and petty requests with which he is bombarded, his tenants reply, 'Sure the agent will do as well, and no more about it. Mr M'Leod will do every thing the same way as usual' (194). Glenthorn, however, is unwilling to give up his feudal fantasy of possessing power 'seemingly next to despotic' (193–4). Reluctant to cede control to his agent, M'Leod, a conscientious Scot to whom he has taken an instant dislike, he likens himself wryly to the King of Prussia, 'who was said to be so jealous of power, that he wanted to regulate all the mousetraps in his dominions' (195). A footnote within the text draws our attention to the source of this remark – Mirabeau's *Memoirs of the King of Prussia*, which was published in France in the year of the revolution and translated into English in 1798 – thus associating Glenthorn's memoir with a French revolutionary critique of monarchical power.

Instead of a delightfully backward feudal estate, remote from 'civilised society' (191), Glenthorn is confronted with the rather less glamorous figure of M'Leod, who handles the estate competently. M'Leod's determination to impress upon Glenthorn the principles of Adam Smith has generated a sometimes violent critical reaction. It has even been claimed that 'the novel is not fiction at all, but an exposition of Lovell Edgeworth's theories of politics, economics, social arrangements, education and morality, and an accompanying exposition of their peculiar appropriateness to Ireland. The vehicle of this instruction is [. . .] M'Leod'.[40] A more politicised response reads these passages as an overt statement of Edgeworth's overweening desire to anglicise Ireland, and therefore as an implicit denunciation of the Irish character. The fact that M'Leod's philosophies are dramatised in encounters with the agent from the neighbouring estate, Hardcastle, is very rarely acknowledged.[41] M'Leod's reliance on the principle of progress, the universal benefits of education and the value of theory is contrasted with Hardcastle's self-satisfied trumpeting of experience and common sense:

> he had nothing to do with books; he consulted only his own eyes and ears, and appealed only to common sense. As to theory, he had no opinion of theory; for his part, he only pretended to understand practice and experience – and his

practice was confined steadily to his own practice, and his experience uniformly to what he had tried at New-town-Hardcastle. (201)

It is Hardcastle, not M'Leod, who dismisses the Irish as incapable of progress. When M'Leod suggests that education is the most effective means of changing a society, Hardcastle objects that 'all this can never apply to the poor in Ireland', that they are 'not like men in Scotland', and that they 'cannot be taught' (203). Of the two scenarios proposed by the agents, one advocating gradual improvement by rational means, and one dismissing the bare possibility of change on the grounds of intractable Irish character, the former is clearly the most progressive, while the latter deals in blind prejudice. M'Leod's patient faith in education and progress fails, however, to persuade Glenthorn, and it should be remarked that this representative of the Scottish Enlightenment disappears from view in the narrative as Glenthorn pursues his own ambitious plans, which are themselves eclipsed first by rebellion and then by Glenthorn's sudden loss of title, property and identity.

Glenthorn's desire for the immediate transformation of his estate into something recognisably English, and therefore manifestly civilised, is symbolised by the cottage he is determined to build for Ellinor. The subsequent disaster is not, as has been sometimes claimed, laid solely at the door of Irish incapacity, as Glenthorn himself admits: 'it would have been difficult for a cool spectator to decide, whether I or my workmen were most in fault; they for their dilatory habits, or I for my impatient temper' (198). Glenthorn's impatient ambitions are, what's more, as much an expression of his own desire to be fashionable as they are focused on improving Ellinor's living conditions: 'I fitted it up in the most elegant style of English cottages; for I was determined that Ellinor's habitation should be such as had never been seen in this part of the world' (199). Glenthorn's treatment of the cottage as a fashion accessory in fact has echoes of Marie Antoinette's infamous dairy at Versailles. When the cottage gradually falls into disrepair and Ellinor refuses to adapt her lifestyle to the grandeur of her new accommodation, Glenthorn's anger and disappointment are such that he promptly abandons all his 'princely schemes' (208). The episode of Ellinor's cottage is crucial to Dunne's argument that Edgeworth's writing is indicative of her project of 'reshaping [. . .] every aspect of Irish life and society on English lines'.[42] Acknowledging Glenthorn's responsibility in the failure of the project, Elizabeth Kowaleski-Wallace provides a more sophisticated argument, suggesting that Glenthorn's subsequent ability to critique his own mistakes 'redeems' him and thus legitimates his perspective: 'although he is initially as foolish as Ellinor, and therefore equally a satiric target, his position is validated in the end'.[43] Kowaleski-Wallace argues that in spite of Glenthorn's faults, the tale is concerned to imagine ways in which he can attain moral and intellectual superiority over his tenants and thus 'master' them.[44] 'In the end' is of course the key phrase: Glenthorn's position is not 'validated' until he has, for instance, discovered that Ellinor is more than a loyal and grateful retainer – she is in fact his mother. In order to become an effective leader, Glenthorn has to be dispossessed of his inherited wealth and status, and acquire the position of leader through effort and work. The tale thus represents political revolution in the form of a folktale or fable.

Ennui's evident interest in exploring the meanings of revolution in an Irish context has been somewhat obscured by its representation of the United Irishmen's rebellion. The most significant emphasis in this representation is on 'party spirit' as a key characteristic of public life at the time. Clearly drawing on her father's experiences of having been attacked for his suspected sympathies with the rebels, Edgeworth portrays Glenthorn as engaging unwillingly in efforts to quell the rising, primarily in order to avoid being branded a traitor: 'it was necessary to take an active part in public affairs to vindicate my loyalty, and to do away the prejudices that were entertained against me' (246). He ultimately derives a kind of stimulation from the enforced activity, but it is clear that he experiences the rebellion as simply another form of entertainment:

> the alarms of the rebels, and of the French, and of the loyalists; and the parading, and the galloping, and the quarrelling, and the continual agitation in which I was kept, whilst my character and life were at stake, relieved me effectually from the intolerable burden of ennui. (247–8)

Although the rebellion rouses Glenthorn temporarily from his 'state of apathy' (244), therefore, it is depicted by Edgeworth as having only transient consequences:

> *Unfortunately for me*, the rebellion in Ireland was soon quelled; the nightly scouring of our county ceased; the poor people returned to their duty and their homes; the occupation of upstart and ignorant *associators* ceased, and their consequence sunk at once. Things and persons settled to their natural level. The influence of men of property, and birth, and education, and character, once more prevailed. [. . .] My popularity, my power, and my prosperity were now at their zenith, *unfortunately for me*; because my adversity had not lasted long enough to form and season my character. (248)

The rebellion may be represented as being of no lasting consequence, but in this story, there is at least one 'poor person' who does not return to his duty and his home once the rebellion is over.

When Glenthorn discovers that he is not a nobleman, but by birth an Irish peasant, changed at nurse by his mother, Ellinor, he insists on changing places with the real Earl, who has been living in ignorance of his true identity, as Christy O'Donoghoe, the village blacksmith. I suggested at the beginning of this chapter that this element in the novel's plot acts as an example of Edgeworth's absorption of popular beliefs about status in Ireland, and the incorporation into her work of popular cultural elements. The combination of these popular beliefs and motifs with allusions to the radical theories of the French revolutionaries and the United Irishmen produces a truly dizzying, destabilising vision as Edgeworth subverts the already subversive popular reading of status in Ireland.

The sudden ennobling of Christy, the former blacksmith, quite clearly reflects the belief among the lower classes in Ireland that they had been wrongfully dispossessed by the current holders of land and power, and that justice would involve the reversal of their respective positions. The idea that the village blacksmith is *really* an earl of noble blood represents this belief with poetic simplicity. But this incident is equally available for another, and very different reading, one which rejects the idea of status as an immutable quality, transmitted through blood. The earl, as he reflects on what action he should take following Ellinor's revelation, makes perfectly clear that his renunciation of wealth and title is voluntary: 'I was not compelled to make such sacrifices' (272). He is confident that Ellinor will keep his secret, and that even if it comes to a lawsuit, 'possession was nine-tenths of the law' (272). In spite of this, he goes ahead with the drastic determination to give up his title and wealth:

> After a severe conflict between my love of ease and my sense of right – between my tastes and my principles – I determined to act honestly and honourably, and to relinquish what I could no longer maintain without committing injustice, and feeling remorse. (272–3)

Having made this difficult decision, Glenthorn is exhilarated:

> My mind seemed suddenly relieved from an oppressive weight; my whole frame glowed with new life; and the consciousness of courageous integrity elevated me so much in my own opinion, that titles, and rank, and fortune, appeared as nothing in my estimation. (273)

This ecstatic description of the renunciation of title and rank and fortune, its association with being relieved of an oppressive weight and with courageous integrity, suggests the iconic figure of Lord Edward Fitzgerald, the son of the Duke of Leinster, whose commitment to French revolutionary principles famously or notoriously lead him to renounce his title, and, subsequently, to join the United Irishmen. The reader may well detect some ironic detachment in the fact that 'titles, and rank, and fortune, appeared as nothing' in Glenthorn's estimation, given that he has never known life without these trifling advantages. But the fact remains that it is only with Glenthorn's loss of title, wealth and position that he becomes something other than the decadent aristocrat whose arrival in Ireland was precipitated by a form of revolution in his own household.

Glenthorn's initial journey to Ireland thus was, as I have suggested above, a form of revolutionary emigration, but the social hierarchy, despite all indications to the contrary, remained stagnantly stable until Glenthorn's core identity was itself subjected to revolutionary transformation. The former Earl then describes himself as being in the position of an 'abdicated monarch' whose subjects, the Glenthorn tenants, persist in bringing him homely gifts of rural produce (296). But 'O'Donoghoe', as he now calls himself, does not cling to his former identity: he begins to create a new identity for himself as a professional relying on application and merit, replicating the progressive paradigms of revolution we have already seen in *Madame de Fleury* and *Emilie de Coulanges*. The obstacles to the realisation of this vision in an Irish context are suggested by the peculiarities of the narrative, including its incorporation of the folkloric, which, at the time of its publication struck many readers as wildly incongruous, and also by the tendency of the plot to keep building to what seems like a climax or denouement, only to be trumped by yet another twist. The former earl's renunciation of his title is the third revolutionary moment in the narrative to that point, following his departure from England and the outbreak of rebellion in Ireland (which, incidentally, involves him as the subject of a failed rebel plot). With the loss of his inherited status, it seems as if revolution can now, finally, be written according to the optimistic vision that characterised Edgeworth's tales of the French Revolution. The force which disrupts this vision is clearly the power of the past, of memory, hence the radical severing of the subject from his past through the device of the child changed at nurse. What makes the tale particularly noteworthy is that it envisions the past being transcended by making use of plot elements and themes derived from Irish popular traditions, thus combining its radical agenda with an indigenous idiom.

Other commentators on this text have suggested that it is conservative, rather than radical, on the grounds that Edgeworth does not repeat the successful formula found in *The Wild Irish Girl*, published only three years before and evidently an influence on Edgeworth's text. The marriage between Glorvina and Mortimer which concludes *The Wild Irish Girl* is so compelling as a symbolic resolution that Robert Tracy dubbed it the 'Glorvina solution'.[45] The Glorvina solution, or the 'national marriage', symbolises the healing of

Ireland's bitter divisions through the marriage of a Gaelic woman and an Anglo-Irish man. These divisions are overcome in part through an imagined reconciliation between past and present: the social hierarchy of the present is legitimated through its claimed affiliation with the past (this, in general terms is exactly how the nationalist state claims its legitimacy). In *Ennui*, Edgeworth raises the possibility of this form of legitimation by introducing the character of the fascinating Lady Geraldine, with whom Glenthorn falls in love – only to dismiss it as peremptorily as Geraldine herself dismisses Glenthorn's proposal. Robert Tracy's initial suggestion that Geraldine is a half-baked Glorvina involves a wider distinction between Edgeworth and Morgan, expressed in terms of Edgeworth's concern with 'legality' and Morgan's desire to establish the 'legitimacy' of the ruling class in Ireland. The distinction is valid in so far as it concerns very different attitudes to the role of the past in resolving real problems of popular alienation from the state in Ireland; what I question, however, is the conclusion that the disappearance of Lady Geraldine indicates a 'colonial' mentality on Edgeworth's part, and that the desire to break with the past is inevitably, as Leerssen and others have suggested, implicated in a conservative politics.[46]

If, as I proposed, Glenthorn's renunciation of his title recalls the dramatic decision of Lord Edward Fitzgerald to embrace democratic principles, Lady Geraldine, through her highly resonant name, makes another and more general reference to the Fitzgerald family, and by extension to the long history of conflict in Ireland. It is ironic that Edward Fitzgerald's revolutionary beliefs, which led him to renounce the position he had inherited as a member of one of Ireland's wealthiest and most influential families, has been interpreted as characteristic of that very family. Tracy for instance remarks that 'from the revolt of "Silken Thomas" Fitzgerald in 1534 to that of Lord Edward Fitzgerald in 1798, that family had often supplied leaders for Irish rebellions against the English'.[47] Tracy's comments are in a tradition established very soon after Fitzgerald's death, as we can see in the comments of Thomas Moore in his biography of Fitzgerald:

> There is, perhaps, no name in the ranks of the Irish peerage, that has been so frequently and prominently connected with the political destinies of Ireland as that of the illustrious race to which the subject of the following Memoir belonged; nor would it be too much to say that, in the annals of the Geraldines alone, – in the immediate consequences of the first landing of Maurice Fitzgerald in 1170, – the fierce struggles, through so many centuries, of the Desmonds and Kildares, by turns instruments and rebels to the cause of English ascendancy, – and, lastly, in the awful events connected with the death of Lord Edward Fitzgerald in 1798, – a complete history of the fatal policy of

England towards Ireland, through a lapse of more than six centuries, may be found epitomized and illustrated.[48]

Fitzgerald's renunciation of his inherited position and his embrace of radical politics results in his posthumous placement firmly within the history of his family, his radicalism interpreted as some kind of tragic inheritance. Moore's claim that the 'complete history' of Ireland (in particular the 'traumatised history' of Irish grievances – the 'fatal policy of England towards Ireland') is contained within the history of a family suggests that if the future is to be different from the past, change must also occur at the level of family history. Glenthorn's loss of aristocratic status coupled with Lady Geraldine's rejection of his marriage proposal can be read as a refusal of the continuous narrative of tragedy. One further jolt to our hero's identity is apparently required to ensure an escape from this violent history, and it involves a renunciation not only of class privilege but of masculine power and authority.

The former earl's reinstatement as the lord of Glenthorn Castle is preceded not only by his marriage to Cecilia Delamere, the heir-at-law to the property, but by his abandonment of the name of O'Donoghoe in favour of his wife's name. He changes his name in order to appease the 'genteel' and arguably sectarian objections of his future mother in law, who balks at his ethnically marked name: 'What a horrid thing it will be to hear my girl called Mrs O'Donoghoe! Only conceive the sound of – Mrs O'Donoghoe's carriage there! – Mrs O'Donoghoe's carriage stops the way!' (306). The association between change of name and accession to property echoes the decision of Sir Patrick O'Shaughlin, who inherited the Rackrent estate on the condition that he 'take and bear the surname and arms of Rackrent',[49] and in both cases there is an allusion to the limitations enshrined in the Penal Laws on the rights of Catholics to own, inherit and bequeath property. The Penal Laws had the curious effect of making highly visible the connections between the public and the private spheres as they intervened in 'family matters' in the interests of state policy. For Edmund Burke, the best-known critic of these laws, the threat implied by this convergence of the political and the domestic, and the consequent unsettling of traditional relations of power between men and women, proved as disturbing as the injustices they visited on Catholics as a group.

As with almost every society in the known world, the holding and transmission of property in Ireland was at this period a system based on gender, and was originally introduced by the early English settlers, who regarded the absence of primogeniture in Ireland as a factor in its supposed developmental lag. The Penal Laws, however, created an entirely novel situation by making religion the most important qualification for property ownership, thus dealing an unintended blow to patriarchy. Burke dwells on this fact at great length, imagining all the ways in which the laws could possibly interfere with the traditional family structure, to the extent that the maintenance of 'proper' relationships of power between men, women and children emerges as the most important factor in maintaining social order. He first expresses horror at the way in which the laws, by allowing a child who conformed to the established church to assume legal rights over property, can undermine the authority of a father: 'the paternal power in all such families is so very much enervated, that it may well be considered as entirely taken away'.[50] A wife can also, according to these laws, similarly subvert her husband's power:

> If in any Marriage settlement the husband has reserved to him a power of making a Jointure, and if he dies without settling it, her conformity to the established religion executes his powers and executes them in as large an extent, as the Chancellor shall think convenient. [. . .] If, therefore, a Wife chuses to ballance [*sic*] any domestick misdemeanours to her husband, by the public merit of conformity to the protestant religion, the Law will suffer no proof of such misdemeanours to be brought to invalidate its presumption. She acquires a provision totally independent of the favour of her husband; and thus deprives him of that source of domestick Authority, which the common Law has left in families, that of rewarding, or punishing by a voluntary distribution of his Effects, what, in the opinion of the Husband, was the good or ill behaviour of his Wife.[51]

Part of the subversive effect of the laws, in Burke's view, is to give women a public identity which takes precedence over their domestic or private role: conformity to the protestant religion gives a woman 'public merit' against which her husband's desire to confirm her identity as merely or purely private is powerless. The measures taken to impose Anglicanism as the established religion in Ireland are thus interpreted by Burke as having destroyed what he regards as the natural relations between the sexes and their relation in turn to social order. The assumption in all these cases is that either women or children assume unnatural and illegitimate power by converting to Protestantism. The conversion of fathers and husbands and the consequences for their wives and children are thus implicitly regarded as unproblematic, because in these cases 'paternal power' and 'domestick Authority' are not compromised. It is thus very hard to avoid the conclusion that Burke's *primary* concern is with the maintenance of traditional, patriarchal systems of power.[52]

Beginning with Ellinor's substitution of one child for another, and ending with the creation of Mr Delamere, the plot of *Ennui* could be described as Burke's worst nightmare – a scenario in which 'paternal power' is utterly non-existent. Thomas Bartlett has written that in the period 1695–1730, given the wide range of restrictions and disabilities in place, 'to have ambition at all one had to conform to the Established Church'.[53] The fact that the Penal Laws were the source of injustice, hardship and oppression for Irish Catholics is not in question. The scarcity of gendered analyses of Irish culture in this period has made it possible to read the successive transformations visited on the Earl of Glenthorn simply as Edgeworth's plea for or endorsement of continued Protestant dominance in Ireland. Can it not be argued, however, that one function of the novel's extraordinary plot is to offer a challenge to a narrative of Irish history based on a roll call of fathers and sons?

In conclusion, *Ennui* represents Ireland as a country which is in need of the social restructuring that can be achieved through revolution, of the kind depicted in *Madame de Fleury* and *Emilie de Coulanges*. Ireland, however, is characterised by a habit of historical memory which threatens to overwhelm any move towards radical change. The events of 1798 and their aftermath suggested that even the most radical, forward-looking social theory could be appropriated for a narrative of endlessly recurring crisis and tragedy, as the treatment of the 'life and death of Lord Edward Fitzgerald' (to quote Thomas Moore) illustrates. The convoluted and controversial plot of *Ennui* is on the one hand an acknowledgment of the power of memory in Ireland, and on the other a means to overcome it. This Edgeworth does in the most radical way possible, by creating a narrator whose identity changes in the middle of his own narration. The message of *Ennui* seems to be that revolution in Ireland cannot be achieved without fundamental changes at the level of subjective consciousness, and these changes include new configurations of gender.

CHAPTER FOUR

German and Irish Heroes in 'Patronage' and 'The Absentee'

→>◅←

In 1813, Maria Edgeworth spent several months in Britain, including a six-week stay in London where she was considered 'one of the "lions" of the season', an important literary figure whom hostesses were keen to invite to parties.[1] The second series of *Tales of Fashionable Life* had been published the previous year and Edgeworth's literary star was as high as it had ever been. Another literary celebrity visited London in 1813, whom Edgeworth was clearly anxious to meet. She wrote to Sophy Ruxton in May 1813:

> I fear Madame de Stael's arrival may be put off till we have left Town. I hear now that she is not to come till the beginning of June. The Edinburgh Review of her last book has well prepared all the world for her arrival. It is a flourish of trumpets before her entrance on the stage. I think the praise of transcendent genius indisputably hers and no more is given to her in that Review than is justly due [. . .].[2]

In the review of *De la littérature* to which Edgeworth refers, the *Edinburgh Review* called Mme de Staël 'decidedly the most eminent literary female of her age'.[3] The review was swiftly followed by the publication of *De l'Allemagne* and its review in the *Edinburgh* in October 1813. In England at any rate, Staël's moment had certainly come. This was undoubtedly due in part to Staël's pronounced opposition to Napoleon and her pro-British politics. Having dwelt at length on the special qualities of English literature in *De la littérature*, Staël ostensibly turned her attention to another representative of 'Northern' culture in *Germany*. From an English perspective, however, the books contained very similar messages. John Claiborne Isbell argues that Staël's Germany is 'both a paradigm for Germanic nations and an ersatz for their true leader, England',[4] while David Simpson notes the existence in *Germany* of England as an 'unspoken ideal'.[5] Staël's focus on Germany does not therefore diminish her portrayal of England as the ideal nation; it perpetuates it in another form. This idealisation of England, in so far as it disposed her towards uncritical support of the government, was not popular in the largely Whig and liberal circles in which she moved whilst in England, and, as Robert Escarpit has noted, resulted in her giving her support to a party which was in fact ill suited to her liberal opinions.[6]

Staël stayed in England for eleven months, returning to France in May 1814 following the restoration of the Bourbon monarchy. Edgeworth, meanwhile, had arrived back in Ireland in the summer of 1813, and had there completed her longest novel, *Patronage*, which was published in December 1813, with an official publication date of 1814. *Patronage* has rarely been reprinted, has not been widely read, and has received very little critical attention. It is surprising therefore to realise that it is a highly political novel, which is explicitly located in the context of the Napoleonic wars and contains some very critical reflections on English institutions and the state of English public life, which caused 'a great *combustion* in London'.[7] Edgeworth's inclusion of an important German character, Count Altenberg, suggests that, like Staël, she was interested in the opposition to Napoleon in Europe. Altenberg, however, functions very differently from the Staëlian representation of the German character: whereas behind Staël's 'Germany' lies the 'unspoken ideal' of England, Altenberg's function in *Patronage* seems to be to awaken some of the English characters to a clearer recognition of patriotism and public virtue. As we have already seen, Staël's promotion of England as an ideal was complicated by her insistence on the subordination of English women and their confinement to the private sphere. Nowhere is this more evident than in her novel of 1807, *Corinne; or, Italy*, in which England features, in the words of one critic, as 'the evil empire of patriarchy'.[8] Edgeworth's writing, on the other hand, is characterised by a blurring of the boundaries between public and private, and a subversion of the gendered oppositions used to represent England and Ireland. In order to explore further how this inflects her representation of English and Irish national character, this chapter uses Staël's *Germany* and *Corinne* as texts through which to read *Patronage* and *The Absentee*, respectively.

The value of reading *Patronage* and *The Absentee* in conjunction with one another has been proposed by W. J. Mc Cormack, not least because *The Absentee* developed out of a discarded sub-plot in *Patronage*, which concerned an Irish absentee family living in London.[9] The genesis of *The Absentee* in the margins of *Patronage*'s capacious plot is reflected, for instance, in the fact that the two novels share several themes, notably that of (il)legitimacy. *The Absentee* has long been one of Edgeworth's most popular novels, and has a much longer history of reprints and editions than *Patronage*. Critical responses to the novel root it firmly in the context of Anglo-Irish relations, suggesting, for instance, that it endorses the Union and, inevitably, that it seeks to legitimate Ascendancy leadership. The role of *The Absentee* and Edgeworth's other Irish fictions in constructing Ireland and Irishness is widely acknowledged; what is missing from the discussion is the awareness that all over Europe, nations and national identities were 'under construction'. Staël is most famous for creating a nation, in textual form, out of the disunited and disparate German states, but her works also contain a very distinct construction of Englishness, as well as portrayals of Spanish and Dutch national character (*Delphine*'s Léonce and M. Lebensei). Edgeworth's England is not Staël's England – it is less insular, less masculine, and in greater need of reform – not least because Edgeworth had to confront the anomaly of Ireland's position within the British multi-national state. The representations of England and Ireland in *Patronage* and *The Absentee* are thus in relationship with one another, and are constructed in the context of a Europe-wide shift towards a new definition of the 'nation' and its significance. Staël's *Germany* is recognised in European romantic studies as one of the most important texts in this shift, one which offers a vivid insight into the political and military backdrop against which 'romantic' versions of the nation and national culture were articulated.

Germany departs fundamentally from *De la littérature* in so far as union, which had in the earlier text featured as the means whereby to achieve progress and perfectibility, is in *Germany* represented as a destructive force which must be resisted:

> Difference of language, natural boundaries, the recollections of common history, contribute all together to give birth to those great individual existences which we call nations; certain proportions are necessary to their existence, they are distinguished by certain qualities; and if Germany were united to France, the consequence would be, that France would also be united to Germany, and the Frenchmen of Hamburg, like the Frenchmen of Rome, would by degrees effect a change in the character of the countrymen of Henry the Fourth: the vanquished would in time modify the victors, and in the end both would be losers.[10]

The explosive political implications of passages such as these were clearly registered by Napoleon, whose police seized the entire first edition, published in 1810, and almost succeeded in completely destroying it.[11] The republication of *Germany* in 1813 coincided with what came to be known as the German War of Liberation, in which Napoleon's armies were driven from the German territories, culminating in French defeat at the Battle of Leipzig in October 1813. In *Germany*, Staël promotes culture as a form of resistance that mirrors military resistance:

The ascendant obtained by French manners has perhaps prepared foreigners to believe them invincible. There is but one method of resisting this influence; and that consists in very decided national habits and character. From the moment that men seek to resemble the French, they must yield the advantage to them in everything. (I, 91–2)

The political message of passages such as these was clearly apparent to contemporary readers – not least the French censor, who originally deleted the first sentence of this paragraph. The English, in Staël's view, are the ideal opposition to Napoleonic France because of the intransigent stubbornness with which they adhere to their own cultural and social mores. In *De la littérature* the English tendency to dismiss or ignore the cultural products of other nations was referred to as an obstacle to progress and enlightenment – here it is hailed as a virtue. Staël's investment in this idea was such that it featured as a significant theme in her novel *Corinne*. The English hero's initial infatuation with Italy and Corinne (in the tradition of the national tale, Corinne embodies the foreign culture that the hero experiences) is repudiated: he returns to England to marry an Englishwoman, and Corinne dies.

The Staëlian paradigm is highly problematic when viewed from an Irish perspective. It is in fact a near impossibility, from this perspective, to celebrate England as the champion of national distinctiveness. Ireland had at this stage been part of the United Kingdom for over a decade, and there was little sign that the 'vanquished' had modified the 'victors' in this case. Union had not produced some new and improved blend of qualities, as Staël's original thesis in *De la littérature* had predicted, but nor was it possible, in the context of the Union, to endorse intransigent and insular nationality as a political virtue. Edgeworth's reflection on German, English and Irish nationalities in this period thus acts as an alternative to Staël's enthusiastic and highly politicised construction of a Europe of nationalities. This is achieved through a reworking of the relationships between gender, national character, and the public and private spheres. Staël's England, as we shall see, is both highly conscious of its national distinctiveness and characterised in terms of a masculine public sphere. The England of Edgeworth's *Patronage*, on the other hand, is depicted in terms of a public sphere that requires reform: in this text, the domestic sphere becomes a place from which to challenge official ideologies of patriotism and national character. Critiquing England is not exactly the same as addressing the dilemma of Irish nationality in this period, however. Turning to the representation of Irishness in *The Absentee* in the second part of this chapter, I propose that one response to the impossibility of promoting Staëlian nationalism in post-Union Ireland was to suggest, in the figures of Colambre and Grace Nugent, an Irishness that is fluid and anti-essentialist. This does not suggest a postmodern construction of identity. The fluid identities of Grace and Colambre in *The Absentee* are mirrored in *Patronage* in Mr Henry, a character whose obscure origins involve a confusing story of mysterious suffering and exile, whose ultimate source is 'Ireland's troubles'. The mystery of Mr Henry's parentage is eventually solved – but not before his story suggests that Irish origins are in some way synonymous with suffering and exile, a fate from which he is ultimately released. The disappearing and reappearing quality of Irishness that we find in both these texts suggests that identity takes shape in the context of real and palpable power differences. This is a conclusion not unlike that which is offered by the story of 'The Irish Incognito' in *Irish Bulls*, but the difference here is that in this new Europe of nationalities there is simultaneously a demand for the production of Irishness as well as an impulse towards its suppression.

Patronage has more often been considered in terms of its morality than its politics. It is, moreover, the most conspicuously ignored of Edgeworth's novels – conspicuous because its enormous length and complexity contrast particularly sharply with the brevity of critical comment. The neglect could almost be described as an embarrassed silence, because *Patronage* is of Edgeworth's longer texts the one most open to the charge of a crippling didacticism. Edgeworth herself remarked that in this novel 'the moral *saute aux yeux* at every turn'.[12] Most damning of all could be the fact that the utilitarian reformer Jeremy Bentham was said to be 'enchanté' with the novel.[13] Marilyn Butler speaks for most twentieth-century critics when she writes that *Patronage* is 'as a whole the least readable of the Edgeworth novels'.[14] Until recently the only exception to this damning consensus was the maverick enthusiasm of James Newcomer, who claims that *Patronage* 'towers with a kind of heavy symmetry for which no apology need be made'.[15] Since the publication of Newcomer's study of Edgeworth, the bibliography of the Modern Languages Association lists only two articles relating to *Patronage*: Dinwiddy's brief account of Jeremy Bentham's response to the novel, and Mc Cormack's essay.[16] The novel's appearance in the recent edition of Edgeworth's selected works, with an up-to-date and informative introductory note represents the only other recent contribution towards the novel's rehabilitation.

In the simplest terms, *Patronage* deals with the contrasting fates of two families, the Percys and the Falconers. Both are families of landed property, but the Percys aim to give their sons (Godfrey, Albert and Erasmus) and daughters (Caroline and Rosamond) a modern education on rational principles, such that the sons will be fit to pursue professional careers and the daughters will be able to recognise worth as a personal quality, rather than relying on an index of wealth or fashion when choosing a husband. The Falconers, by contrast, rely on their ability to win favour with the fashionable and influential in order to 'push' both their sons and daughters to positions in which they can gain access to income, or income in the form of a wealthy suitor, in the easiest possible manner. The families, who are in any case cousins, are linked in the plot through the figure of Lord Oldborough, who was in his youth a friend of Mr Percy's, and has in latter days become a somewhat reluctant patron to the Falconer family. The gradual recovery and rise of the Percys following the loss of their estate through the unfortunate mislaying of a deed, and the manner in which they attain not only to prosperity but to happiness, is contrasted with the increasing misery of the Falconers and their children, Maria, Georgiana, Buckhurst and Cunningham.

To summarise the novel in these terms, however, is to give a false impression of its simplicity and didacticism. James Newcomer estimates that there are 65 characters who play a part in the plot of *Patronage*, presenting 'a polychrome of personality and morality'.[17] It is a mistake moreover to separate the novel's moral lessons from the political background which Edgeworth goes to great lengths to depict. References to campaigns, actions and battles pepper the pages of this novel. The Percys' close friend Mrs Hungerford has two sons, one in the navy and one in the army. These combatants are not merely referred to: they make their way into the narrative. Mrs Hungerford receives a letter from her younger son written ten minutes after an action at sea with the French, while her elder son returns from service on the Continent for three weeks' leave of absence and enthrals the assembled company at Hungerford Castle with tales of his military experiences. Meanwhile, the Percys' eldest son Godfrey, having joined the army, is sent to the West Indies, from where he writes several letters detailing conditions. At the novel's close his return and reunion with his family is delayed owing to the capture of his transport by the Dutch; he is subsequently detained in Amsterdam for several weeks.[18] Examples of this kind, in which Edgeworth draws on the events of the war to furnish both central and peripheral plot devices and details, could be multiplied.

The plot of *Patronage* is, to a considerable extent, driven by its wartime setting. The novel opens with a shipwreck, and the rescue of the French diplomat, M de Tourville, who mislays an encrypted document in the subsequent chaos. The opportunistic Mr Falconer recognises immediately that 'something might be made of this intercepted dispatch', and earns Lord Oldborough's favour by putting the document in his hands and offering to decode its contents.[19] The Falconers therefore succeed in their desire for advancement through the manipulation of current events to their advantage. Mr Percy, by contrast, suffers owing to his refusal to make of the '*existing circumstances*' (vi, 60) an excuse for unethical behaviour. Mr Percy's principles seem to be based on those of R. L. Edgeworth, according to Maria, who wrote of her father that 'the maxim, that extraordinary times call for extraordinary measures, he considered to be a principle, dangerous as it is vague'.[20] By taking the part of a tenant who is being harassed in the courts on the pretext of owning an unlicensed dog, Mr Percy earns the dangerous enmity of the unscrupulous attorney Sharpe. Sharpe utters the following cynical admonition:

> for his part, he did not pretend to be a reformer of abuses; he thought in the present times, that gentlemen, who wished well to their King, and the peace of the country, ought not to be forward to lend their names to popular discontents, and should not embarrass government with petty complaints. – Gentlemen could never foresee where such things would end, and therefore, in the *existing circumstances*, they ought surely to endeavor to strengthen, instead of weakening the hands of government. (VI, 60)

Enraged by Mr Percy's opposition, attorney Sharpe subsequently takes pleasure in depriving the Percys of their estate once the loss of a crucial deed is revealed. Edgeworth thus makes the war an actor in her plot in manner designed to irritate nationalist feeling: she suggests that in these circumstances the honourable and virtuous are likely to suffer, while the venal and self-seeking are provided with opportunities for advancement.

Patronage could in fact be regarded as belonging to a distinct moment of reformist and radical protest in Britain, the period 1807–12, in which 'four distinct strands of radicalism appeared and interacted'.[21] *Patronage* contains criticism of some measures specific to the war period, such as press-ganging, the practice whereby any man could be forced to serve in the British Navy. By drawing attention to the practice of press-ganging, Edgeworth was addressing an issue which had been the cause of popular disturbance in many parts of Britain: riots in Essex, for instance, took place among the Irish community, who reacted to the impressment of a number of Irishmen living locally.[22] It is interesting to speculate on whether or not Edgeworth had heard of this incident, as she centres her attack on the press-gang system around the supposed seizure of an Irish labourer, O'Brien, and Erasmus Percy's attempts to have him released. Criticism of the activities of the press-gangs were also voiced in the memoirs of the radical MP, Samuel Bamford, who was jailed for a year after the Peterloo massacre in 1819.[23] The *Quarterly Review* responded to Edgeworth's 'diatribe' on the subject of impressment by remarking that it was 'a subject which faction itself has hitherto left untouched', and implying that the criticisms were of the kind designed to stir up discontent:

> [Impressment is] a subject [. . .] which under proper management may one day ripen into a first-rate grievance, and become the parent of as numerous a progeny of patriots as the borough-mongering system itself.[24]

The satirical use of the word 'patriot' is of particular interest: the reviewer, John Ward, completely dismisses the idea that the desire to change or reform existing practices and institutions could be motivated by a genuinely 'patriotic' desire to improve one's country. In wartime, the only patriotism possible is apparently unquestioning support of the government and the *status quo*.

Edgeworth's criticism is, moreover, considerably more far reaching than the issue of press-ganging. The crisis of the novel occurs when Lord Oldborough realises that Mrs Falconer has been raising money by selling positions, apparently under his name. In his review of *Patronage*, Francis Jeffrey suggested that 'the more loyal' among his readers might 'discover, in Mrs Falconer's forging, and sale of commissions, the nauseous detail of Mrs Clarke's plot and correspondence with the Claverings and Fitzgeralds'.[25] The scandal to which Jeffrey refers, that of the sale of commissions by the Duke of York's mistress, Mrs Clarke, was brought to light initially by the *Independent Whig* in 1808, following which a 'full-blooded attack on corruption rocked the ministry';[26] this was the major scandal of the period, and was fully exploited by radical journalists such as William Cobbett and Leigh Hunt.[27] Edgeworth's engagement with themes and concerns such as these placed her in a position of extreme liberalism, close to radicalism – the scandal on the sale of commissions resulted in a temporary coalition of interests between liberals and radicals in Parliament. This can be gauged partly from the *Quarterly's* unusually critical response to the novel, but also from a letter to *The Examiner*, edited by the radical Hunt brothers, signed 'A Pupil of Miss Edgeworth's'. According to John Dinwiddy, this letter was 'evidently written by Jeremy Bentham', and draws attention to an example of corruption among British officers in Barbados.[28] Bentham plays on the fact that Major-General Clay, the officer in question who was tried with misappropriating government money, shares a name with two characters from *Patronage*, brothers known as 'French Clay' and 'English Clay'. The charges of misconduct were brought against Clay by an officer of an inferior rank, and while Clay was dealt with extraordinarily leniently, his accuser was subsequently dismissed from the army. Bentham's argument, as Dinwiddy points out, is that 'this case illustrates in a most revealing manner the real character and *modus operandi*, not only of the army, but of "the whole official establishment."'[29] Thus not only did Edgeworth's novel, in Bentham's view, encompass a critique of 'the whole official establishment', it also contributed after its publication to a climate of opposition and liberal comment via the public sphere of print.[30]

The figure of Count Altenberg provides another layer to the critique of wartime England in *Patronage*. According to *Germany*, one of the differences between England and Germany lay in the inability of German men to participate in public life, largely owing to the fragmentation of the German lands into tiny states and principalities. This rendered their characters 'purer' than those of Englishmen, but resulted also in a fatal inability to act effectively. In a chapter that was ultimately excluded from the published text of *Germany*, Staël turned her observations of and theories about German character to the task of speculating on the traits of 'a German hero'. Staël based this sketch on a young Austrian whom she met in 1805, Count Maurice O'Donnell.[31] As his name suggests, O'Donnell was the descendant of the Ulster O'Donnells who were among the 'Wild Geese' who left Ireland following the disastrous Battle of Kinsale. He was the son of Count Joseph O'Donnell, who served as finance minister in the difficult period following the Napoleonic invasion. What Staël has in mind in describing a German hero is the hero of a novel – an alternative title which she considered for the chapter. Noting that the male heroes of her two novels, Léonce in *Delphine* and Oswald, Lord Nelvil, in *Corinne*, were judged by most readers to be patently unworthy of the heroines, Staël claimed that if she were ever to depict a 'perfect' hero, he would have to be German, rather than Spanish, like Léonce, or 'English', like Oswald.[32] Admitting that the imperfections of her heroes are essential if her plots of female tragedy are to have any force, Staël nonetheless varies masculine faults according to the nationality of the hero. Thus Léonce shares Oswald's concern with social judgements, but Léonce's refusal to countenance social disapproval is associated with his 'Spanish' aristocratic pride, whereas Oswald's springs from a supposedly English reverence from tradition, embodied in the will of the father. The 'German' hero approaches perfection owing to what Staël describes as a lack of 'prejudice', which enables the idealised German man, in stark contrast to Oswald and Léonce, to stand apart from social convention and opinion. In an inverse description of the central tragedies of *Delphine* and *Corinne* Staël writes that when creating a German hero 'one could imagine to oneself a character who was proud without being severe, who did not censure according to received rules, but only according to the impulse of the heart'.[33]

While the German hero approaches perfection owing to his ability to rise above social conventions and live life as an individual guided by heart and conscience, his potential flaws lie in an inability to perform an active role in society. In order to underline the contrast between German and English character in this specific area, Staël suggests that, were he to live in England, the German man would be unable to fix on a course of action, in the excess of opportunities that such a society offers. She predicts that he would confine himself to a private, domestic existence, but would be perpetually troubled by restlessness due to the failure to exercise his abilities.[34] What she is suggesting, therefore, is that the 'ideal' German man actually lacks sufficient masculinity to perform in Britain's masculine public sphere, and will be frustrated by his confinement to the feminine domestic sphere. Although Staël consistently expressed admiration for the achievements of British public life, she was ambivalent as to the corollary, which, according to her, limited women to an entirely domestic role. Her insistence on the characterisation of England as a 'masculine' country is evident in all her works, not least *Corinne*. Edgeworth's England as depicted in *Patronage* differs fundamentally from Staël's, not only for its criticism of the conduct of public life, but also for the way in which Edgeworth insists on the feminisation of English national character. The contrast is especially evident in the figure of the novel's German hero, Count Altenberg, who decides at the close of the novel to make his life in England with his English wife.

It is clear that Edgeworth shared Staël's opinion as to an affinity between the English and the Germans, and that this opinion is in Edgeworth's case also driven to a certain extent by the contemporary political situation. Mentioned in passing at the opening of the narrative, Altenberg is subsequently absent throughout the whole of the first volume and much of the second, until he eventually appears in person, at a particularly charged moment, protesting to an English navy captain about the manner in which his servant has been 'pressed' into naval service. Altenberg's 'foreignness' makes his protest against this practice potentially inflammatory, and it is significant that the captain initially mistakes him for a Frenchman, and puts on 'the surly air, with which he thought it for his honor, and for the honor of his country to receive a Frenchman' (VI, 238). Upon discovering that the Count is in fact German, the Captain's manner changes instantly:

> 'Ah, Ha! [. . .] I thought you were not a Frenchman, or you could not talk so well of English law, and feel so much for English liberty – And now then, since that's the case, I'll own to you frankly, that in the main, I'm much of your mind'. (VI, 239)

Altenberg is unquestionably a hero, a man one could reasonably call perfect, and, unlike Staël's heroes, eminently worthy of the heroine. From early on, the reader becomes aware that Caroline Percy, exemplary eldest daughter of the Percy family, has rather high standards when it comes to suitors. A relative of Mr Percy's, Lady Jane Granville, despairs at the reluctance of the Percys to launch their daughters on the fashionable marriage market, and warns them not 'to puff up Caroline's imagination with a parcel of romantic notions' (VI, 129); she warns further that Mr and Mrs Percy will be disappointed if they 'expect a genius to descend from the clouds express for your daughters. Let them do as other people do, and they may have a chance of meeting with some good sort of men, who will make them as happy as . . . as happy as their neighbours' (VI, 129). Caroline subsequently turns down a proposal from a Mr Barclay, a man of fortune and family, and reveals that she possesses a number of 'romantic notions' as she explains her refusal to her sister Rosamond:

> 'Mr Barclay appears to me incapable of that enthusiasm, which rises either to the moral or intellectual sublime. I respect his understanding, and esteem his principles, but [. . .] there is a want of the higher qualities of the mind. He shows no invention, no genius, no magnanimity – nothing heroic, nothing great, nothing which could waken sympathy, or excite that strong attachment, which I think I am capable of feeling for a superior character – for a character at once good and great.' (VI, 169)

Caroline's desire for a lover whose character encompasses enthusiasm, genius and the capacity for heroism marks her out as, indeed, unusually 'romantic' in the context of Edgeworthian heroines, and her discovery of these qualities in Altenberg confirms the position that Germany came to occupy as a site of romantic values. It is significant that the first acquaintance the Percys make with Altenberg is through the report of a French diplomat, a M de Tourville, posted to the German court of which Altenberg is a member. M de Tourville relates that Altenberg lost the favour of the Prince by his refusal to connive at a sexual intrigue carried on by the Prince with an actress. Whereas M de Tourville represents Altenberg as '*une tete exaltée*, a young man of a romantic Quixotic enthusiasm' (VI, 14), the Percys conclude that the anecdotes and incidents related by Tourville are 'proofs of his [Altenberg's] independence of character, and greatness of soul' (VI, 14). The schema proposed by Staël in *De la littérature* and developed in *Germany* reflects this characterisation of the French as particularly indifferent to the promptings of individual conscience and the heart, in direct contrast with the inhabitants of the North. Thus far Edgeworth's portrayal of the German hero seems to mirror that of Staël's. However, Altenberg is not flawed in the way that Staël deemed characteristic of the German hero, and this divergence is highly significant.

Altenberg's decision to settle in England is rendered more plausible by the fact that his mother was English and that he has always regarded England as a potential home. This revelation is made in a more or less strategic way, however, and no elaboration on the potentially hybrid nature of his identity is made. In fact, Altenberg is frequently referred to as a foreigner, and his function, at numerous points in the novel, is to provide the perspective of an intelligent and sophisticated external observer, a 'philosophical traveller', on aspects of English life, including customs, law, landscape and architecture. Thus it is noted when Altenberg visits Clermont Park, Lord Oldborough's country seat, that it is 'one of the really magnificent places in England, which an Englishman may feel proud to show to a foreigner' (VII, 15). More telling than Altenberg's appreciation of the pleasures of English country life is his unbiased appraisal of English womanhood. Mrs Falconer's design of making a match between her daughter Georgiana and the glamorous German visitor is, she fears, jeopardised by his friendliness with the Percy family:

> by those of the [Percy] family whom she saw this day, she judged of Caroline, whom she had not seen; and she had tact sufficient to apprehend, that the conversation and manners of Mrs Percy and of Rosamond were such, as might, perhaps, please a well-bred and well-informed foreigner, better, even, than the fashionable tone and air of the day, of which he had not been long enough in England to appreciate the conventional value. (VI, 270)

Altenberg's superior nature thus resides partly in his ability to recognise similar superiority in the Percys, and more specifically in Caroline Percy. The influence of an emergent romantic sensibility is also suggested by Altenberg's apparent lack of interest in 'conventional value'. One might contrast this with Clarence Hervey in *Belinda*, whose pursuit of what is natural and sweeping dismissal of 'what everybody knows' is portrayed with ironic distance. Caroline's character has features which are, it is very subtly implied, more 'permanent' than the fashion and convention which governs Georgiana. How do we interpret the fact that not alone is Altenberg, of all the characters in the novel, judged to approach the 'moral and intellectual sublime' that Caroline seeks, but that he, as a 'well-bred and well-informed foreigner' is best placed to appreciate the English feminine perfection that Caroline herself represents? Caroline's virtues are only half of the story: their recognition by Altenberg alters the meaning of those virtues, suggesting that the best 'English' characteristics are not necessarily those valued in the England of the day.

The politically charged nature of this mutual recognition of virtue is underlined by several more explicit incidents and allusions throughout *Patronage*. Altenberg's objection to press-ganging has already been mentioned: the incident is, however, even more inflammatory of patriotic opinion in view of the fact that Erasmus Percy fails to make any reasonable defence of the practice. Altenberg points out the inconsistency between English opposition to the slave trade and the practice of impressment, and forces Erasmus to admit its inhumanity. Erasmus, as he relates in a letter to his family, is driven to defend the measure 'on the plea of necessity':

> "'Necessity!" said the Count – "pardon me if I remind you, that Necessity is the tyrant's plea."
>
> 'I mended my plea, and changed Necessity, into – Utility – general utility. It was essential to England's defence – to her existence – she could not exist

without her navy, and her navy could not be maintained without a press-gang – as I was assured by those who were skilled in the affairs of the Navy.

'The Count smiled at my evident consciousness of the weakness of my concluding corollary, and observed, "that by my own statement, the whole argument depended on the assertions of those who maintained, that a navy could not exist without a press-gang." – He urged this no further, and I was glad of it'. (vi, 239–40)

The references to England's 'defence' and her 'existence' remind us that this exchange takes place firmly within the context of England's war with Napoleonic France.

In his review of *Patronage*, cited above, John Ward makes a sidelong reference to the claims of liberals and radicals critical of the government to be motivated by patriotism. Edgeworth's 'patriotism' is surely even more calculated to irritate conservative feeling, since the German Altenberg, already acknowledged as the embodiment of virtue, proceeds to instruct Englishmen in the meaning of the virtue of patriotism. Edgeworth portrays Altenberg and Caroline Percy in confrontation with the extremes of English national prejudice on the one hand, and utter indifference to nationality on the other, in the persons of 'English Clay' and 'French Clay'. In spite of their obvious shortcomings, the two brothers are being 'managed' by Mrs Falconer as potential husbands for her two daughters, should nothing better present itself. French Clay is a frenchified Englishman, of a type that occurs more than once in Edgeworth's fictions, but in *Patronage*, the 'Frenchness' that French Clay seeks to imitate has a very particular sense of indifference to homeland that is not evident in Edgeworth's earlier work. French Clay announces that: "'it is quite indifferent to me, whether England be called England or France. – For", concluded he, [. . .] "after all I have heard, I recur to my first question, what is country – or, as people term it, their native land?'" (vii, 42). The context of the Napoleonic Wars is implicit in Altenberg's response that attitudes such as those of French Clay have been 'the precursors of the ruin, disgrace, destruction of the princes and nations of Europe' (vii, 42). Altenberg is astonished that it is 'in England, and from an Englishman' that he has heard these views. The 'patriotic' views of English Clay are not likely to reassure him. English Clay's patriotism is compounded of bigotry, ignorance and a self-confessed indiscriminacy when it comes to 'English' culture:

'I have every edition of Shakspeare [*sic*], that ever was printed or published, and every thing that ever was written about him, good, bad or indifferent, at Clay-Hall. I made this a principle, and I think every Englishman should do the same. – *Your* Mr Voltaire', added this polite Englishman, turning to

Count Altenberg, 'made a fine example of himself, by *dashing* at *our* Shakspeare?' (VII, 42–3)

Altenberg's response is to refer English Clay to Elizabeth Montagu's *Essay on Shakespeare*, and to suggest that national prejudice may be a peculiarly masculine quality:

> 'Even Voltaire had some tinge of national prejudice, as well as other men. It was reserved for women, to set us an example in this instance, as in many others, an example at once of superior candor, and superior talent.' (VII, 44)

Altenberg manages to combine a slight to English Clay with a gallant compliment: English *women*, rather than English men, represent the best qualities of the nation. As far as Count Altenberg is concerned there is of course one particular English woman who epitomises the best qualities of the country:

> In his own country, at the court where he had resided, in the different parts of the continent which he had visited, Germany, Poland, Swisserland, France, he had seen women celebrated for beauty and for wit [. . .] It was reserved for Count Altenberg, to meet in England . . . in England, where education, institution, opinion, manners, the habits of society, and of domestic life, happily combine to give the just proportion of all that is attractive, useful, ornamental, and amiable, to the female character . . . It was reserved for Count Altenberg, to meet in England a woman, who to the noble simplicity of character, that was once the charm of Swisserland, joined the polish, the elegance, that was once the pride of France [. . .] It was reserved for Count Altenberg, to meet in England with a woman of sensibility, exquisite, generous as any German romance could conceive, yet without exaggeration in expression, or extravagance in conduct [. . .]. (VII, 51–2)

On one level, this is an assertion of English superiority over all the other nations of Europe. But it should be noted that what makes Caroline so special, in the eyes of Altenberg, the sophisticated foreigner, is that she combines a variety of qualities, typical of different nationalities.

Altenberg's decision to marry and settle in England with Caroline is deferred, however, not once, but twice. Firstly he must extricate himself from a match arranged by his father in his absence, and then he is forced to leave England immediately after his marriage, following reports of 'revolutionary symptoms' at home. At this point, it is assumed that Altenberg and Caroline will live in Germany, so that Altenberg can pursue his political career. However, the 'revolutionary symptoms' turn into an invasion by the French, connived at by the Prince's successor, and Altenberg returns to England, satisfied that loyalty no longer requires his presence at court:

seeing that, under such a successor to the Government, no means of serving or saving the country remained, he at once determined to quit it for ever. Resolved to live in a free country, already his own half by birth, and wholly by inclination, where he had property sufficient to secure him independence, sufficient for all his own wishes, and for the still more moderate desires of the woman he loves. Where he can enjoy, better than on any other spot now in the whole compass of the civilised world, the blessings of real liberty, and of domestic tranquillity and happiness. (VII, 230)

This apparently unequivocal declaration of faith in England's superiority, symbolised by her unique resistance to Napoleonic tyranny, is belied by the novel's 'massively comprehensive account of cynicism'.[35] The fact that the Percys act as the embodiment of all imaginable virtues has been viewed as an index of Edgeworth's didacticism, in that character appears to be sacrificed to the constant need to point a moral, by contrasting the admirable Percys with the behaviour of those around them. However, it has not been noted that the Percys appear to be almost alone in their pursuit of independence and virtue, both public and private. Following the loss of their estate, the family retire to a small residence, all that remains of their property. With the exception of the loyal Hungerfords, 'society' at large promptly forgets their existence. The rise of the Falconers, meanwhile, is facilitated by the corruption and venality of the social and public world. Edgeworth received criticism for precisely this tendency to depict the wider world of fashion, society and politics as an almost unavoidably corrupting influence. In the *Quarterly*, Ward objected to Edgeworth's quiet insistence on widespread corruption among the fashionable:

> She produces an erroneous impression [. . .] by drawing too many favourable specimens from some classes, and too many unfavourable ones from others. This is a most successful, and when it is intentional, a most insidious mode of misrepresentation, because it is not liable to a direct charge of falsehood.[36]

In *Patronage*, Lord Oldborough is portrayed as the slave of ambition who, in spite of his respect for Mr Percy's independent life as a country gentleman, cannot wean himself off the intoxication of a life of power. *Patronage* is loud in its admiration for those of ability and talent who serve their country in public life, but the novel nevertheless ends with Lord Oldborough's decision to retire from public service and acquaint himself with the pleasures of domesticity. In the words of the closing quotation, he 'please'd resign'd/To tender passions all his mighty mind' (VII, 252).

Far from acting to exclude the public sphere from the domestic, however, this recurring theme functions as a protest against the construction of a feminine domestic space designed to exist in parallel with but without reference to the masculine world of politics, industry and the professions. Rather than conclude that the public sphere is portrayed as an unsuitable place for a woman, it might be said that the domestic as imagined as a man's world. The novel's exemplary men, Mr Percy and Count Altenberg, choose the life of an 'independent country gentleman': virtue and independence are portrayed as being incompatible with a political career. Edgeworth goes so far as to suggest that genuine patriotism is threatened by the demands of public service, while it flourishes among those who lived a retired, domestic life:

> [Lord Oldborough] sometimes nodded, and sometimes smiled, as Mr Percy spoke of public men or measures; but when he expressed any sentiment of patriotism, or of public virtue, Lord Oldborough took to his snuff-box, shook and levelled the snuff, and if he listened, listened as to words superfluous and irrelevant. When Mr Percy uttered any principle favorable to the liberty of the press, or of the people, his lordship would take several pinches of snuff rapidly to hide the expression of his countenance; if the topics were continued, his averted eyes and compressed lips showed disapprobation, and the difficulty he felt in refraining from reply. (VI, 19)

Count Altenberg suggested that English women led the way in demonstrating that love of one's 'native land' could be expressed without bigotry. Here Edgeworth claims that patriotism flourishes in the domestic sphere, thus questioning the gendering of that sphere as female, and undermining England's claim to the unique position of a masculine public sphere that symbolised national virtue.

Patronage is clearly a novel written in the shadow of the ongoing Napoleonic campaigns. This context is not limited to the allusions to military and naval engagements, and the invasion of the German lands by the French, but is reflected in the novel's heightened concern with nationality, national prejudice and patriotism. This is most evident in Edgeworth's creation of a German hero. In contrast to Germaine de Staël's imaginary German hero, the character of Altenberg forms part of a critical reflection on the potential for the corruption of public life with specific reference to the demands of militarism. *The Absentee* can also be read in this context, as it explores the possibilities for the expression of Irish identity in this volatile political climate.

As it is in *Patronage*, feminine patriotism is an important theme in *The Absentee*. When Grace Nugent refers to herself as a 'friend to Ireland', her aunt Lady Clonbrony replies irritably: 'I hate to hear people, women especially, and young ladies particularly, talk of being friends to this country or that country. What can they know about countries?'[37] The novel goes on to suggest that women can indeed 'know about countries' and that that this is a positive virtue. Critical comment has focused on the fact that Grace Nugent's repeatedly affirmed relationship with Ireland is belatedly severed, when she is revealed to be an English heiress, the granddaughter of a Mr Reynolds, of Suffolk. The text itself highlights and plays with the sudden changes that take place in Grace's identity; the fact that she acquires two new names in the course of the narrative does not go unnoticed, and is pointed out by the observant lady's maid, Mrs Petito:

> 'I beg you'll make my humble respects acceptable to the *ci-devant* miss Grace Nugent that was; and I won't *derrogate* her by any other name in the inter-regnum, as I am persuaded it will only be a temporary name, scarce worth assuming, except for the honour of the public adoption; and that will, I'm confident, be soon exchanged for a viscount's title, or I have no sagacity or sympathy.' (186–7)

Mrs Petito is amazed at 'the *metamorphoses* that have taken place, though by what magic I can't guess' (186). Grace Nugent is thus much more than a watered-down version of Morgan's Glorvina. References to 'magic', 'meta-morphosis', and Grace's own exclamation at the disclosure about her identity, 'I am still as if I were in a dream', all suggest that the ambiguity that surrounds Grace's birth and nationality is deliberate and purposeful, rather than merely evasive. Marilyn Butler has suggested that 'Edgeworth's allegorical Irishwomen are a particularly strange variant of an insufficiently discussed type – the figure of a woman as a symbolical national leader'; representatives of this type include of course the heroines of Morgan's novels, but also of Staël's and Mary Shelley's.[38] In *Corinne*, the heroine's tragedy is that she cannot reconcile her hybrid identity as half-Italian and half-English, largely because she discovers the English to be intolerant of difference. *Corinne*, therefore, like *The Absentee*, focuses on a female character whose identity is not contained within a unitary national cate-gory, but whereas this is the source of tragedy in *Corinne*, *The Absentee*, through the younger generation of characters, Lord Colambre and Grace Nugent, con-structs an Irish identity which is characterised by being elusive and adaptive.

Corinne opens with Oswald's departure from Britain, under a mysterious cloud of guilt and melancholy. His father has recently died and it is intimated that Oswald's gloom relates to a rupture between himself and his father which was unresolved before his father's death. He journeys to Italy, hoping to recover his health, but almost immediately upon his arrival he becomes acquainted with Corinne, whom he has seen being crowned at the Capitol, and he is captivated by her. The romance between Corinne and Oswald is played out against the backdrop of Roman art and antiquities and the Italian countryside, as Corinne seeks to hold her admirer's interest and to banish his native distrust of the foreign, and foreign womanhood. Corinne herself is possessed of a secret, which, it is hinted, would conclusively destroy any hope of a marriage between the two. Oswald's unease about Corinne centres not on her foreignness, but on the *ambiguity* of her nationality: although the inhabitants of Rome boast that her perfect Italian could only be the speech of a native Roman, he is startled to discover that she also speaks English 'with the pure native accent that can almost never be reproduced on the Continent'.[39] This inimitable speech convinces Oswald that Corinne must have spent some years in England, and that it may even have been her native land, a thought that gives him much disquiet, since he cannot conceive how she could have left England for Italy were this the case.

Oswald's melancholy is rooted in the fact that he disobeyed his father and pursued a romance with a Frenchwoman, ignoring paternal pleas to return to Scotland, until it was too late: his father died before the two could be reconciled. His passion for Corinne is a source of pain because he knows that his father had planned for him to marry Lucile Edgermond, the daughter of his oldest friend. Although Oswald is not engaged to Lucile and is thereby not in breach of any promise, he feels instinctively that it would have been his father's wish for him to marry an Englishwoman. The lovers' relationship reaches a crisis when Corinne reveals that she is Lord Edgermond's elder daughter, the product of his first marriage to an Italian woman. On her mother's death Corinne was left to finish her education in Rome under the care of an aunt, and arrived in England for the first time aged 16 to live with her father, his new wife and her stepsister, Lucile. Corinne's motive in postponing this revelation lies in her knowledge that the late Lord Nelvil had originally intended a marriage between her and his son, but that he decided against it. The lovers part and Oswald returns to England to visit the Edgermond estate in Northumbria, ostensibly with the intention of persuading Lady Edgermond to recognise Corinne and thereby to 'legitimise' her; he also wishes to discover what objections his father had raised against a marriage with Corinne. Once removed from Italy Oswald quickly resumes the habits and ideas which characterise the English, who are, as one of Corinne's admirers once warned her, 'slaves to the customs and habits of their country' (49). The blonde, blushing beauty of Lucile Edgermond, together with her extreme innocence, modesty and reserve, begin to strike Oswald as more captivating than Corinne's brilliance and genius. He also learns that his father expressly objected to a marriage with Corinne on the grounds that she 'would inevitably lead my son away from England, for such a woman can never be happy here, and Italy alone is right for her' (329). Marriage to Corinne, in the late Lord Nelvil's eyes, would result in and be synonymous with 'expatriation' (330). Corinne, meanwhile, distraught because she has not heard from Oswald, decides to travel to England. Observing him from a distance, Corinne becomes convinced that Oswald has fallen in love with Lucile, and writes him a note releasing him from the relationship. She returns to Italy and Lucile and Oswald ultimately marry. The novel concludes with Oswald's return to Italy, accompanied by his wife and daughter Juliette. Their marriage has been blighted by Oswald's guilt and Lucile's jealousy of Corinne and also her anger at her husband's cruel treatment of his former lover. In Florence they learn that Corinne now lives there in seclusion. Corinne refuses to see Oswald, but begins to educate his daughter Juliette, who bears a close resemblance to her, and also instructs Lucile as to how to regain her husband's love. The novel closes with Corinne's death.

The simple identification suggested by the title – that Corinne *is* Italy – is as we can see immediately undermined by Corinne's mixed parentage. She describes herself as possessing a unique dual identity, saying that 'Thanks to the rare combination of circumstances that had given me a dual education and if you will, two nationalities, I could think myself destined for special privileges' (264–5). The evidence of the novel suggests, however, that Corinne's dual identity guarantees not special privileges, but tragedy. The sound of her perfect English accent shocks Oswald into a new perception of the figure whom he had regarded initially as a foreign spectacle: it 'naturalised all of Corinne's charms' (33). The combination of the exotic or foreign and the homely and familiar proves irresistible to Oswald. However, this combination of characteristics is also what dooms the relationship between the two. Corinne's unsuitability as a wife for Oswald lies not only in her foreignness, but also in her revolt from her 'fatherland', quite literally the land of her father, which she cannot bear to live in. Oswald is somewhat shocked by her manner and way of living, which would be unthinkable for an Englishwoman, but it is this figurative betrayal of the father which horrifies him most. Oswald's guilty reverence of his own father is such that it overturns natural succession. He declares: 'happy are the children who die in their father's arms, [. . .] and who meet death in the bosom of the one who gave them life!' (80).

The reasons for Corinne's inability to live in England can be summarised in two different ways: firstly, it is a society in which the maintenance of the domestic sphere is all important, and unusual or striking talents in women are thus discouraged. Secondly, English national character is portrayed as resolutely insular and resistant to foreign influence. When Corinne arrives to live with her father in Northumberland he counsels her to avoid appearing unusual or unconventional: 'you would never find anyone to marry you if people thought your tastes were foreign to our customs' (253). The late Lord Nelvil's objections to the marriage between Oswald and Corinne focus on the virtue of English insularity; he forecasts that

If my son married Miss Edgermond he would surely love her very much, for no one could possibly be more charming; therefore, to please her, he would try to introduce foreign ways into his household. Soon he would lose that sense of nationality, those prejudices, if you will, that bind us together and make of our nation one body, a free but indissoluble association that cannot perish until the last one of us is dead. (329–30)

This portrayal of England (which must surely have been influenced by Burke) implies that it is a nation incapable of absorbing or accepting non-native elements, a trait which led Corinne to abandon the country initially and ultimately leads to her tragedy.

In contrast to Staël's insistence that English women live an entirely secluded life in which afternoon tea with neighbouring ladies represents the highest point of sociability and entertainment, *The Absentee* opens with a vivid scene involving the Duchess of Torcaster and the other English ladies who are leaders of the 'ton' – not only are they occupying a public space, but in their cruel dismissal of Lady Clonbrony and what they deem her social pretensions, they are clearly demonstrating their status and power as social arbiters. It is in fact possible to read *The Absentee* as operating on the basis of a series of contrasts which recall *Corinne*, but reverse the patterns of the earlier novel. Grace's ambiguous nationality may echo Corinne's, but she is essential to the hero's desire to return to his homeland, while Corinne, by contrast, threatens to draw Oswald away from England. Oswald is fascinated by the mixture of notoriety and mystery which surround Corinne: 'the combination of mystery and public notice – this woman everyone discussed without even knowing her real name – seemed one of the wonders of the singular country he had come to visit' (*Corinne*, 20). Colambre falls in love with Grace observing her while she cares for his mother in a darkened sick-room 'where often he could but just discern her form' (*The Absentee*, 35), yet he is confident that this sketchy figure 'with plain, unsophisticated morality, in good faith and simple truth, acted what she professed, thought what she said, and was that which she seemed to be' (36).

Although Grace's 'shadowiness' obviously contrasts with the image of Corinne standing in the capitol in the brilliant Roman light, the contrasts in the representation of the hero, Colambre, are of equal importance. Colambre for instance, has no difficulty in refusing to go along with his parents' plan to marry him to an heiress, and eventually succeeds in morally governing his parents, while Oswald is tortured by the idea of posthumous filial disloyalty. Colambre should not only be considered in relation to Oswald, however. Like Corinne, Colambre is the beneficiary of a dual education. Having spent his childhood in Ireland, he attended school and university in England, and emerges the perfect hybrid: 'The sobriety of English good sense mixed most advantageously with Irish vivacity: English prudence governed, but did not extinguish, his Irish enthusiasm' (9). Unlike his mother, Colambre can 'pass for English': the Duchess of Torcaster declares that he is "not an Irishman, I am sure, by his manner"' (6). Other characters express the desire of being incognito, but it is Colambre who successfully masks his identity when travelling through the family estates in Ireland. What differentiates Colambre from Corinne is the success of his hybrid identity. Colambre can pass for English, but unable to conform to the rigid conventions of English life, Corinne must instead, in order to spare her family in England from disgrace, 'pass for dead' (267). Colambre differs from his parents in this ability: it is suggested that both his mother and father possess only one true identity, and it is Colambre's function to persuade them to recognise this. Lady Clonbrony is only laughable because she attempts to hide her true nature:

> A natural and unnatural manner seemed struggling in all her gestures, and in every syllable that she articulated – a naturally free, familiar, good-natured, precipitate, Irish manner, had been schooled, and schooled late in life, into a sober, cold, still, stiff, deportment, which she mistook for English. (8)

Towards the novel's conclusion Colambre engages in some impassioned pleading in order to persuade his mother that the family would be best off at home; this, he assures her, would 'restore' his father 'to himself' (154).

Colambre's visit to Ireland is central to the novel's meaning. The citation of a number of key texts in the tradition of colonial discourse on Ireland at the beginning of this visit clearly raises questions about how we are to read Colambre's impressions. Colambre's tour, according to some critics, is a device to depict Irish conditions in such a way as to justify the application of modernising, implicitly English methods and practices. The citation of the tradition of colonial discourse is interpreted accordingly: 'like Spenser, she presented a stereotype of the native Irish, which suited her recipe for the anglicisation of all aspects of Irish life'.[40] It seems significant, however, that these texts, 'from Spenser and Davies to Young and Beaufort' are described as including 'representations and misrepresentations of Ireland' (65). Katie Trumpener argues instead that the role of the national tale in undoing misrepresentations is fundamental to its structure and its aims. *The Absentee* seems to suggest, however, that what makes the difference is not the 'truth', which is relative and open to a number of interpretations, but personal choice. The initial references to texts are replaced by personal experiences, which prove to be just as confusing as textual 'representations and misrepresentations'.

The first great comic scene in the Irish section of *The Absentee* takes place in 'Tusculum', the villa of the *nouveau riche* 'grocer's lady', Anastasia Raffarty.

While the other dinner-guests feel free to laugh at their hostess's absurd pretensions, Colambre realises miserably that 'what she was to them his mother was to persons in a higher rank of fashion' (72). The spectacle of 'Irish' tastelessness and vulgarity, as embodied by Mrs Raffarty's over-elaborate dinner and aesthetic obtuseness is tempered by Colambre's realisation that the scene, no matter how distasteful or ridiculous, cannot be dismissed as foreign or alien. Like his experiences at Tusculum, Colambre's experience of Ireland is mediated largely by women. As the men return to Dublin they encounter Lady Dashfort, an Englishwoman in Ireland on a mission to marry her daughter, Lady Isabel, to an Irish nobleman. In spite of the warnings of his friend Sir James Brooke, Colambre finds himself being ensnared in Lady Dashfort's marriage plot, part of which involves the 'misrepresentation' of Ireland, contrived so that Colambre will give up his plan of becoming resident in Ireland. She manipulates situations to an extraordinary degree, and manages to introduce him to people who 'give him a worse idea of the country, than any other people who could be produced' (84); she takes care 'to draw them out upon the subjects on which she knew that they would show the most self-sufficient ignorance, and the most illiberal spirit' (84):

> No one could, with more ease and more knowledge of her ground, than Lady Dashfort, do the *dishonours* of a country. In every cabin that she entered [. . .] she could distinguish the proper objects of her charitable designs, that is to say, those of the old uneducated race, whom no one can help, because they will never help themselves. To these she constantly addressed herself, making them give, in all their despairing tones, a history of their complaints and grievances [. . .]. (85)

Even when, having finally discerned Lady Dashfort's motives and the true character of her daughter, Colambre is free of her manipulative 'misrepresentations', it emerges that no form of representation is in fact adequate, and that Colambre's ultimate decision is to choose to see the Ireland that he wants to see. Having witnessed the chaos and unfairness that accompanies the renewing of leases on the Clonbrony estate, 'the smell of tobacco and whiskey, [. . .], the din of men wrangling, brawling, threatening, whining, drawling, cajoling, cursing, and every variety of wretchedness' (125), Colambre exclaims to himself:

> Is this Ireland? No, it is not Ireland. Let me not, like most of those who forsake their native country, traduce it. Let me not, even to my own mind, commit the injustice of taking the speck for the whole. (125)

Colambre dismisses metonymic representation – 'taking the speck for the whole' – as an injustice, but does not propose any alternative answer to the question of how Ireland could be justly represented. It seems to be primarily a matter of choice: Colambre ultimately chooses to identify 'Ireland' with the household in the cottage of the Widow O'Neil, whose son is engaged to a young woman named Grace, after Grace Nugent.

There has understandably been a considerable emphasis on Colambre's fact-finding journey to Ireland, largely because it situates *The Absentee* in a rich and controversial tradition. If his journey refers to one means whereby knowledge of cultures and places could be gathered and disseminated, the text provides another version of the same process in its treatment of Lady Clonbrony's gala. Whereas Colambre's journey is characterised by an earnest purpose and anchored in a textual tradition, the gala is, on first appearance, a very different manifestation of the desire of the metropolis for the visual and surface effects of the exotic and the foreign. This gala presents the sophisticated guests with a series of scenes straight out of imperialist and orientalist fantasy. The reception rooms are transformed into a Turkish tent, a mock Alhambra and a Chinese pagoda, with the aid of Mr Soho, a fashionable decorator and upholsterer who provides fabric and wallpapers, from Egyptian hieroglyphic to 'Trebisond trellice', and all the fittings, including 'josses, jars and beakers', 'sphynx candelabras' and 'phoenix argands', which are supposed, rather implausibly, to produce a '*tout ensemble*' or total effect (14). What should be Lady Clonbrony's social triumph, however, is ruined by the assurances of her fashionable guests that she has been swindled into accepting second-class goods, previously turned down by the Duchess of Torcaster 'in consequence of sir Horace Grant, the great traveller's objecting to some of the proportions of the pillars – Soho had engaged to make a new set, vastly improved, by sir Horace's suggestions, for her grace of Torcaster' (30). The consumption of highly fashionable products based on exotic cultures is in fact directly linked to the kind of travel on which Colambre was engaged – but, as we shall see, strict distinctions are made between producers and consumers.

Everyone agrees that Lady Clonbrony has been 'shamefully imposed' upon by Mr Soho, and her 'being a stranger, and from Ireland, makes the thing worse' (30). To Lady Clonbrony's mortification, her fashionable guests maliciously imply that as an Irish woman, she is not properly qualified for the élite forms of consumption which are reserved for metropolitan subjects and which are based on knowledge acquired by the large number of travellers – military, commercial, scientific, diplomatic – who regularly departed from the metropolitan centre and returned to it with their notes and observations. Lady Clonbrony tours her elaborately decorated rooms, nervously assuring herself that everything 'is correct, and appropriate and quite picturesque' (32); she has, however, mistaken what is actually correct and appropriate for her in the metropolitan setting, and that is to be a provider, not a consumer, of cultural commodities. Shortly after this unsuccessful extravaganza Lady Clonbrony finds herself forced to offer Irish dried salmon as a gift, or more accurately a bribe, in order to gain an invite to the Duchess of Torcaster's party. This is not the only occasion on which the text makes reference to Irish 'specialities': at Halloran Castle Colambre and his companions are treated to 'Irish ortolans', of which it is remarked that they 'are worthy of being transmitted a great way to market', and 'Irish plums', which are apparently 'the thing the queen's so fond of' (95). The emphasis on Ireland as the source of produce that can be transformed into fashionable and exclusive consumables in London (no less a person than the queen enjoys 'Irish plums') echoes Staël's word of warning to 'small nations' seeking to be fashionable:

> French milliners export to the colonies, to Germany, and to the north, what they commonly call their *shop-fund (fonds de boutique)*; yet they carefully collect the national habits of the same countries, and look upon them with very good reason, as very elegant models. (1, 95–6).

Grace's possession of a pair of gloves made from Limerick lace symbolises her awareness that the imitation of fashionable London dress and manners is a futile pursuit; equally symbolically, Colambre's enraptured exclamation at the sight of these gloves is enough to betray his passion to the ever-observant Mrs Petito: '"Limerick!" said he, quite loud enough to himself, for it was a Limerick glove, my lady – "Limerick! – dear Ireland! she loves you as well as I do!" – or words to that effect' (83). Colambre has already noticed the arresting contrast between Grace's beauty and the garish surroundings at Lady Clonbrony's gala:

> The only object present on which his eye rested with pleasure was Grace Nugent. Beautiful – in elegant and dignified simplicity – thoughtless of herself – yet with a look of thought, and with an air of melancholy, which accorded exactly with his own feelings, and which he believed to arise from the same reflections that had passed in his own mind. (25)

With its smoked salmon, Limerick lace, and Irish plums and ortolans, Ireland is represented as possessing the basic requirements for membership of a Europe of nations, but the bathetic failure of Lady Clonbrony's gala is a clear warning that not all nations are equal. *The Absentee* thus provides an equivocal perspective on the Staëlian notion of 'very decided national habits and character' and their role in resisting Napoleonic imperialism. Lady Clonbrony's experience suggests that for Irish people to attempt to be anything other than Irish is futile and misguided – but this is elaborated in a context in which metropolitan fashion dictates what one can and can't be, rather than deriving from essentialist conceptions of identity. Complications also arise in the context of Ireland's military involvement in the battle against Napoleon, given the dual role that Ireland has played at various points, as both Britain's ally and her adversary.

Irish involvement in the campaign against Napoleonic France is raised at the level of possibility, but dismissed almost immediately. While he is convinced that Grace's birth was illegitimate, Colambre plans to leave Ireland and join the army – a decision which, it is made explicit, will involve service in 'a campaign abroad' (172). Count O'Halloran approves of his decision, and reflects that

> The life of an officer is not now a life of parade, of coxcombical or of profligate idleness – but of active service, of continual hardship and danger. All the descriptions which we see in ancient history of a soldier's life, descriptions which in times of peace appeared like romance, are now realised; military exploits fill every day's newspapers, every day's conversation. (172)

But these apparently worthy and noble plans have barely been formulated when Colambre discovers that Count O'Halloran has information that confirms Grace's legitimacy: 'all the military ideas, which but an hour before filled his imagination, were put to flight: Spain vanished, and green Ireland reappeared' (175). Like Count Altenberg, who finds conveniently that there is no longer a role for him in his country's resistance to Napoleon, Colambre is more than happy to put his military ambitions to one side and to focus instead on the role of landlord and husband. Colambre's briefly entertained military ambitions acknowledge the role of the Irish in the British army fighting a war on the European continent. There are, however, other connections between Ireland and Europe which feature in both *The Absentee* and *Patronage* and draw the two texts together, acting to destabilise the terms in which British and Irish national character tended to be articulated. Both Count O'Halloran and Grace Nugent's father, Mr Reynolds, served in the Austrian army, a fact which recalls Staël's 'German hero', Maurice O'Donnell, and to which I shall return shortly. The ending of *Patronage* draws Ireland into its frame of reference in two different but related episodes, both of which suggest similar connections between Ireland and Europe.

Patronage's Caroline and Rosamond Percy, temperamentally different but loving and united sisters, could be argued to symbolise the potential for a sisterly union between Ireland and Britain. The image of 'Hibernia' and 'Britannia' as sisters was an image more current in the eighteenth century than in the post-Union period, but it is clearly hospitable to Edgeworth's desire to recast the idea of national identity in a more feminine and domestic mould.[41] Towards the end of the novel, the Percy family sit in their garden discussing literature, including 'Scotch and English ballads' and Thomas Percy's *Reliques of Ancient English Poetry*. The sisters, Rosamond and Caroline, each have a different favourite poem, but both are by the same author, Thomas Campbell. Rosamond's favourite is 'The Exile of Erin' and Caroline's 'Ye Mariners of England'. 'Ye Mariners of England' was written and published in 1801 in direct response to the wars with France, and as its name suggests, it presents a stirring image of the undaunted English navy, who 'guard our native seas', and refers to specific heroes of the recent conflict, including Admiral Nelson.[42] Rosamond's favourite, 'The Exile of Erin', written in 1800 and also published in 1801, is by contrast an exercise in melancholy. The poem itself is located in an unspecified time and place, and repeated references to harps and bards, along with the insertion of the Gaelic phrases 'Erin go bragh' (Ireland forever) and 'Erin mavournin' (Ireland my darling), add to the impression of a vague and generalised 'Irish' gloom, almost as if to be Irish were synonymous with picturesque depression. The only clue as to a cause for the exile's misery is that 'once, in the fire of his youthful emotion/He sang the bold anthem of "Erin go bragh!"'[43] This suggests that the subject is in fact a *political* exile, and an editorial note indicates that this is in fact the case. In spite of the poem's carefully generalised and dehistoricised quality, Campbell was prompted to write it having met a certain Anthony McCann, a former United Irishman exiled in Hamburg.[44] On one level, therefore, the sister's choices are an acknowledgement of the deep political divisions between Britain and Ireland and of the traumatic elements within Irish history. On another level, however, the novel actually subverts the stark opposition of Britain (imperial and victorious) and Ireland (conquered and tragic) which these two poems suggest. Anthony McCann was not alone in settling in Hamburg – it was a significant centre for United Irish activities following the defeat of 1798, owing to the large number of exiles settled there, and this fact is registered elsewhere in the pages of *Patronage*, in one of the accounts of the birth and upbringing of Mr Henry.[45]

We first encounter Mr Henry at the beginning of the novel, when he is introduced as a member of Godfrey Percy's army regiment. He subsequently leaves the army to pursue a career in business and commerce, and we hear rather little of him until the closing pages, in which the facts of his birth are revealed and explained extremely rapidly. Mr Henry is thus drawn from the novel's margins to its centre in a rather violent manner. James Newcomer comments ironically of Mr Henry that 'under the chastening influence of employment in business, he assures his financial future, wins marriage with an heiress, and – lo and behold! and hardly to the artistic credit of the author – is discovered to be heir to one of the noblest titles and fortunes in all England'.[46] The discovery that Mr Henry is in fact Lord Oldborough's son contains shock value quite distinct from its obvious convenience as a means to tie up loose ends. He is illegitimate, the product of a love affair between Lord Oldborough and 'an Italian lady of transcendent beauty' whom he had met while travelling on the continent as a young man (VII, 248). The affair ends, due to Oldborough's unjust suspicious of his lover's fidelity, and she retires to a convent while he returns to England. The first he learns of his son is upon receipt of a letter from his former lover, written on her deathbed, and delivered to his hand by a Neapolitan abbé. The letter informs him that 'the boy was sent when three years old to England or Ireland, under the care of an Irish priest, who delivered him to a merchant, recommended by the Hamburgh banker, &c' (VII, 249). This reference to 'the Hamburgh banker' is rather mysterious because it is never properly explained – why *the* Hamburgh banker? He has not been referred to before and is never actually specified. It is worth noting that Oldborough's affair with the transcendently beautiful Italian woman recalls Oswald's infatuation with Corinne, while the awkward reference to Hamburg, with its well-known colony of political exiles, signals the possibility of political insurgency in Mr Henry's background. Hearing this description Mr Percy immediately recognises that the boy must be Mr Henry, who, according to his son Godfrey, had been taunted about the circumstances of his birth while in the army. Godfrey's account of the scant facts that Mr Henry himself has about his parents contains a more explicit reference to Irish insurgency:

> 'he really does not know to what family he belongs, nor who his mother and father were; but he has reason to believe, that they were Irish. He was bred up in a merchant's house in Dublin. [. . .] The merchant [. . .] said, that Henry was not his nephew, nor any relation to him, but hinted that he was the son of a Mr Henry, who had taken an unfortunate part in *the troubles* of Ireland, and who had *suffered*, – that his mother had been a servant maid, and that she was dead.' (VI, 85–6)

The reader learns at a very late stage that Mr Henry was not in fact the son of a man who was involved in 'Ireland's troubles', but the possibility stands for most of the novel. The fact that Mr Henry's allowance is sent to him regularly from 'the Hamburgh banker' allows the association with political exiles from both Ireland and France to linger. Mc Cormack claims that 'the exclusion of the Irish troubles [in *Patronage*] must be regarded as a major motive force in the novel', given that 'it compensates for sexual irregularity in a great minister'.[47] However, rather than compensating for his sexual irregularity, Oldborough's assumption of paternity draws these disruptive elements into the heart of the novel. 'Fresh and strong' corroborating evidence of Mr Henry's parentage is provided by the fact that he is recognised by an Irish priest officiating at the deathbed of Erasmus Percy's patient, the Irish labourer, O'Brien (VII, 250). Mr Henry's filial relation to Lord Oldborough thus becomes clear in the dim light of the Catholic ceremony of Last Rites.

In the case of both Mr Henry and *The Absentee*'s Grace Nugent, the confusions surrounding their birth and parentage involve illegitimacy (in Grace's case, feared, but in Mr Henry's case actual), birth abroad, the intervention and agency of Catholic clerics, and, finally, the imputation of political insurgency.[48] At one level of symbolism, therefore, Mr Henry is the 'Exile of Erin', who at the close of the novel is repatriated to England, following a series of associations with Italy, Germany and Ireland. He is like Corinne the child of an Italian mother and an English father, but unlike Corinne he finds a place in his father's home. It is finally entirely possible to read Count Altenberg as being, like Maurice O'Donnell, a German hero who is on one level Irish. As *The Absentee* indicates, Edgeworth was familiar with the fact that Irish Catholics served in the Austrian army and it is unlikely that she was not aware of Count Maurice O'Donnell and his father Count Joseph, who occupied a highly public and influential position as finance minister in this period. The Napoleonic wars had performed an extraordinary transformation, turning families such as the O'Donnells from exiled rebels into valued allies. This reading of Altenberg is supported by the scene in which he arrives back in England, at the Percy household, in order to declare his love for Caroline and propose to her. He arrives just at the moment in which she is reciting Campbell's 'Ye Mariners of England':

> Caroline fixed the attention of the company on the flag, which has
>
> > 'Brav'd a thousand years the battle and the breeze,'
>
> when suddenly her own attention seemed to be distracted by some object in the glen below. She endeavoured to go on, but her voice faltered, her color changed. (VII, 189)

Altenberg's arrival thus disrupts Caroline's recitation of the poem, making her 'voice falter'. The previous discussion of *Patronage* suggested that Altenberg's 'Germanness' enabled a critical rather than a celebratory account of English public life; here his arrival clearly disrupts the rather simple-minded patriotism of Campbell's poem. Rather than discussing either Altenberg or Mr Henry in terms of the 'exclusion' of subversive aspects of Irish history, one could potentially regard these hybrid and highly mobile characters as transformations, sharing some of the magical quality of Grace Nugent's 'metamorphoses'. 'Suppressions' such as these are in any case less problematic in my view than the parallel demand for the *production* of an Irishness that can be consumed in the metropolitan centre, in the form of smoked salmon and 'Irish plums'.

The Absentee and Patronage engage in the same field of ideas as Staël's *Germany*, but imagine radically different possibilities. The type of romantic nationalism which Staël's text did so much to popularise insisted on the identification between person and place, hence the seeming perversity of the idea of the Frenchmen of Hamburg or Rome. Edgeworth's texts on the other hand allude to the fact that the history of Anglo-Irish conflict had resulted in various waves and forms of emigration, from the Wild Geese to Catholic clerics, to soldiers serving in foreign armies and the exiles of 1798. The suggestion in the texts is that the realignments of the Napoleonic period provided an opportunity for the 'repatriation' of these exiles, but this repatriation involves a fundamental reimagining of the British nation, rejecting militarism and chauvinism, and insisting, characteristically for Edgeworth, that a reformed nation required the creation of a space in which the genders could meet on equal terms.

CHAPTER FIVE

The Language of an Irish Gentleman
in 'Ormond'

-+>-<+-

No well-bred gentleman would put a foreigner out of countenance by openly
laughing at [. . .] a [linguistic] mistake: he would imitate the politeness of the
Frenchman, who, when Dr Moore said, 'I am afraid the expression I have just
used is not French', replied, 'Non, monsieur – mais il mérite bien de l'être'. It
would indeed be a great stretch of politeness to extend this to our Irish neighbours:
for no Irishism can ever deserve to be Anglicised, though so many Gallicisms have
of late not only been naturalised in England, but even adopted by the most
fashionable speakers and writers. The mistaking a feminine for a masculine noun,
or a masculine for a feminine, must, in all probability, have happened to every
Englishman that ever opened his lips in Paris; yet without losing his reputation
for common sense. But when a poor Irish haymaker, who had but just learned a
few phrases of the English language by rote, mistook a feminine for a masculine
noun and began his speech in a court of justice with these words: 'My lord, I am
a poor widow', instead of 'My lord, I am a poor widower'; it was sufficient to
throw a grave judge and jury into convulsions of laughter.[1]

E dgeworth has been acknowledged as a faithful and innovative recorder of
vernacular speech, particularly in an Irish context. More recently, critics
have drawn attention to the fascination with language that characterises all her
writing, whether set in Ireland or not. When we encounter Mr Soho, the
interior decorator in *The Absentee*, or Lame Jervas, whose experience as a
mine-worker is reflected in the large number of specialised words and phrases
he uses, we are reminded that Edgeworth's desire to record the distinctive
speech of the common Irish was motivated by an interest in the ways in which
language was a record of experience. This interest, it has been pointed out,
does not imply any 'romantic commitment to the primitive, the unsophisticated or the democratic'.[2] Edgeworth's evident fascination with vernacular
speech of all sorts has in fact been characterised as an assumption of superiority

with regard to speakers whose language was so clearly marked by region or trade, in contrast to the imagined universality and neutrality of educated upper-class speech.[3] The extract from *Irish Bulls* above, however, gives a strikingly different perspective on Edgeworth's attitude to the Irish language and, indeed, to language in general. What distinguishes this portrayal is the authors' awareness of the Irish language itself as a foreign language, rather than primarily as a factor influencing the speech of people in Ireland. Speakers of Irish are, here, equated with speakers of French, apparently in order to make a point about linguistic competence: it is not normally assumed that speakers will be perfectly competent in a second language, a language which is foreign to them. The example given makes uncomfortably clear the fact that speakers of Irish and speakers of French are *not* in fact equal. Whereas inter-action between speakers of English and speakers of French takes place in the context of 'polite' conversation among 'well-bred gentlemen', the speaker of Irish is a 'poor haymaker' who is addressing a judge in a court of law, and who must expect to be judged by a jury. The situations of Dr Moore and the anonymous haymaker could hardly be more different. Edgeworth's example illustrates the gulf between what has been termed 'elite multilingualism' and the more common but less widely recognised non-elite multilingualism which results from social and economic necessity.[4] The laughably poor English of the Irish haymaker has much more in common with the English spoken, for instance, by hispanic migrant workers in California, than it has with Dr Moore or his modern-day equivalent – the English-speaking student spending a 'year abroad' in Paris, or Madrid, or Rome. The text's insistence on equating Irish speakers with speakers of other foreign languages has the paradoxical effect of highlighting the disparities in power and prestige between the speakers: as is painfully apparent, the reason the 'grave judge and jury' laugh at the man's mistake has everything to do with his economic and social position, and very little to do with language.

There is more to the comparison than its striking inappropriateness, however. The French language, as the extract here indicates, was undergoing a shift in perception at this period. The imagined situation of an Englishman in Paris, attempting to converse in the language of his hosts and being met with impeccable politeness, positions French as the language of international elite society and culture – a status which it held for most if not all of the eighteenth century. It also serves to remind us that the French were regarded as masters of politeness: the Frenchman's response to Dr Moore is given in the original, rather than in translation, which suggests, moreover, that this polite-ness inheres in the language itself, not merely in the content of the remark. But in remarking that 'so many Gallicisms have of late not only been naturalised in England, but even adopted by the most fashionable speakers and writers', the passage simultaneously expresses other, more contemporary and more anxious perceptions of French culture and language. In contrast to the idealised image of well-bred gentlemen communicating with exemplary politeness across cultures, the reference to the 'naturalisation' of French expressions in England suggests a desire to maintain a 'pure' cultural environment within the boundaries of the nation state. The suggestion that the Irish haymaker is comparable to an Englishman speaking French is heavily loaded with potential political meanings that have very little to do with the nuts and bolts of second language acquisition. The overt aim of the comparison appears to be to humanise the stereotype of the ignorant Irishman by reminding educated readers of their own experience of learning a second language; it is, however, too strange and too politicised to function adequately at this level. Instead, it has the potential to put readers in mind of less favourable comparisons between the Irish and the French, and by extension to question what place the Irish occupy in the British state, which, as we know, was (and is) a multi-national state rather than a nation state: the extract seems to suggest that their 'place' is in the dock.

In *Ormond*, the last Irish tale that Edgeworth wrote, the French language plays a crucial role in ways that are frankly surprising, given the date of the novel's publication. As we have seen thus far, Edgeworth found ways to retain the idea of France as a positive resource in her writing, but there is no doubt that reference to France were a volatile ingredient, and this volatility increases rather than diminishes as the century progresses. In *Ormond*, however, published in 1817, only two years after the final defeat of Napoleon at Waterloo, Edgeworth presents us with an Irish hero whose education culminates in an extended stay in Paris, where he acquires the kind of *savoir faire* that would have adorned the manners of a mid eighteenth-century gentleman, but which seems strangely out of keeping with the temper of the times in which it was published, even taking into consideration the fact that the events described are set in the 1770s. *Ormond*, having been out of print for decades, has recently begun to attract much greater attention from critics, a number of whom have focused on the text's exploration of identity, both personal and national. *Ormond* represents a perhaps surprising close to Edgeworth's career as a novelist of Irish themes given that, as Katie Trumpener has commented, with the death of the enormously lovable King Corny, Edgeworth 'moves into the mode of national elegy, to mourn what is lost with Corny's passing'.[5] For Trumpener, *Ormond* aligns Edgeworth, however briefly, with the values and representative strategies of cultural nationalism. For others, *Ormond* displays continuity with Edgeworth's earlier work, retaining a view of identity as constructed and 'pragmatic' rather than essential.[6] This chapter explores the question of identity and identity construction in *Ormond* by focusing on language and the use of the French language specifically as an aspect of the formation of identity and character. Connections between Ireland and France have increasingly attracted the attention of scholars, particularly historians of this period, but the function of the French *language* in Irish texts of this period is a theme with rich potential which has barely been explored.[7] My discussion of *Ormond* aims to point out some of the directions this exploration could take.

The extract quoted from *An Essay on Irish Bulls* tells us that the French language itself was, for Edgeworth, far from being a neutral means of communication. It is clear that French means something, no matter what is actually being said, whether it is the fashionability associated with 'Gallicisms' or the famed politeness of *ancien régime* society. What French means is heavily – perhaps entirely – context-dependent. Its meaning changes according to your class, your gender, and, most certainly, your nation. The French language is therefore both central to this discussion and, at the same time, a way of tackling themes which are not restricted to language. To illustrate what I mean by this, I shall refer to a phrase from 'Letter to a Gentleman' already quoted in chapter 1 (p. 36). In a section of the Answer in which the enlightened father is ostensibly pointing out how ideals of feminine beauty and behaviour change as society changes, he observes that 'If, some years ago, you had asked a Frenchman what he meant by beauty, [. . .] he would have referred ultimately to that *je ne sçais quoi*, for which Parisian belles were formerly celebrated.'[8] The use of the French phrase is of crucial importance in creating the meaning of this statement. In contemporary English-language culture, the phrase 'je ne sais quoi' functions almost as a signifier for the French language itself. One can't say whether 'je ne sais quoi' had quite the same emblematic function in 1795, but the inclusion of an untranslated French phrase, as in the extract quoted from *Irish Bulls*, implies that the phrase is untranslatable, and that the concept to which the phrase refers is peculiarly and essentially French. In this way, the sentence refers to an assumed knowledge of the mores of pre-revolutionary France (the phrase would have been used 'some years ago', 'formerly'), in particular the role played by women, and creates an unspoken connection between France, femininity and decadence.

As this example illustrates, the French language had a distinct and potentially problematic character in relation to femininity and feminine behaviour, as it did in relation to Ireland. The use of the French language had particular and politicised significance in Ireland's case. Sylvie Kleinman has recently provided a fascinating account of Theobald Wolfe Tone as a 'motivated learner' of French: his motivation was indeed considerable, as he was required to negotiate in French with key figures in the Directory, in an attempt to persuade them to send an invasion force to Ireland to aid in the rebellion.[9] The attractions of French, from an Irish perspective, could range from political radicalism to fashionability, but there are also anecdotes concerning cases of

Irish people living in Britain who assumed a French identity in order to mask their Irishness. The practice indicates that Irishness and Frenchness were on the one hand equivalent as 'foreign' identities, but were also clearly distinguished in terms of status – an accent influenced by the French language was clearly more advantageous than an accent influenced by the Irish language. The advantages and disadvantages of cloaking an Irish identity with a French identity are referred to, with specific reference to femininity, in *The Absentee*, when Lady Clonbrony urges her ward, Grace Nugent, to cloak the '*iricism*' of her name by giving it a French gloss in the form of 'de Nogent'.[10] Grace of course refuses, one indication among many of her emotional attachment to Ireland. The assessment of many critics is that Edgeworth, representative of the mainstream of British opinion in the post-revolutionary period, employed the idea of France and Frenchness, particularly in regard to femininity, as signifiers of moral and social corruption. Grace's refusal to 'frenchify' her name is read as a way of portraying a commitment to Ireland that is specifically distinguished from Frenchness. The context of the post-rebellion period provided some dramatic examples of cases in which the suppression of Irish identity and the assumption of French identity made the difference between life and death: in the aftermath of the rebellion, stories circulated about Irish insurgents who escaped execution by passing themselves off as French. In one very famous case, this attempted suppression of Irishness was unsuccessful. Following the surrender of the French ship on which he had served in 1798, Tone, the diligent student of the French language, was brought ashore in Donegal, because a violent storm prevented the journey of the ship to Portsmouth: 'but for the storm', Marianne Elliott comments, 'Tone would have ended up in an English prisoner of war camp with the other French officers, all of whom were taken directly to England and eventually exchanged back to France'.[11] Tone clearly preferred to think of himself as a French soldier rather than an Irish traitor, a self-conception that was not supported by his captors: 'in the view of his captors, for Tone to stand on his dignity and insist on receiving the respect due to his rank in the French army was arrogant, and an aggravation of his offence'.[12]

The association between France and political subversion, so dramatically and poignantly illustrated in Tone's case, is, for some critics, an adequate basis from which to interpret all references to France in Edgeworth's fiction as uniformly negative. Hence Hollingworth justifies his claim that 'Edgeworth presents France, and uses nomenclature and symbols related to France, very negatively in her later Irish stories' using the following rather circular logic:

> Edgeworth is labouring here [in The *Absentee* and *Ormond*] to confirm the Union. In this she is confirming the Protestant Ascendancy which her own family represented, and, for her, the greatest threat this order faced was France.[13]

Although Grace's 'St Omar' legacy and the ensuing anxieties about her legitimacy – and her suitability as a wife for Colambre – clearly refer to the subversive and revolutionary connections between Ireland and France, it is simply reductive to 'explain' every reference to France according to this single political imperative. Elsewhere, Hollingworth describes Edgeworth's attitude towards France, 'overall' as 'wildly varying',[14] which is one way of dealing with the very positive representations of France to be found in tales such as 'The Good French Governess', *Madame de Fleury* and *Emilie de Coulanges*, as well as the ample evidence of Edgeworth's close and productive connections and contacts with writers and intellectuals in France. As the readings of *Letters for Literary Ladies* and *Belinda* in chapter 1 sought to establish, Edgeworth's texts frequently feature a strategic defence of France which facilitated a recuperation of socially influential femininity. *Ormond* represents another possible configuration of gender and national identity by using the French language to construct a masculine identity that is informed by traces of femininity and criminality, becoming 'Irish' in the process.

One of Edgeworth's earlier novels, *Leonora*, like *Ormond*, features dense references to France, including quite extensive treatment of language. *Leonora* was written shortly after Edgeworth's return from her visit to Paris, and much of the detail in the representation of life in the French capital is drawn from Edgeworth's own experiences and observations. While in Paris, Edgeworth experienced at first hand the sensation produced by Germaine de Staël's novel *Delphine*, and was clearly intrigued by the fact that a novel by a woman writer could have such an impact.[15] *Leonora* is a contemporary and topical text, which situates itself in the context of the renewed hostilities between Britain and France, and discusses, for instance, the controversial introduction of divorce law in France. It is an epistolary novel set in contemporary England, concerned with the threats posed to an English marriage by a 'frenchified coquette', and has been read as a reflection of counter-revolutionary ideology in Britain, putting a domestic and sexual spin on the French threat to the English way of life.[16] Although there is insufficient space here to debate this reading fully, it may be useful in the context of a discussion of Harry Ormond's French education to point out that *Leonora* also, somewhat surprisingly, reveals that for men – even English men – facility in the French language can be advantageous.

In *Leonora*, when Olivia and her bosom friend, Gabrielle, Madame de P, break off their friendship, Gabrielle writes to Olivia in the frostiest tones, saying:

Adieu, my charming Olivia! I embrace you tenderly, I was going to say; but I believe, according to your English etiquette, I must now conclude with

I have the honour to be,
Madam,
Your most obedient,
Humble Servant,
Gabrielle de P –.[17]

Gabrielle's preferred expression, 'I embrace you tenderly' is of course a direct translation from the French 'je t'embrasse', which means not 'to embrace' but 'to kiss', and is in French a conventional way of closing a letter to a friend. The rift between the Frenchwoman and her English friend is expressed in terms of language and nationality. Now that Gabrielle no longer considers Olivia a friend, she insists on the difference in their national affiliations: in reference to Olivia's request to have her various gifts and keepsakes returned, Gabrielle remarks scornfully that 'with *us Parisians*, this returning of keepsakes has been out of fashion since the days of Molière and *Le Dépit Amoreux*' (125, my emphasis). This fictional exchange bears a striking similarity to the awkward cooling of the short-lived friendship between Frances Burney and Germaine de Staël. In this case as well, according to Margaret Doody, Staël signalled her coolness through her use of language. Having previously been willing to use her imperfect English, and thus risk exposure by making mistakes and expressing herself awkwardly, Staël abruptly reverted to writing in French, except to address Burney patronisingly as 'my dear Miss', and to advise her to read Voltaire – if she were allowed to.[18] One of the things that these episodes remind us of is that language is anything other than a transparent medium, and that the meanings it conveys are part of a dense network which involves interpersonal relationships, literature, cultural knowledge and the political sphere.

Leonora is composed in letters written both by speakers of French and speakers of English. The French language is present in two different ways in this text. It is indicated by the presence of French words and phrases in a text which is otherwise in the English language. It is also signalled through uses of English which appear to have been influenced by the French language, such as Gabrielle's use of the phrase 'I embrace you'. In the case of the letters exchanged between Olivia and Gabrielle, it is unclear whether we are to understand that they are written in French or in English. The use of the phrase 'I embrace you' could signal either that Gabrielle is writing in French, or that she is writing in an imperfect English in which she has made the understandable and characteristic error of language-learners, where she has relied on what is called a 'false friend' for a translation from one language into the other. These possibilities imply, however, that the boundaries between languages are reasonably secure, whereas the border that separates English from French has been at times remarkably porous. English of course owes its modern form and a sizeable portion of its vocabulary to the French language. It is perhaps for this reason that the use of French words and phrases in English (the 'naturalisation' of 'Gallicisms') is and has been a reasonably common feature with some speakers. The correspondence of Leonora and Gabrielle is a perfect example of a language in which actual foreign words and phrases are embedded within an English which seems in any case highly influenced by 'foreign' ideas and sentiments – what Nicola Watson has called the 'sentimental "French" discourse of the letter'.[19] In *Leonora*, the occasions on which French words are used are predictable, relating to stereotypes which characterise the French as preoccupied with sexual intrigue. A typical example would be Olivia's remarks on Leonora's inability to coquette: 'nothing *piquante*; nothing *agaçante*; nothing *demivoilée*' (95). The vast majority of usages involve remarks on love affairs, fashion, and other women: 'un peu passé', 'l'erreur d'un moment', 'le besoin d'aimer', 'intrigante', 'elegante', 'bel esprit', 'mise à ravir'. The absence of such phrases in letters written by the other female characters, and the contexts in which that language is used suggest the function of the language's presence in the text is to underline the association between France and a feminised and therefore unstable social and political culture.

Olivia and Gabrielle are not, however, the only characters who have frequent recourse to the French language in order to express themselves. Mr L—'s correspondent, General B—, has recently returned from Paris and makes use of French words and phrases. General B—'s use of French is in some instances similar to that of Olivia and Gabrielle, such as when he quotes a gentleman of his acquaintance in Paris, who remarked of Olivia, 'with an unanswerable French shrug', 'Tout le monde sait que R*** est son amant; d'ailleurs c'est la femme la plus aimable du monde' (38). Making a direct and unveiled reference to Olivia's (presumed) infidelity is apparently easier in French. General B— is, however, not usually lost for words in any language and is characterised by frank and unambiguous expressions. He is by his own description 'a man of the world' (134) who has recently returned from a trip to Paris, and whose firm moral principles are coupled with a worldly unshockability. He does not engage in or condone immoral behaviour, but his response to his friend's dilemma is to treat him like a fool rather than a moral reprobate. On hearing of Mr L—'s decision to leave his wife and take Olivia as his mistress he remarks 'Call a demirep an angel, and welcome; but remember that such angels are to be had any day in the year' (89). It is worth noting that this cool remark is facilitated by the use of a 'naturalised' French phrase to describe Olivia's tarnished moral reputation.

General B—'s account of his stay in Paris bears strong resemblance to the Edgeworths' experiences there. He had the 'good fortune to be admitted into the best *private societies* in Paris' which were made up of 'the remains of the French nobility, of men of letters and science, and of families, who, without interfering in politics, devote themselves to domestic duties, to literary and social pleasures' (26–7). Significantly, the General says that he has no comment to make on the revolution and the violence associated with it: 'Of the cruelties of the revolution I can tell you nothing new. The public have been steeped up to the lips in blood, and have surely had their fill of horrors' (26). The General thus refuses to add to the association of France with 'blood' and 'horrors'. In spite of his obvious appreciation for French culture and his apparent fluency in the French language, General B— is portrayed in markedly masculine terms. His characteristic style, as examples already given will indicate, is direct to the point of bluntness. His language is endowed with a kind of obvious masculinity through the use of phrases such as 'damn' and 'God knows where', and when he remarks that one of his friend's letters, having travelled after him for a number of days 'caught me at last with my foot in the stirrup' (89), it is a detail which suggests Edgeworth's desire to underline his status as a man of action.

The deeply rooted association, prevalent in England, between the French language and effeminacy is discussed by Michèle Cohen, who observes that

> The relation of English to French was [. . .] 'sexualized', discursively constructed as a relation of seduction and desire, positioning English as male and French as female. But because desire and seduction were held to be effeminating, this relation threatened the manliness of the English tongue.[20]

The eighteenth-century 'fop' represented the derided figure of an Englishman so caught up with the refinements of French manners and culture as to lose all claims to masculinity. Cohen, however, argues that the English perception of French language and culture as effeminate or feminising was based on a fundamental misconception about the role of mixed-gender sociability and conversation in France:

> The English 'translation' and representation of French gallantry and *l'art de plaire* missed the point: the aim of the social practices around conversation was not the seduction of women so much as the fashioning and perfecting of *men*.[21]

The portrayal of General B— in *Leonora* thus runs counter to the popular view of the French language in Britain by suggesting that exposure to French culture and language does not automatically 'effeminate'. General B— is in fact much more clear headed and has much better judgment than the unfortunate Mr L—, who might not have mistaken a 'demirep' for an angel if he had had the same experience of French language and culture as his friend.

Ormond takes a still more radical approach to the construction of masculine identity, suggesting that the French 'art de plaire' still has a role in the perfection of the gentleman: Harry Ormond is made a gentleman by the company of women and his exposure to French culture. It is necessary to emphasise how profoundly this configuration departs from what we have come to regard as the 'norm' in the cultural politics of the period. By this I do not mean simply that it is unusual to portray France positively, or even that it is unusual to suggest that men would benefit from a little French polish. Ordinarily, the *Bildungsroman* is predicated on the norm of masculinity: the representation of life as a series of choices increasing in complexity, requiring and producing an increasingly autonomous and self-determining individual, is based on a masculine subject who has the basic freedom to *make* key decisions autonomously. Hence the initial appearance of the novel of courtship and marriage as the form through which to express female subjectivity, as the choice of marriage partner was for many women the only area in which their choice played any significant role. The comparative cultural dimension to Ormond's education contributes to the development of a feminine subjectivity, whilst the novel at the same time insists that this is the story of the education of an ideal Irishman. In this vein, Susanne Hagemann uses Linda Alcoff's concept of 'positionality' to interpret the significance of the choices made by Ormond during his stay in Paris:

> If Alcoff asserts that, on the one hand, women's subjectivity and identity are constituted by their position within a given society, but, on the other hand, a woman 'is part of the historicised, fluid, movement, and she therefore actively contributes to the context within which her position can be delineated', the same applies to Ormond.[22]

Hagemann's use of the concept of positionality accords with my own view that Ormond's identity is constructed along feminine as well as masculine lines. Like the hero of a conventional *Bildungsroman*, Ormond does of course make choices, but these are from within a specific range, and often amount to the choice of influence (not least the influence of women), which conflicts with the presentation of choice as the determining action of a completely autonomous subject. The fact that so many of Ormond's choices relate to cultural environments positions the individual clearly at the intersection of the discourses of gender and nationality. My focus, therefore, on Ormond's education does not detach this theme from historical and political concerns. Claire Connolly, a recent editor of the novel, has pointed out that the narrative of the hero's education and development is located in a rich cultural and political context, which incorporates, for example, the 1798 rebellion and the French revolution, as well as more distant echoes such as the life of the first Duke of Ormond, who accompanied Charles II into exile.[23] Connolly concludes that *Ormond* is concerned with providing alternative 'prophecies' for the future of Ireland, to replace the apocalyptic and millenarian prophecies of the past. Although my discussion does not engage directly with the dense historical allusions to which Connolly refers, my concern is precisely with the broad political implications of the kind of formation that the text imagines – one that arises from highly specific political and cultural locations.

Ormond opens with a crisis in the life of its young hero, the orphan Harry Ormond, who is gifted with 'natural genius' and has an 'extremely warm, generous, grateful temper'. His education has, however, been totally neglected and he is as a consequence 'ungovernable', except by his guardian Sir Ulick O'Shane, and 'rude, even to insolence, where he felt tyranny or suspected meanness'.[24] These flaws of character have a catastrophic outcome when he and Sir Ulick's son, Marcus, become involved in an altercation with Moriarty Carroll whom Ormond then shoots accidentally, in the midst of a scuffle. From this opening, the novel then proceeds to chart how the young hero finally achieves wealth and happiness, learning to overcome his own flaws and the external obstacles that he encounters.

Ormond's horror at the potentially fatal consequences of his uncontrollable temper makes him for the first time question his actions; his determination to develop his character and his intellect is, however, motivated to a considerable degree by the interest shown in his fate by Lady Annaly:

> 'Is it possible,' repeated Ormond, in unfeigned astonishment, 'that your ladyship can be so very good, so condescending, to one who so little deserves it? But I *will* deserve it in future. If I get over this – interested in *my* future fate – lady Annaly!' (27)

Not only does Lady Annaly's attention encourage Ormond to rethink the way in which he has been living his life, she also provides him with the motivation and the means to learn French. Lady Annaly sends him as a gift 'an excellent collection of what may be called the English and French classics':

> the French books were, at this time, quite useless to him, for he could not read French. Lady Annaly, however, sent these books on purpose to induce him to learn a language, which, if he should go into the army, as he seemed inclined to do, would be particularly useful to him. (55)

The 'appropriateness' of French in an Irish context is further underlined by Lady Annaly's observation that

Mr Ormond, wherever he might be in Ireland, would probably find even the priest of the parish a person who could assist him sufficiently in learning French; as most of the Irish parish priests were, at that time, educated at St Omer's or Louvain. (55)

French is thus represented as a key feature of a gentleman's education (it is after all supposed to fit him for a career in the decidedly masculine armed forces) and as being particularly accessible in an Irish context. It is suggested that knowledge of French is more widespread in Ireland because its largely Catholic clergy, of necessity, study abroad. The text thus acknowledges, rather than represses, the special cultural and political circumstances which link Ireland to France.

The importance of women in the formation of the gentleman is also emphasised by Harry's reaction to Richardson's *Sir Charles Grandison*:

In sir Charles Grandison's history he read that of a gentleman, who, fulfilling every duty of his station in society, eminently *useful*, respected and beloved, as brother, friend, master of a family, guardian, and head of a large estate, was admired by his own sex, and, *what struck Ormond far more forcibly*, loved, passionately loved, by women – not by the low and profligate, but by the highest and most accomplished of the sex. (56; second emphasis mine)

The formation of the gentleman here proceeds on lines very different from those represented as dominant in early nineteenth-century Britain. Harry's desire to be 'loved, passionately loved' by women, and his immersion in French language and culture, might be expected to produce a ludicrous fop, but the text insists instead that these all contribute to shaping an ideal Irish gentleman.

Sir Ulick exploits Ormond's involvement in the fracas with Moriarty Carroll as a means to remove him from Castle Hermitage, in the hope that his absence might facilitate the making of a match between Marcus O'Shane and Lady Annaly's daughter, Florence. Ormond is offered a home and a refuge in the 'Black Islands' by Sir Ulick's cousin Cornelius O'Shane, otherwise known as King Corny. Thus commences a period in Ormond's life in which he struggles to educate and improve himself in a less than ideal environment. He has to learn to resist the temptations of his host's hospitality and to avoid succumbing to sexual temptation in the form of a village beauty, Peggy Sheridan. His position is complicated still further with the return of Corny's daughter Dora, in the company of her aunt, Miss O'Faley. Ormond looks forward to Dora's arrival, which he anticipates will provide him with much-needed opportunities to acquire some social refinement:

she should teach him French, and drawing, and dancing, and improve his manners. He was conscious that his manners had, since his coming to the Black Islands, rusticated sadly [. . .]. His language and dialect, he was afraid, had become somewhat vulgar; but Dora, who had been refined by her residence with her aunt, and by her dancing-master, would polish him, and set all to rights, in the most agreeable manner possible. (59)

As Dora is already engaged to 'White Connal', a wealthy grazier, as a result of a drunken oath sworn by Corny and Connal's father, Ormond considers that he can be in no danger from her company. His confidence is, however, misplaced, partly because of his own susceptibility, partly because of Dora's flirtatiousness and partly because of the selfish agenda pursued by Miss O'Faley, her aunt.

'*Mademoiselle* – as miss O'Faley was called, in honour of her French parentage and education' (59) is a singular and striking individual whose bilingualism in French and English results in a unusual speech pattern in which she mixes the two languages in a phenomenon referred to by linguists as 'code-switching' or 'code-mixing'.[25]

> In her gestures, tones, and language, there was a striking mixture or rapid succession of French and Irish. When she spoke French, which she spoke well, and with a true Parisian accent, her voice, gestures, air, and ideas, were all French; and she looked and moved a well-born, well-bred woman: the moment she attempted to speak English, which she spoke with an inveterate brogue, her ideas, manner, air, voice, and gestures were Irish; she looked and moved a vulgar Irishwoman. (60)

Mlle O'Faley is thus both-Irish-and-French, and neither-Irish-nor-French, a fact which is reflected in her appearance:

> Mademoiselle was dressed in all the peculiarities of the French dress of that day: she was of that indefinable age which the French describe by the happy phrase of 'une femme *d'un certain age*,' and which miss O'Faley happily translated, 'a woman of *no particular age.*' [. . .] She wore abundance of rouge, obviously – still more obviously took superabundance of snuff – and without any obvious motive, continued to play unremittingly a pair of large black French eyes, in a manner impracticable to a mere Englishwoman, and which almost tempted the spectator to beg she would let them rest. (59–60)

Mademoiselle's 'happy translation' of the phrase 'un femme *d'un certain age*' is not entirely correct, and so also it seems her French fashions, and rouge, and, most of all her 'large black French eyes' have a jarring effect. Brian Hollingworth claims that Mlle O'Faley's 'ungrounded idiolect, her uncertain registers, the lack of integrity in her vocabulary and idiom, all express the deeper political concerns of the narrative'.[26] She is determined to find a way for herself and Dora to settle in Paris – the only place, apparently, in which one can live ('else-where people only vegetate' [63]) – and is prepared to do more or less anything to achieve her aim. Ormond appears to her an ideal means to this end. If Dora's engagement to White Connal can be broken off, and Ormond substituted as her lover and fiancé, Mlle O'Faley imagines that her plan of settling in Paris will finally come off, given that Ormond appears 'to hang very loosely upon the world; no family connexions seemed to have any rights over him.' (63).

Mlle O'Faley, undoubtedly, calls to mind certain connections between France and Ireland. She is described as 'continually receiving letters, and news, and patterns, from Dublin, and the Black Rock, and Paris. Each of which places, and all standing nearly upon the same level, made a great figure in her conversation' (62). Mlle O'Faley thus links Ireland to France, whilst excluding Britain (London plays no part in her network); in addition, the mention of Blackrock, then a seaside village outside Dublin, amounts to a subterranean reference to Lord Edward Fitzgerald, whose mother, Emily, Duchess of Leinster, built a house in Blackrock for the specific purpose of providing her children with a healthy upbringing in accordance with the precepts of Rousseau.[27] Fitzgerald of course married a Frenchwoman – and Mlle O'Faley, with her curious dual identity, is herself a product of the marriage between and Irish man and a French woman. It is not at all clear, however, that her Franco-Irish identity, as expressed in her strangely mixed speech, is indicative of 'deeper political concerns', if what is meant by that is connections with revolutionary politics. Mlle O'Faley's greatest weakness appears instead to be her conviction that refinement and 'living' are to be found only in Paris. This is a prejudice shared by 'Black Connal', who arrives in the Black Islands following the death of his brother, as a rather cold-blooded potential suitor. Having served for many years in the Irish brigade of the French army, Black Connal, or 'M. de Connal' as he is now known, represents, for Mlle O'Faley, an ideal prospective husband, who shares her own preference for life in Paris. M. de Connal shares with Mlle O'Faley a strangely compelling manner of speech marked by a mixture of Irish and French influences:

[M. de Connal] went on conversing with mademoiselle, and with her father, alternately in French and English. In English he spoke with a native Irish accent, which seemed to have been preserved from childhood; but though the brogue was strong, yet there were no vulgar expressions: he spoke good English, but generally with somewhat of French idiom. Whether this was from habit or affectation it was not easy to decide. It seemed as if the person who was speaking thought in French, and translated it into English as he went along. The peculiarity of manner and accent – for there was French mixed with the Irish – fixed attention [. . .]. (92)

Connal has a clear hierarchical sense of place – one in which Paris is superior to all other places. He confides to Ormond that he is 'philosophic' and has 'thought profoundly' (100). This he imagines, is a specifically French trait: 'Every body in France *thinks* now', he assures Ormond, whilst 'taking a pinch of snuff with a pensive air.' (100). Philosophic reflection, in Connal's eyes, is dependent on location – 'I own I am surprised to find myself philosophising here in the Black Islands' (100). Connal associates Enlightenment ideas with fashion, and with the habits of a narrow social circle: the narrative of Harry Ormond's gradual path to maturity suggests, however, that Enlightenment can be accessed regardless of location, and that one can, indeed, philosophise in the Black Islands.

At this point, Harry is compelled to leave the Black Islands and to continue his uncertain path elsewhere. The impending marriage of Dora and Connal has already made his presence at Corny Castle uncomfortable, and his kind guardian has resolved to procure him a military commission as soon as possible, but Corny's sudden death in a hunting accident leaves Ormond once more in search of a home, 'hanging loosely upon the world'. Before Ormond has embarked on his chosen military career, he discovers that the death of his half-brother, his father's son by a second marriage, has provided him with a substantial fortune. Ormond regards this sudden accession to wealth more in the light of a challenge than as a stroke of good luck. Having already reflected on what it means to be a 'gentleman', he considers that having 'the fortune of a gentleman' brings a certain responsibility: 'now that I have every way the means, I will, by the blessing of Heaven, and with the help of kind friends, make myself something more and something better than I am' (129). Aside from avoiding making some major errors of judgment with respect to women, however, Harry does not in fact make any great progress toward this laudable goal until he decides to take a trip to Paris to visit M. and Mme de Connal. This is represented in part as a narrative 'wrong turn': he makes the decision in haste, having jumped to the conclusion that Florence Annaly, for whom he feels a passionate attachment, has accepted an offer of marriage from a Colonel Albemarle. Leaving Ireland (as was the case with *The Absentee*'s Colambre) appears to be associated with disappointment and loss. It quickly becomes apparent, however, that this experience represents the final and perhaps the most important stage in Ormond's education as an Irish gentleman.

In spite of his supposedly broken heart, Ormond displays a great deal of interest and enthusiasm upon his arrival in Paris; he is evidently keen to make a good impression and to enjoy whatever is on offer. He submits happily to Connal's prescriptions on the changes that must be made in his dress and appearance, which involve new outfits, new shoe buckles, the attention of a *chapelier* and an urgent appointment with a hairdresser. He is rewarded with the approving remark of M. Crepin, the 'valet de chambre', 'no contemptible judge in these cases', that 'M. Ormond looked not only as if he was *né coiffé*, but as if he had been born with a sword by his side' (199). Ormond's effortless transformation is in stark contrast with the figure usually made by a 'Milord Anglois', 'lost in the crowd, or stuck across a doorway by his own sword' (198). Aside from his poise, good looks and fashionable appearance, Ormond also differs from the average English visitor because of his facility with French and his ability to make pleasing conversation. Back in the Black Islands, Ormond had succeeded in learning a considerable amount of French, and had surprised Mlle O'Faley by 'the quickness with which he acquired the language, and caught the true Parisian pronunciation' (63). Conversation is, according to Connal, one of the keys to success in Paris:

> 'Talk, at all events, whether you speak ill or well, talk: don't aim at correctness – we don't expect it. Besides, as they will tell you, we like to see how a stranger "plays with our language"'. (190)

One might note here that Ormond's speech in French – described as a form of play – is thus as 'ungrounded' as the speech of Mlle O'Faley, which according to Hollingworth marks her as politically undesirable. Ormond's facility in French conversation means that he is once again explicitly distinguished from English visitors:

> 'You would pity us, Ormond,' cried [M. de Connal] 'if you could see and hear the Vandals they send to us from England with letters of introduction – barbarians who can neither sit, stand, nor speak – nor even articulate the language.' [. . .]
> 'It is really too great a tax upon the good-breeding of the lady of the house,' said Mad. de Connal, 'deplorable, when she has noting better to say of an English guest than that "ce monsieur là a un grand talent pour le silence."' (198)

Ormond is soon an acknowledged part of the Parisian social scene, and is referred to as '*le bel Anglois*' (201); this, however, is altered by Dora, who prefers to call him '*mon bel Irlandois*' (201). The experience of being assumed to be English is a common one for Irish people travelling abroad, other than in Britain. The Parisian indifference as to whether Ormond is English or Irish is in marked contrast to the story of Phelim O'Mooney in *An Essay on Irish*

Bulls, who discovers that it is almost impossible for an Irish person to travel 'undetected' in England. In Paris, Ormond can choose to identify himself and be identified as Irish. Although 'Irlandois' is initially distinguished as Dora's private term of affection for Harry, subsequent uses imply that it replaces 'Anglois' as the term by which he is known more generally: 'The two friends, le bel Irlandois, as they persisted in calling Ormond, and la belle Irlandoise, and their horses, and their horsemanship, were the admiration of the promenade' (204). It seems significant that 'the two friends' are identified as Irish – this suggests that Irishness is something which acquires meaning only in the context of community and relationships.

The claim that France represents a threat to Ormond's moral fibre, that he is 'confused and seduced by the blandishments of French society',[28] is difficult to sustain, given the emphasis on the benefits he derives from his stay. The de Connal household may well intend to involve Ormond in financial and sexual schemes, but they are rather toothless villains. The narrator informs us that Connal's motive in courting and flattering Ormond is to induce him to gamble, and thus rob him of his fortune. He is also exposed to moral danger because of his attraction to Dora and the relatively sterile nature of her 'typically French' marriage. His financial and moral security are brought into conjunction one evening when he explains to Connal that he will no longer play, because he had privately determined to stop gambling altogether once he had lost £500. Dora then takes him aside to tell him that she and her aunt have a significant financial interest in the 'faro bank' and that he too could profit by it. Her offer is made in such a way as to emphasise the involvement of her feelings and her desire to keep him close to her: 'O Harry, my first, my best, my only friend, I have enjoyed but little real happiness since we parted' (213). Ormond is, however, as much concerned for Dora's reputation as he is distracted by his own passions – his motive in having a private conversation with her is to warn her that the attentions paid to her by the comte de Belle Chasse have begun to be gossiped about. As he kneels before her, he catches sight of a ring containing some strands of her father's hair; this reminder of his beloved benefactor is enough to recall Ormond to himself, and to encourage Dora to adhere to the moral code she has been taught:

> 'He would see you, Dora, without a guide, or friend; surrounded with admirers, among profligate men, and women still more profligate, yet he would see that you have preserved a reputation of which your father would be proud.' (214)

It is thus difficult to read Ormond's time in Paris as the kind of dip in the moral cesspool that certain readings would suggest. Paris is, moreover, represented explicitly as the home of Enlightenment, which Ormond experiences at first hand through his acquaintance with André Morellet, who has been described as 'one of [the] most representative' figures of the French Enlightenment, and with whom Maria Edgeworth and her father were personally acquainted.[29] Impressed by the discovery that Ormond desires more than to be fashionable and flattered, Morellet arranges for him to attend a literary breakfast. Although (apparently) Voltaire is out of the country and Rousseau 'who was always quarrelling with somebody, and generally with everybody, could not be prevailed upon to go to this breakfast', Ormond meets Marmontel, Marivaux and 'the great d'Alembert' (208). Through his fortunate introduction to these literary and intellectual circles, Ormond experiences 'some of the really good company of Paris' (210). He goes to a variety of salons, including those of Mme Geoffrin, Mme de Tencin and Mme du Deffand, and learns, amongst other things that 'there is such a thing as conjugal fidelity and domestic happiness' in Paris (210).

Thus far one might say that Ormond's French education has created an idealised version of the eighteenth-century gentleman – differentiated from his English contemporaries in degree rather than kind by his superior success in acquiring the most polished refinements of a cosmopolitan culture. One could also argue that the recent defeat of Napoleon made the potentially subversive portrayal of an Irishman as the toast of Paris less problematic than it might otherwise have been. The associations between Irishness and criminality are, however, vividly brought to life once more by the chance meeting between Ormond and Moriarty Carroll:

> Just as [Ormond] was crossing the Pont Neuf, some one ran full against him. Surprised at what happens so seldom in the streets of Paris, where all meet, pass, or cross, in crowds with magical celerity and address, he looked back, and at the same instant the person who had passed looked back also. An apparition in broad daylight could not have surprised Ormond more than the sight of this person. 'Could it be – could it possibly be Moriarty Carroll, on the Pont Neuf in Paris?' (214)

The description of the incident includes a classic comic 'double take' and an evident relish in the incongruity of the meeting. Being Irish ('Moriarty Carroll') is constructed as absolutely other to being French ('Pont Neuf'); but the 'otherness' is comic rather than hostile. The incongruity which is part of the comic effect clearly implies a kind of inequality between Moriarty and the cosmopolitanism of the location, which reminds us of the difference in status between the poor Irish haymaker, struggling to speak English, and the English gentleman visiting Paris. The difference between elite and non-elite multilingualism is relevant here, in so far as the collision between Ormond and

Moriarty represents, similarly, a collision between elite and decidedly non-elite visitors to Paris. In stark contrast to Ormond's '*succès*' and his identification as 'le bel Irlandois', Moriarty is in Paris because he has escaped from jail, having been wrongly convicted of theft and sentenced to transportation to Australia (or Botany Bay, as the penal colony was then known). Paris thus acts as a refuge for an Irish felon – once again recalling the most famous recent Irish visitor to France, Theobald Wolfe Tone, who lived in France from 1796 to 1798 (acting as an official agent in Paris for the United Irishmen, 1796–7), when returning to Ireland would have meant being tried for treason.[30] So, the text acknowledges the subversive potential of Franco–Irish relations, but chooses instead to insist on their non-threatening character – Moriarty is technically a criminal, having been convicted, but is in fact innocent of the charges against him. This highly symbolic meeting thus brings together two apparently very different Irishmen – the criminal on the run and the educated, cosmopolitan gentleman. In doing so, it provides two different versions of how France relates to Irish identity. I suggested at the outset of this chapter that Edgeworth's linguistic example in *An Essay on Irish Bulls* served to underline the gulf of difference between the bilingualism of the lower-class Irish migrant worker and the educated visitor to Paris. The collision on the Pont Neuf, however, brings these two very different types of speaker together and claims their shared identity as Irish.

The fact that Ormond is not actually distinguished from Moriarty, but identified with him instead, on the basis of common Irishness, suggests an even more radical possibility, which is that Ormond and Moriarty are in fact two aspects of the same person. Taken together, Ormond and Moriarty display a number of the features of possibly the most popular character in eighteenth- and nineteenth-century literature in Ireland – the 'Irish Rogue'. *Ormond*, as is well known, makes explicit reference to two key eighteenth-century novels, Fielding's *Tom Jones* and Richardson's *Sir Charles Grandison*, but it also contains distinct echoes of Cosgrave's *A history of the most notorious Irish tories, highwaymen, and raparees* (commonly known by its abbreviated title of *Irish rogues and raparees* or *Irish rogues*), first published in 1747 and constantly reprinted throughout that century and well into the nineteenth century. This suggestion seems less unlikely when we consider that the high/low distinction between these two examples of intertextuality is in any case far from watertight – given both Fielding and Richardson's use of popular forms such as criminal biographies and familiar letters, and the similarity between the picaresque wanderings of Fielding's hero and those of the heroes of popular romances and chapbooks. As Niall Ó Ciosáin remarks, '*Irish rogues* illustrates the fact that 'popular' culture cannot be distinguished from 'elite' or 'learned' culture on the grounds of content, but that broader practices need to be borne in mind'.[31]

The longest and best-known story in this collection was that of Redmond O'Hanlon, a notorious Irish 'tory' of the seventeenth century, who is represented by Cosgrave as a noble figure brought low by political misfortune:

'Redmond O'Hanlon was the son of reputable Irish gentleman who had a considerable estate . . . The nation being reduced by the English forces, several Irish families who had a hand in the wars of Ireland were dispossessed, and their lands forfeited; by which means a very great alteration was made in this family, and several of the O'Hanlons were obliged to travel in hopes of retrieving their fortunes . . . ; poor Redmond [was] in this unhappy condition.'[32]

In Cosgrave's highly idealised and sanitised account, O'Hanlon is forced into the condition of an outlaw by '"happening to be at the killing of a gentleman in a quarrel."'[33] The similarity between this opening and the opening of *Ormond*, with Ormond's accidental shooting of Moriarty and his subsequent banishment from his guardian's house to the isolation of the Black Islands, is striking. Critical attention to date has tended to focus on characters in Edgeworth's fiction who allude very obliquely to violent and subversive aspects of Irish history, such as Mr Henry in *Patronage*, and Grace Nugent's 'St Omer' inheritance in *The Absentee*, only for these connections to be disavowed as the novel concludes. Criminality as a persistent feature of Irish identity is, however, highlighted in the characters of Phelim O'Mooney and the Irish haymaker in *An Essay on Irish Bulls*, as it is I suggest in *Ormond*. The connections between France and criminality and France and femininity are radically reconfigured in this novel, through the doubling of the upper and lower-class characters and through the emphasis on the role of a French education in producing, not a rebel or a felon, but a perfect husband and gentleman.

Ormond's highly symbolic meeting with Moriarty brings an abrupt end to his stay in Paris: by warning Ormond of the imminent failure of Sir Ulick O'Shane's bank, Moriarty is able to prevent the loss of his fortune and provides the immediate motivation for Ormond's departure from Paris and his eventual return to Ireland. He rushes to London to stop Sir Ulick using his power of attorney to cash in all his stock, and then returns to Ireland to help clear Moriarty's name. While in Ireland he learns to his joy and surprise that Florence Annaly has refused Colonel Albemarle's offer of marriage. The possibility of reconciliation with Florence puts paid to any plans he may have had of returning to Paris and travelling in Europe. Now, with the education and the fortune of a gentleman, and the prospect of a happy marriage, Ormond is at last able to find a place of his own – he buys the Black Islands estate from M. de Connal, thus taking his place as the heir of King Corny.

Ormond's return to Ireland does not indicate the repudiation of his experiences in France, however.[34] Upon his return from Paris Ormond has benefited from a number of significant experiences, almost all of which could only be regarded as positive. He has had the gratifying experience of being socially successful and has enjoyed all that Paris has to offer – from the theatre to the gaming table and the flattery of attractive women. He also has the morally gratifying sense of not being overly impressed by these superficial pleasures, and has enjoyed the distinction paid to him by some of the most celebrated authors of the day. The 'moral dangers' of Paris also seem to have few terrors for Florence and Lady Annaly, in spite of their status as moral exemplars. Ormond evidently feels that it is incumbent on him to articulate the conventional criticisms of French morality, to signal, perhaps, that he has not been contaminated by any dubious French influence:

> He was glad of this opportunity to give, as he now did with all the energy of truth, the result of his feelings and reflections on what he had seen of the modes of living among the French; their superior pleasures of society, and their want of our domestic happiness. (233)

The two women, however, seem much more focused on the ways in which Parisian influence has enhanced his external appeal:

> While Ormond was speaking, both the mother and the daughter could not help admiring, in the midst of his moralizing, the great improvement that had been made in his appearance and manners. (233)

At the end of the novel, therefore, Ormond has succeeded in his goal of turning himself into a gentleman who is, in addition to all his other worthy qualities, thoroughly approved of by women.

Critical debate on *Ormond* focuses for the most part on what the novel might have to say about issues of leadership and governance. The role of the landlord is of course present in the novel: Florence's brother Sir Herbert Annaly, with whom Ormond had an opportunity to become acquainted before he left for his trip abroad, functions as the explicit ideal of an Irish landlord, and Ormond reflects that 'by the time I am his age, why should not I become as useful, and make as many human beings happy as he does?' (162). As the novel closes, the narrator explains how it was that Harry came to acquire the Black Islands estate where 'he might do a great deal of good, by carrying on his old friend's improvements, and by farther civilizing the people of the Islands' (234). Thomas Flanagan's early assessment of Ormond's accession to Corny's 'kingdom' as 'a resolution so impossible of acceptance as to become a mocking epitaph'[35] is reiterated by Hollingworth who describes it as an 'implausible device' and 'a piece of Ascendancy wishful thinking increasingly irrelevant to the social realities of 1817.'[36] Other critics focus on *Ormond* as representing a significant shift in Edgeworth's thinking. For Trumpener, this conclusion is of a piece with aspects of the novel such as the warmly affectionate portrayal of Corny and the references to Sheelagh's knowledge of herbal remedies and 'their Irish names', and signals a shift towards a model of leadership legitimated by affiliation with cultural tradition.[37] Meredith Cary comments similarly on *Ormond*'s accommodation of 'traditional' ideas around status and leadership:

> In *Ormond* [Edgeworth] devised an 'Irish nation' which solves the Ascendancy's identity problems by guaranteeing to members the status she considered requisite. In this novel, true 'Irish aristocrats' express their identity as Europeans, scorning England and establishing claim to Irish land through both gift and purchase. The change makes room for more 'lifelike' character pictures than Edgeworth offered in any other work.[38]

Note that for Cary the imaginative construction of a unified rather than a divided nation is the precondition for the creation of 'lifelike' characters, a comment which actually reflects the ideology of nationalism itself, but which does grasp some of the qualities that distinguish *Ormond* from Edgeworth's earlier Irish tales. In my view, however, *Ormond* is not an end-point in Edgeworth's evolution towards sympathy with cultural nationalism, as Trumpener and Cary imply. It is, rather, a transitional text which for the first time in Edgeworth's fiction detaches the individual from the social role, but which imagines the construction of individual identity in a culturally specific and radical way.

The attention given to Ormond's role as a landlord within the text is very perfunctory when compared to *Ennui* and *The Absentee*, and to the emphasis on the interdependence of private and public in *Patronage*. The information as to Ormond's desire to settle in the Black Islands and continue Corny's plans for the people is marked specifically by the narrator as being intended for 'those who wish to hear something of estates, as well as of weddings' (234). The almost self-mocking remark – Edgeworth had after all been taken to task in reviews for her lack of emphasis on romantic love – is profoundly significant. Edgeworth's earlier works, from *Letters for Literary Ladies* onwards, had insisted on a metonymic relationship between the private and the public. Here they are brought into conjunction – 'as well as' – but they are not *necessarily* in conjunction, thus dissolving the basis on which a complex web of gendered and national identities could be held in a finely balanced tension.

What we find in *Ormond* is arguably more radical, however, in that the text destabilises the boundaries of femininity and masculinity in specific relation to Irish identity. The final lines of the novel are, highly significantly, from the perspective of Lady Annaly, who is 'rewarded [. . .] for that benevolent interest which she had early taken in our hero's improvement, by seeing the perfect felicity that subsisted between her daughter and Ormond' (235). France and the French language play a vital role in redeeming an 'Irish rogue', thus both raising the spectres of subversion and effeminacy (we might note that Moriarty seems to Ormond like an 'apparition in broad daylight'), and banishing them at the same time. In this novel France and the French language carry the widest possible range of signification – Catholicism, Enlightenment, criminality, politeness, femininity, superficiality – conflicting and often subversive influences, all of which, however, are resolved in the 'lifelike' character of Ormond. The potentially conservative implications of this psychologically plausible and 'unified' character are offset by the primacy that is given to its shaping according to feminine desires. By contrast, Edgeworth's last novel, *Helen*, also creates a disjunction between 'weddings' and 'estates', but unlike *Ormond* it associates these spheres decisively with unambiguous gender identities and national identities, with consequences that are both aesthetically and politically conservative. As we shall see in the following and final chapter, *Helen* is thus something of an anomaly in terms of Edgeworth's writing, but by virtue of its appearance so late in her career its reversals act to confirm the distinctively challenging configurations of gender and nationality which characterise her writing.

CHAPTER SIX

'Après nous le déluge'

The Woman Writer in the Age of O'Connell

-+->-<-+-

*H*elen, Edgeworth's last full-length fiction, is much less well known than the comments Edgeworth made about that novel, and specifically, the fact that it contains no Irish scenes or characters:

> It is impossible to draw Ireland as she now is in a book of fiction – realities are too strong, party passions are too violent to bear to see, or care to look at their faces in the looking-glass. The people would only break the glass, and curse the fool who held the mirror up to nature – distorted nature, in a fever.[1]

Edgeworth's remarks of 1834 on the impossibility of representing Ireland are arguably her most frequently cited words, whereas the novel she published in that year has received virtually no critical attention.[2] Margaret Kelleher has noted the 'popularity, and perceived relevance, of this extract for readers and critics in the late twentieth century' noting that it features prominently not only in studies of Edgeworth's works, but also in more general cultural studies such as David Lloyd's *Anomalous States* and Terry Eagleton's *Heathcliff and the Great Hunger.*[3] Edgeworth's 'failure' to produce a novel set in Ireland after *Ormond*, which appeared in 1817, and the finality with which she pronounced in 1834 the 'impossibility' of representing Ireland in fiction contribute to the widespread assumption that Edgeworth was a woman and a writer overtaken by events and unable to come to terms with the political changes that transformed Irish reality in the 1820s and 1830s. *Helen* has not benefited from the considerable revival of interest in Edgeworth since the 1970s, which has involved reassessments of her Irish fiction, as well as significant feminist reappraisals, and the exploration of colonial and postcolonial perspectives in a variety of her works. As a novel, *Helen* does not offer the kind of technical innovation that distinguished *Castle Rackrent*, or the intellectual scope and ambition which accounted for Edgeworth's place of honour in the literary reviews earlier in the century; in the narrative of British literary history, therefore, Edgeworth's significance appears to be past by the time *Helen* is published. For Irish literary critics and historians, Edgeworth inaugurated an Irish canon with *Castle Rackrent* and opened a space for the literary representation of Ireland; what is perceived as Edgeworth's ultimate failure to build on her own pioneering achievement means that *Helen* does not figure anywhere in accounts of the nineteenth-century Irish novel.

A disjunction has therefore taken place between *Helen* and the social and political conditions in which it was written, which is exemplified for instance in Michael Hurst's *Maria Edgeworth and the Public Scene*, which treats of Edgeworth's political views from the 1820s until her death in 1849, and contains exactly two references to *Helen*, the major piece of writing produced in this final phase of her life. The few critical treatments of the novel, in their turn, make little if any reference to the social and political changes during the novel's period of composition, which were by any measure momentous. Rather than attempt any kind of synthesis of thought and work, the standard critical response is to accept at face value Edgeworth's assertion that 'it is impossible to draw Ireland as she now is in a book of fiction'. In the case of *Helen*, therefore, the relationship between text and context seems to have mysteriously evaporated.

The idea that *Helen* is the logical result of Edgeworth's political and imaginative limitations has, understandably, done little to enhance the novel's reputation. However, as Marilyn Butler has remarked, Edgeworth was if anything *more* politically conscious and critical at this late stage in her life than she had been at the height of her career.[4] In a comparatively short span of time the political landscape of Ireland was transformed by the eventual granting of Catholic emancipation, by parliamentary reform and by the campaign for repeal of the Union. Michael Hurst suggests that the combined result of these changes was that 'the political ground of moderate Whiggery was suddenly swept from beneath Maria's feet';[5] within a few years the only sizeable Unionist support lay within the Tory party, and Edgeworth, along with her family, found herself in a new alignment with those who opposed both repeal and reform. It is impossible to imagine that a shift of this kind could find no reflection in a novel written in the wake of Catholic emancipation and the rise of O'Connell, and throughout the period of agitation for reform. That readers and critics have been able to divorce Edgeworth's last novel from this profound alteration in her political sympathies indicates the extent to which commentary on Edgeworth assumes that Irish content is synonymous with political content. The silence (from Irish literary historians and critics of Irish literature in particular) expresses a generally held belief about the novel, explicitly articulated by Marilyn Butler, who argues that 'when she found irreconcilable conflicts in life, her reaction was first to write in order to propose remedies, second to fall silent; rather than depict the country in turmoil, she allowed her career as an Irish novelist to come to an end'.[6] This comment suggests that the milieu in which *Helen* is set – that of the English gentry and aristocracy – provided Edgeworth with a background for a novel of personal relationships, untroubled by conflict or turmoil. This assumption is bolstered by the powerful tendency within criticism to limit Edgeworth's engagement with history to her Irish texts – creating an identification of England with the feminine and domestic.

Critical comment that does *not* dismiss *Helen* on the grounds of its perceived political irrelevance focuses on the extent to which Edgeworth manages to create rounded characters with psychological depth, noting the departure from her earlier plots and praising her achievement in sustaining character-driven interest. Both approaches to the novel fail to recognise that this turn to character and psychology in an autonomous zone of 'personal relationships' is in fact politically determined and reflects changed perceptions of the public sphere and the woman writer's relationship to that sphere. Edgeworth's career flourished in the period between the passing of the Act of Union and the achievement of Catholic emancipation. The long delay in granting emancipation had effectively disabled the emergence of a bourgeois public sphere in Ireland and, as we have seen, created the conditions for women writers such as Edgeworth and Morgan to produce texts which addressed 'masculine' themes like history, politics, economics, but which, in very different ways, 'feminised' these themes and concerns. O'Connellism, however, was triumphantly successful in creating a political nation, and in this context the more typically feminine concerns of *Helen* can be read as a reflection on the disappearance of the anomalous Irish public sphere in which Edgeworth had begun her writing career. This shift was underlined by the eventual passage of the first electoral Reform Act in 1832, which heralded the advent of democratic politics in both Britain and Ireland.

Edgeworth spent an extended period of time in England in 1830–1, witnessed at first hand the civil unrest that preceded the passage of the Reform Bill, and had contact with prominent Whigs and Tories – all this while she was planning and drafting *Helen*. In a period in which fears of revolution in England were rife, and not entirely without foundation, it does not follow, therefore, that Edgeworth's decision to set her novel among the gentry and aristocracy of that country was motivated by a desire to avoid controversy. While the achievement of Catholic emancipation and the subsequent campaign for repeal of the Union in Ireland, orchestrated in O'Connell's radical, populist style, was the political phenomenon which dominated Irish life at the time of *Helen*'s publication, it is imperative to read the novel in the context of the 1832 Reform Act. The two are in any case connected, in substance and in style: both parliamentary reform and the O'Connell's success in mobilising mass support, typified in the later 'Monster Meetings' of the Repeal campaign, indicate a profound shift in the location of power.

The perception at the time was that Britain was on the brink of an unprecedented political change that was revolutionary in scope. Marilyn Butler has noted that around 1830, 'as pressure for political reform built up, the minds of Englishmen returned to the topic of the French Revolution'.[7] Edgeworth was acutely conscious of the role played by counter-revolutionary ideology in prescribing what was appropriate or natural for women, and from the outset of her career, as we have seen, she had written with a lively aware- ness of how vulnerable women were to changes in political and social structures, and the ability of men to 'enforce their decrees' regarding women, as she com- mented in *Leonora*.[8] The focus on the interior lives of women in *Helen* derives from a conviction that the social and political changes of the 1830s were indeed revolutionary, leading to the creation of an exclusively masculine public sphere. There is moreover evidence to suggest that Edgeworth's reading of English culture and politics in this period was informed by her reaction to the transfor- mation of Irish public life that preceded O'Connell's election to Westminster.

In the 1820s Edgeworth was anxious to see the granting of Catholic eman- cipation and was convinced of the benefits it would bring to Ireland. She and other Irish Whigs, such as Thomas Spring Rice, with whom she corresponded, were perhaps curiously optimistic about the combination of progress and stability that they expected would issue from the granting of emancipation. In 1825 Edgeworth wrote to Rachel Mordecai Lazarus, 'If this [Catholic emancipation] be done, the people will be contented and quiet'.[9] It must also be emphasised, as Butler remarks, that Edgeworth's eagerness to correspond with Spring Rice and her willingness to express political opinions is in itself noteworthy, and is in contrast to the reticence on political matters she displayed in earlier life. During the brief Canning administration in 1827, Spring Rice accepted office; Edgeworth was thus closer than she had ever been to the centre of political power, and was afforded insight into its operations by Spring Rice's correspondence.

The efforts of liberal Protestants to effect emancipation through persuasion were unsuccessful. It was O'Connell's Catholic Association, which based its strength firmly on the ability to mobilise large numbers, and to demonstrate loyalty through the willingness of all classes of Catholics to pay the Association's fee (known as 'Catholic rent'), that eventually swung the issue. The role played by the Catholic rent in creating a cohesive political movement was greeted with alarm in Protestant circles, being described as 'in truth, an Irish Revolution.'[10] Edgeworth deplored O'Connell's methods, feeling that they relied on the intimidation of the poor and ignorant by priests, and represented an implicit threat of civil disorder.[11] What is more, O'Connellism did not end with emancipation. Oliver MacDonagh has remarked that O'Connell's unique achievement from 1830 to 1845 was to transfer the organisation and strength that had been harnessed for the emancipation campaign to the much more generalised, even amorphous aims of 'Repeal'; he thereby 'pioneered not only popular participation and manipulation on a huge scale, but also the various tactics of deploying the forces he had conjured up against governments'.[12] It is not hard to imagine how O'Connell's success in depriving the landlords and gentry of their traditional leadership role was feared and deplored by those such as the Edgeworths, who had at all times taken this leadership role extremely seriously.

The manner in which 'O'Connellism' transformed the Edgeworths' political landscape is illustrated by the election of 1831, in which two Tory candidates ran in Longford, opposed by two O'Connellites, Luke White and a local canal engineer named Mullins, whom Mrs Edgeworth described unceremoniously as a 'vulgar fellow'.[13] Lord Forbes, one of the Tory candidates, was a friend of the family, and it was perhaps this connection that persuaded Lovell that he should give his support to a member of his circle and class rather than to candidates who appeared antithetical to everything the Edgeworths stood for. The comments of one tenant, however, recorded by Mrs Edgeworth, suggest that Lovell's tenants were of a different opinion. Garret Keegan affirmed that he would vote for Lord Forbes, but:

> There is not another Catholic among them [the tenants] will vote for him especially. They never could abide him since he dispersed the Anti-Union meeting last January at Longford – and he finished himself by voting against this bill of Reform.[14]

Lovell ultimately succeeded in delivering the support of his tenants for Lord Forbes, who was duly elected along with his Tory running mate. Maria Edgeworth's comments, written in a letter from England, suggest some hesitation at Lovell's unprecedented decision to support the Tory candidate:

> I like Lovells address to the tenants and am very glad that his tenants all adhered to him so well. Indeed he deserved it from them – a kinder landlord cannot be. [. . .] It is so difficult to tell what is best for these countries at present that I am sure I should not know whether to vote for or against *the bill and the whole bill and nothing but the bill* if a pistol were held to my brains this minute.[15]

What strikes one immediately about this comment is how Edgeworth links the changed political landscape in Ireland in the wake of O'Connell's election with the debates on parliamentary reform. Edgeworth was broadly in favour of reform, but the combination of an increasingly politicised Catholic constituency and the impact of parliamentary reform transformed politics in Ireland in ways which she clearly found alienating. In 1832, when an election followed the Reform Act, Edgeworth was both angry and upset that almost the entire tenantry voted for the O'Connellite candidates. The tone of her comments is unusually uncompromising and bitter: 'Now at least we know whom we cannot trust – and we have experienced the force against us. The evil will not stop at this election. It is not, as in former times, only losing an election.'[16] Edgeworth's fears regarding O'Connell were in the first instance focused on his impact on Ireland, specifically – she perceived, accurately enough, that the tendency of his politics was incompatible with the system of landlordism. Repeal of the Union would not have meant a return to the (briefly independent) pre-Union parliament, effectively a Protestant Parliament for a Protestant People, but would usher in an entirely new era of populism and democracy. The evidence of Edgeworth's letters from England during the period of the reform debates, however, suggests that O'Connell's recent rise to prominence in Ireland coloured her view of events in England so that it exacerbated her fears of the radical threat in England itself, to the extent that she openly spoke of her fear of revolution.

Marilyn Butler has noted that Edgeworth's lengthy stay in England during the period of *Helen*'s composition meant that she had an opportunity to observe contemporary high society, a fact which is seen as contributing to the greater naturalness of tone in this, her final novel.[17] In July 1831 while staying with family friends in Hamstead Hall, Edgeworth wrote to her sister Fanny that 'Helen has been going on in my head I assure you through all and several things I have seen here and several I have heard will turn to profit to her account'.[18] Participation in and observation of high society involved political assessments, however, as well as those of character, conversation and style. When Edgeworth wrote this letter to her sister in London, she had just arrived at Hamstead Hall after an extended stay in London, during which she had frequent contact with men then actively engaged in the debates on Reform: she was on several occasions the guest of Lord Lansdowne, a leading Whig, but also met Murray and J. G. Lockhart, publisher and editor of the *Quarterly Review*, who were active in the same debates on the Tory side. Edgeworth was on good terms with Lockhart and through him came into contact with many of those who contributed to the debate on England's impending 'constitutional revolution'.[19] In 1831 the *Quarterly* carried an article on reform, and Edgeworth was sufficiently close to the publisher, editor and contributors to be given a piece written by Philip Henry Stanhope (Lord Mahon), which was intended for but not published in this number.[20] The letters that Edgeworth wrote at this period are vivid and detailed, suggesting that the dramatic events in the House of Commons, the precariously balanced state of the parties and outbreaks of civil unrest ensured that conversation revolved around politics.

In April 1831, following the dissolution of Parliament by the Whigs, she remarked to her stepmother, 'Oh it is impossible to give you an idea of the talking and hurry-flurry about elections at this moment',[21] but went on to give an account of discussion at Lansdowne House, concluding optimistically that the next ministry, whether Whig or Tory, would introduce a measure of reform. It is characteristic of Edgeworth, although until very late in life a Whig, not to adhere to one party on any given issue – she was firm in her belief that one's obligation was to place the substantive issue at the centre of any debate, and to disregard party loyalties or antipathies. Shortly before the dissolution of parliament, Edgeworth speculated that 'If they [the Whigs] went out Peel would come in and it is said would bring in a moderate yet *real* reform bill giving representatives to large towns that want them and not allowing the £10 qualification.'[22] Edgeworth was supportive of the cause of Reform – she deemed it 'absolutely necessary'[23] – but like many of her class at that time was concerned about the manner in which the reform issue appeared to have mobilised the population at large into a potentially threatening 'mob'. When asked to state her position on the Bill by a hearty gentleman engaged in carving a slice of 'the roast beef of old England', Edgeworth recounts: 'I gave him my *opinion* in a bumper toast "Reform without Revolution if possible".'[24] This (rather incongruous) image belies the concern that Edgeworth in reality felt about the possibility of popular violence and revolution in England at this time.

Edgeworth had arrived in England in mid-October 1830, and by mid-November serious agricultural riots had broken out in Kent, in the very neighbourhood in which her brother Sneyd was then living. On 17 November she felt that she had to reassure her family that there was no danger: 'We are all here safe and well – and it is well to begin with telling you so, as the exaggerated reports we see in the E[nglish] papers of the mobs and burnings in Kent may have reached you.'[25] These 'Captain Swing' riots were, in the opinion of historians, prompted by economic rather than political issues and grievances, but in the eyes of contemporary observers they were precipitated by the second Revolution in France, the fall of Charles X in 1830, 15 years after the restoration of the Bourbon monarchy.[26] Edgeworth herself made an explicit connection between civil disorder and the pressure for reform:

> If the ministry change as from this majority against them seems inevitable those who come in *must* see what they can do for reform and then all the grievances must come before Parliament in constitutional form. I think it is absolutely necessary. Otherwise there would be *risings* and revolution.[27]

Edgeworth's sense of the need for parliamentary reform is expressed in terms of the danger of formlessness, in the amorphous body of the mob: 'If any step be gained by the *mob* – all is lost – for there is no saying to the mob any more than to the sea so far shalt thou go and no further.'[28] In place of the formless and boundless sea, a reformed parliament is figured here as a safe space which can contain 'all the grievances in constitutional form'. The space needs to be expanded – literally, as the extension of the franchise would have the effect of making the parliament bigger by creating additional members. Within this larger space grievances are made safe by being given a specific form. Edgeworth's description echoes the nineteenth-century trend towards specialisation: 'politics' becomes a specialised activity directed at the containment of disruptive forces in society. Without politics, society is threatened by a constant tendency towards collapse, towards 'risings and revolution'. There was of course no question of women participating in this increasingly large and important arena, as either electors or elected representatives, so the channelling of power to parliamentary politics involves a highly problematic gendering of the forms of government. There is, moreover, a connection between the emergence of a specifically masculine sphere of politics and Irish conditions, suggested by Edgeworth's use of the word 'risings'. The word is emphasised in the same way that words specific to Irish speakers of English are emphasised and typographically marked in her novels, implying that 'risings' are an Irish phenomenon that may be transmitted to England. Edgeworth's sense of the need for an enlarged and more powerful zone of politics appears therefore to relate to her experience of specifically Irish instances of social unrest and violence.

Edgeworth herself appeared to think that repeal of the Union was a distinct possibility. Immediately following the election of December 1832 she recorded her intention to write to Lord Lansdowne to 'waken in time his fears for his Irish territories, which if there be (and what is to prevent) a dissolution of the Union will soon cease to afford him rents and presently pass into other hands'.[29] In 1835 she expressed the hope that Peel's Conservative administration would 'prevent a revolution' in Ireland.[30] Edgeworth's sense that the location of power in Ireland had shifted dramatically and irrevocably did indeed make it impossible for her to represent Ireland in fiction: the assumptions on which her representations had rested were fatally undermined. These assumptions are not confined to her desire to see Protestant landowners as the locus of power and authority in Ireland, as so many critics have claimed. Equally as significant was the fact that the advent of populist democracy made it impossible to continue imagining the forms of female social influence that had been so central to her thinking. *Helen*, which is on the surface at least a drama of personal relationships set in an idealised England, is thus a projection of Edgeworth's sense of loss and displacement as an Irish woman. One of the last letters Edgeworth wrote before she left England in 1831 contains a striking aside in which she apostrophises England: 'Wonderful England! With all your industry and all your prosperity I hope you will not be revolutionised – especially in our time. Après nous le déluge.'[31] This Burkean lament sounds a very new note in Edgeworth's writing.

The *Dublin University Magazine* was founded, as is well known, in 1833 in the wake of the Great Reform Bill to defend Tory, Unionist and Protestant principles in Ireland. The issue that carried a review of *Helen* led with an editorial that commented in cataclysmic terms on the impact of the Reformed parliament. 'The constitution has been capsized', it declared, and 'a race of legislators has been called into being whose notions of good government are essentially different from those of all who went before them'.[32] The article laments at length the passing of the 'salutary influence of the upper classes on the lower'.[33] I argue that *Helen* addresses the disappearance of this 'salutary influence', focusing in large part on the experience of upper-class and aristocratic women. *Helen* can be described as a conservative text, but it is remarkable for the way in which it articulates and reveals the ideological underpinnings of its conservatism. Its tendency is on the one hand to naturalise established relations of gender and power, but, paradoxically, also to reveal their constructed quality.

Helen concentrates on three principal characters and the complex relationships of intimacy through which they are drawn together, and which threaten to divide them. As the novel opens Helen Stanley is a girl of 19, left an orphan on the death of her uncle Dean Stanley, who had been her guardian since the death of both parents when Helen was an infant. A home is offered to her in Clarendon Park, with her childhood friend, Lady Cecilia, who has recently married General Clarendon. Also a member of the household is Cecilia's mother, Lady Davenant, a highly intelligent and talented woman who acted as a mother to Helen when she was a child, and whom Helen still regards with a mixture of love and awe. The household into which Helen moves thus almost replicates that of her childhood, but with the significant difference that she must now comes to terms with the somewhat formidable General Clarendon. Clarendon is described as having a 'high-born, high-bred military air', and as 'English decidedly – proudly English. Something of the old school'.[34] His qualities of breeding and 'Englishness' are not without complication, as in spite of his impeccable manners and politeness Helen cannot feel at ease in his company. Helen seeks advice on how she should behave towards Clarendon, and in what way she might gain his approval, from her childhood mentor, Lady Davenant. The problem is temporarily solved when it emerges that Clarendon had gathered from Cecilia that Helen had promised many years before to live with Cecilia after her marriage, should she herself remain unmarried. Cecilia had used this bogus promise as a means of vetoing her husband's plan of bringing his sister Esther to live in Clarendon Park. Helen's courage in confronting Clarendon's displeasure and her subsequent honesty win his admiration and enable Helen to live at ease once more. It is, however, significant that Helen's peace of mind is dependent on Clarendon's estimation of her. He assumes the role of judge and arbiter of feminine behaviour, embodying a typically patriarchal authority – it is surely no coincidence that he shares the name of Edward Hyde, first Earl of Clarendon, a prominent Royalist of the Civil War period and author of the well-known *History of the Great Rebellion*. Edgeworth's Clarendon, unlike the more complex historical figure from whom he takes his name, is strongly ideologically committed to the idea of aristocracy and inherited status.[35] Whereas his ward, Granville Beauclerc, favours the continued and increased diffusion of knowledge, and enthusiastically proclaims the fact that a man of abilities can rise to almost any rank in England, regardless of birth, General Clarendon maintains a strong aristocratic bias: 'the march of intellect was not a favourite march with him, unless the step were perfectly kept, and all in good time' (83).

Before his marriage to Cecilia, Clarendon had the reputation of a man who could never be satisfied in a wife, as he had 'specially resolved against marrying any travelled lady, and most especially against any woman with whom there was danger of a first love' (24). Miraculously, Cecilia Davenant fulfils his demand for beauty, intelligence and perfect virtue and truth. However, danger lies in the fact that 'the idol he adores must keep herself at the height to which he has raised her, or cease to receive his adoration' (25). Clarendon's judgement and reasoning are, however, compromised by his pride, as Lady Davenant astutely remarks:

> 'General Clarendon is too proud to be jealous of his wife. For aught I know, he might have felt jealousy of Cecilia before she was his, for then she was but a woman, like another; but once HIS – once having set his judgment on the cast, both the virtues and the defects of his character join in security for his perfect confidence in the wife "his choice and passion both approve"'. (25)

Helen notes that Clarendon speaks in a tone of command – the household over which he presides is one in which things must conform to his will; however, since his will must depend on his judgement, this command quickly becomes an entrapment, as his pride cannot accommodate the possibility of error. In his household, Lady Davenant is reduced to the status of advisor to her 'daughter', Helen, whose fate depends ultimately on the male father figure of Clarendon. Lady Davenant is in addition absent for the central section of the narrative, leaving Helen at the mercy of Cecilia's self-seeking dishonesty and Clarendon's harsh judgement.

The central position that Clarendon occupies indicates an almost complete reversal of the symbols and structures of Edgeworth's fiction. It is Clarendon, rather than Helen, or any of the female characters, who represents what it is to be English. In the tradition of Germaine de Staël, this Englishness is not only masculine but is aggressively so, in that it threatens the female characters' happiness and peace of mind. *Helen* thus differs profoundly from *Patronage* and the other works of Edgeworth's earlier career in that it portrays women as subject to a patriarchal structure. Maggie Gee writes that 'the heart of the novel is the intricate and shifting relationships' between the three principal female characters. Clarendon and the other male characters she dismisses as being almost 'puppets'.[36] This is I feel a radical misreading of the novel. Whilst the reader is almost certainly focused on the female characters, the action of the plot is determined by Clarendon. The relationships between the women are circumscribed by his rigidity and his vastly over-confident judgement. Caroline Gonda argues that the novel 'maintains a strong sense of women's agency and of their moral responsibility for what they write, say, or do'.[37] My account will demonstrate, however, that the choices available for women as moral agents do not include those which will benefit both them and the society which they inhabit. This marks a distinct departure for Edgeworth.

Although Cecilia's dishonesty and cowardice are the root causes of the collapse of Helen's hopes, Clarendon's role in acting as her judge is decisive. When he suspects Helen of having received letters from a Colonel D'Aubigny, he impresses her with the need to hear the 'plain truth' and the 'plain fact', without which he cannot esteem her. Clarendon is unaware that his wife, Cecilia, has persuaded Helen to accept these letters as hers, in order to preserve Cecilia from her husband's anger. When Helen miserably states that she is not in a position to offer such truth or such facts, she is conscious of 'how sunk she was in his opinion, – sunk for ever, she feared!' (285). Yet although an apparent adherent of plain facts, Clarendon's judgement is far from being as impartial as he would like to believe. He accepts unquestioningly an evasive answer from Cecilia as to the handwriting on the letters, not realising that, on a literal level, Cecilia has not frankly denied that the handwriting is hers. A similarly worded reply from Helen provokes only his scorn. When he asks if she burned the originals of the letters Helen replies, as truthfully as possible, that 'They are burned', thus concealing that it was in fact Cecilia who burned them. Clarendon draws from her response only the inference that she wishes to deny responsibility for herself: 'They are burned [. . .] that is, you burned them: unfortunate' (285). Clarendon's confidence as to his own ability to discern the truth of the matter is revealed to be no more than a series of over-confident assumptions in which he is led more than he could possibly know by his love for Cecilia. When she sees the extent of her success in manipulating her husband, Cecilia realises with horror that he has become a 'dupe': 'his credulous affection had blinded his judgment' (350).

The figure of Clarendon suggests a gender politics characterised by inequality and relations of dominance and subservience. Any discussion of gender and power in *Helen* must, however, consider the role played by Lady Davenant, whose remarks on women and politics form one of the more frequently cited passages from the novel:

> 'Women are now so highly cultivated, and political subjects are at present of so much importance, of such high interest, to all human creatures who live together in society, you can hardly expect, Helen, that you, as a rational being, can go through the world as it now is, without forming any opinion on points of public importance. You cannot, I conceive, satisfy yourself with the common namby-pamby little missy phrase, "ladies have nothing to do with politics"'. (214)

The comments on politics that make up such a significant part of Edgeworth's correspondence in the 1830s suggest that Lady Davenant's views are very close to those of the author, who, after all, did not shirk from giving her '*opinion*, in a bumper toast'. Lady Davenant's description of the emergence of politics as an important subject suggests that this has not always been the case – the word 'now' is used twice in the passage. This recalls Edgeworth's own sense that the expansion of the zone of the political was a necessary response to a changed social context. The passage has sometimes been read as indicative of a late-emerging radicalism on Edgeworth's part, in supposed contrast to the 'caution' of her earlier position on women and politics. I would suggest, however, that what it really reflects is the realisation that 'politics' was not only increasingly important, but was increasingly positioned as alien to the concerns of 'ladies' and namby-pamby little misses.

Elsewhere, Lady Davenant's description of women's relation to politics is actually very limited. She affirms that 'female influence [...] should always be domestic, not public – the customs of society have so ruled it' (214). In *Letters for Literary Ladies*, published almost forty years before, Edgeworth had carefully avoided challenging the prohibition on women's participation in the public sphere, but she had attempted to reimagine the domestic as a micro-cosm of the public, not as defined by its difference from the public. Lady Davenant's observation that the 'customs' of society determine what women's roles are to be, moreover, involves a striking alteration in Edgeworth's vocab-ulary. Whereas *Letters for Literary Ladies* challenged the Burkean rhetoric of custom and prejudice, *Helen* accepts its terms. The emphasis on the greatly increased significance of the political evidenced in Lady Davenant's remarks to Helen, though combined with a comment on women's increased 'cultivation', ultimately indicates that women's potential sphere of influence is reduced. This is borne out by Lady Davenant's account of her own path from 'female politician' to ideal and cultivated wife.

As she does in *Belinda*, Edgeworth presents a compelling account of the suffering caused by an unhappy marriage, which in Lady Davenant's case is caused by her wilful manipulation of her husband's affection for petty 'political' ends. Lady Davenant is in some ways a more impressive and powerful character than *Belinda*'s Lady Delacour. She gains insight into her errors, and displays a self-generated ability to alter her behaviour once she realises that she and her husband are becoming increasingly estranged. Her happiness is not threatened by her wit and intelligence, but eventually secured by these characteristics. Lady Davenant could therefore be said to represent a 'progression' in terms of Edgeworth's portrayal of older women. Lady Davenant relates the story of her life early in the novel, however, and is subsequently absent from its most dramatic scenes, reappearing only in the final chapters, where it is strongly indicated that she is near death. Edgeworth thus creates one of the strongest female characters in her entire œuvre, only to relegate her to peripheral significance.

The manner in which Lady Davenant recedes from the centre of the novel is programmed by a series of allusions to France and the French Revolution which occur throughout *Helen*. Lady Davenant's role model in her attempts to become a 'female politician', and play a distinguished part in society is Mme de Staël: she is inspired to create a salon when she reads Staël's *Considerations on the French Revolution* (1818), in particular her comments on the limited role played by English women in social life:

> She asserts that, though there may be women distinguished as writers in England, there are no ladies who have any great conversational or political influence in society, of that kind which, during *l'ancien regime*, was obtained in France by what they would call their *femmes marquantes*, such as Madame de Tencin, Madame du Deffand, Mademoiselle de l'Espinasse. This remark stung me to the quick, for my country and for myself, and raised in me a foolish, vain-glorious emulation, an ambition false in its objects, and unsuited to the manners, domestic habits and public virtue of our country. I ought to have been gratified by her observing, that a lady is never to be met with in England, as formerly in France, at the Bureau du Ministre; and that in England there has never been any example of a woman's having known in public affairs, or at least told, what ought to have been kept secret. Between ourselves, I suspect that she was a little mistaken in some of these assertions; but, be that as it may, I was determined to prove that she was mistaken [. . .]. I set about, as soon as I was able, to assemble an audience round me, to exhibit

myself in the character of a female politician, and I believe I had a notion at the same time of being the English Corinne. (59–60)[38]

The desire to emulate the social leadership of French women is misguided and futile, she now judges, because such a role is incompatible with English manners and institutions. It is also futile because, as Staël herself repeatedly remarked, the social pre-eminence of women in France was an aristocratic and pre-revolutionary phenomenon. As early as her *De la littérature*, Staël envisaged an entirely new social formation and, as we have seen in earlier chapters, much of her work is coloured by a regret for the loss of a social structure which accommodated and enabled female influence. Edgeworth's previously optimistic view of social change, by contrast, was predicated on the maintenance of an elite class through which women could exercise an influential and reforming role. In *Helen*, however, it is proposed that the preservation of England from 'revolutionising' influences depends on the (voluntary) withdrawal of women from political influence, or pretensions to political influence. The bleak alternative is suggested by the state of affairs in France, which is described in terms of bitter factionalism fuelled by frustrated women. Lady Davenant expresses her fear to a visiting Frenchman that British society may be headed in the same direction:

'No', said the French gentleman, 'English ladies will never be so vehement as my countrywomen; they will never become, I hope, like some of our lady politicians, "*qui heurlent comme des demons*."' (210)

In response, Lady Davenant makes female influence conditional on the maintenance of a highly specific feminine character:

'So long as ladies keep in their own proper character,' said Lady Davenant, 'all is well; but, if once they cease to act as women, that instant they lose their privilege – their charm; they forfeit their exorcising power; they can no longer command the demon of party nor themselves, and he transforms them directly, as you say,' said she to the French gentleman, 'into actual furies.' (210)

The idea of female agency is here drastically circumscribed: if women are to act, they must 'act as women' – the performance of their gender is the only socially useful role they can adopt.

The sense of the recent and rather sudden shift in the location of power is encoded in Lady Davenant's account of her misguided ambitions and her realisation of the error of her ways, which effectively takes us from *ancien régime* France to post-reform Britain in a few pages, as she narrates her conversion from female politician to politician's wife. Her determination to become an agent involves her in increasing ethical and moral dilemmas, as she attempts to influence and manipulate her husband. She thus decides to end her failed career as an active participant and to become instead a well-informed spectator and analyst of people and events. She undertakes a course of reading which is quite different from 'such reading as ladies read', as it is to enable her to 'keep pace with Lord Davenant and his highly informed friends' (66), and she begins to appreciate the truth of the aphorism that 'knowledge is power' (67). Having renounced her aim of wishing to influence action, however, Lady Davenant's desire to acquire 'masculine' knowledge and thereby a form of power is rendered unproblematic and in fact praiseworthy. This period of intellectual cultivation takes place during a period in which her husband's party is in opposition. With a symbolic return to power – which can be interpreted as a post-reform administration – Lady Davenant has an opportunity to put into practice her new plan of behaviour. She states that she 'had learned, if not to be less ambitious, at least to shew it less' (68). Husband and wife are in perfect harmony, and Lord Davenant expresses his appreciation of his wife's intelligent support by claiming that 'every public man who has a cultivated and high-minded wife has in fact two selves, each holding watch and ward for the other' (68). Lady Davenant's retreat is thus completed by a very Victorian emphasis on femininity as the source of male virtue and, consequently, the construction of a purely domestic sphere as the precondition for a viable public sphere.

The 'reformed' political process, and the role subsequently adopted by the aristocracy, is depicted in the most obviously political scene in the novel, Lady Castlefort's party in London, at which Helen and Cecilia are disturbed to find themselves crushed by 'hard unaccustomed citizen elbows' (273). The reason for the presence of so many 'Goths and Vandals' is explained by one of the aristocratic guests: 'in short, one of Lord Castlefort's brothers is going to stand for the City, and citizens and citoyennes must be propitiated' (273). The image of the plebeian and possibly recently enfranchised 'citizens' as 'Goths and Vandals' alludes to Staël's comparison of the invasion of the Roman Empire by the Goths and the Vandals of the North with the seizure of power by the *sans-culottes* in the French Revolution. This invasion of the citizens in Edgeworth's text does not produce the progressive union that Staël envisioned, however. The effect of the mixing of classes at the Castlefort party, according to Helen's observation, is to increase the pride of the 'high-born, high-bred group' and their contempt for the 'unprivileged multitude', thus 'rudely severing' the links between the classes (275). The crowded, chaotic and hostile atmosphere described is one in which little is likely to be achieved in any case by personal contact. The nobility are present, one observer claims, merely as

'baits to the traps [. . .] We are what they are "come for to see"' (273). The entire
nobility, and not simply the women of that class, has been robbed of its power
and reduced to the status of decorative object: two fashionable gentlemen
lounging against a fireplace are for instance described as 'caryatides' – a term
from statuary which normally refers to a female figure. It is significant that
Lady Davenant is not present at this politically motivated gathering. She is
absent from the central section of the narrative, and absent from the kind of
domestic politics described, while accompanying her husband in his position
as ambassador to Russia. Edgeworth thereby suggests that post-reform
politics is a world in which there is no need or no demand for the talents and
intelligence of a woman like Lady Davenant.

In spite of the claims of Lady Davenant that England is less plagued by
factionalism and 'party spirit', and that women are thus able to exercise the
charm of their 'influence', at the Castlefort party the language of factionalism,
borrowed from France, is liberally sprinkled about. Louisa Castlefort, Cecilia
remarks, is an 'ultra exclusive' but has been forced to 'turn ultra liberale, or an
universal suffragist' because of her brother-in-law's marriage to a merchant's
daughter and his political ambitions (278).[39] This prompts the wit, Horace
Churchill, to quote a saying of the French upper classes on the subject of 'low
money-matches': 'mettre du fumier sur nos terres' (spreading manure on our
fields) (278). This phrase is borrowed from Auguste de Staël's *Letters on
England*, where it is used, in contrast to its function in Edgeworth's text, to
suggest the difference between France and England. Staël claimed that
whereas in France marriages between the landed and commercial classes were
regarded with disdain, as indicated by the crude metaphor, in England
tensions and divisions between the two groups were far less acute.[40] Citing
Staël in this context, however, Edgeworth inverts his comment, portraying the
relations between the aristocratic and commercial classes in terms of cynical
dependence and exploitation. The equation of France and England implicit in
this scene seems paradoxical, given the lengths to which the text goes
elsewhere to portray the English way of life as an ideal, explicitly contrasted
with France. What emerges from this seeming paradox is a tension between
the ideal and the actual which is without precedent in Edgeworth's fiction,
involving the construction of the past as the site of the ideal, a move which, as
we shall see, marks *Helen* as the only romantic text Edgeworth ever wrote.

In a highly symbolic episode in the novel, Clarendon leads his wife and
friends on a trip from his estate to the neighbouring estate of Old Forest, the
home of the Forresters, once a 'respectable, good, old English family' (75), now
living abroad and unable to keep up their estate. The romantic ideal of
permanence and community is celebrated in this episode, and in true romantic
mode, this ideal is suggested primarily through the representation of its

antithesis, the spectre of decay and ruin. On the way to Old Forest the party passes through a village on Clarendon's estate, which is described in rapturous terms, as indicative of both English liberty and material prosperity:

> The road led them next into a village, one of the prettiest of that sort of scattered English villages where each habitation seems to have been suited to the fancy as well as to the convenience of each proprietor; giving an idea at once of comfort and liberty, such as can be seen only in England. Happy England, how blest, would she but know her bliss! (81)

The tenants who greet the landlord and his guests are uniformly grateful and deferential, contrasting perhaps with those of Edgeworthstown who had proved themselves unwilling to support even kind and just landlords. The creation of England as an ideal implicitly in contrast with Ireland is however rendered problematic by the hints that present conditions are not actually in harmony with this idealised state. The stretch of the Thames along which they continue their ride is one where 'the black steam-boat never marked the way' and is free from 'the din of commerce' (82). The rural village which is supposed to represent the very best qualities of Englishness is in tension with commerce and industry, and therefore with contemporary reality. The poverty of the present is graphically represented by the scene of devastation that reveals itself when the General's party finally arrive at Old Forest, to find the mansion itself dilapidated and the surrounding parkland destroyed:

> The avenue, overgrown with grass, would have been difficult to find, but for deep old cart-ruts which still marked the way. But soon, fallen trees, and lopped branches, dragged many a rood and then left there, made it difficult to pass. And there lay exposed the white bodies of many a noble tree, some wholly, some half, stripped of their bark, some green in decay, left to the weather – and every here and there little smoking pyramids of burning charcoal. (84)

The family's financial collapse is laid at the door of their involvement in, of all things, politics and, specifically, feminine interference in politics: 'to make herself somebody', Mrs Forrester 'forced her husband to stand for the county. A contested election – bribery – a petition – another election – ruinous expense' (75). Parliamentary politics, a sphere of activity which Edgeworth herself foresaw as increasingly important in containing the forces of social unrest, is here represented as the cause of the collapse of a great house and an 'old English family'.

    W. J. Mc Cormack has commented on Burke's use in *Reflections on the Revolution in France* of the image of the 'Great House', in which 'its recurrent citation is ironic and objective in that Burke uses it primarily as an image of ruination contrasted with a wholeness which historical continuity may afford'.[41] As Mc Cormack and others have argued, Burke's powerful evocations of wholeness and historical continuity can be situated in relation to his concern with the absence of these values in Ireland, an absence which for Burke made Ireland a location of crisis and ruin, vulnerable to revolutionizing influences. In *Helen*, the narrator's observation that England does not recognise its own virtues – 'Happy England, how blest, would she but know her bliss!' – suggests strongly that the idealised image of England is, similarly, driven by Edgeworth's belated anxiety about the instability of the social fabric in Ireland. The ruin at Old Forest could therefore be read alongside other Irish texts of this period, including Sheridan Le Fanu's haunting description of the decayed great house of Bartram-Haugh in *Uncle Silas* (1864) – which, it may be worth noting, was based on a short story published as early as 1838.[42] It need hardly be pointed out that Old Forest forms a sharp and telling contrast with Edgeworth's first fictional ruin, Castle Rackrent, which articulated the comic rather than the tragic meanings of decay, or with the burnt-out shell of Glenthorn Castle, the destruction of which appears as a precondition for the tale's progressive outcome.

Whereas the country house and estate had featured in Edgeworth's earlier fiction as the space in which it was possible to imagine new configurations of gender and power, here the estate is radically reconceived as the site of tradition. The abandonment of earlier models is further underlined by the character of Esther Clarendon. Marilyn Butler has suggested that Esther bears a resemblance to heroines of Edgeworth's earlier fictions, women such as Belinda, and Grace Nugent of *The Absentee*, 'who turned their back on social life in favour of strenuous independence'.[43] Indeed, Esther lives out what Edgeworth's earlier fictions would have proposed as a model existence for a wealthy young woman. She resides on a remote Welsh estate, Llansillen, where she occupies herself by focusing her energies on improving the lot of her tenants through the various means in her power. It is she who offers Helen a refuge when General Clarendon's judgement of her dishonesty makes it impossible for her to remain a member of his household. While recovering from her shock and disappointment, Helen 'followed Miss Clarendon about in all her various occupations, from flower-garden to conservatory, and from conservatory to pheasantry, and to all her pretty cottages, and her schools, and she saw and admired all the good that Esther did so judiciously, and with such extraordinary, such wonderful energy' (342). In spite of her hostess's kindness and manifest virtues, Helen remains unhappy, finding no solace in the useful activities Esther proposes.

Marilyn Butler interprets Edgeworth's altered vision of personal worth and virtue as indicative of an increasing self-confidence on her part. Lady Davenant's culpability in the character flaws of her daughter represents, according to Butler, a rejection of the 'personal ideal that Richard Lovell Edgeworth and Mrs Ruxton [had] taught Maria, the ideal of classical nobility and virtue'. In short, Butler claims, 'Maria rejects her father's heroic, unyielding idea of virtue and replaces it with a softer, more feminine and domestic scale of values'.[44] But on closer examination, *Helen* is a pessimistic tale, in which the happiness of the central characters is retrieved only at the very last moment, and seems even then provisional. Cecilia's eventual confession of her dishonesty clears Helen's name and enables her to accept Beauclerc's offer of marriage, but no absolute guarantee is offered that Clarendon will forgive his wife and abandon his determination to separate from her. Lady Davenant, meanwhile, returns from Russia gravely ill and the conventional happy ending symbolised by the wedding of Helen and Beauclerc is overshadowed by her impending death. Whereas the marriages in Edgeworth's Irish tales as well as in *Patronage* and *Emilie de Coulanges* suggest social and national solutions as well as personal, emotional ones, the same cannot be said of *Helen*. For the first time, Edgeworth is unable to imagine a social role for her fiction. This inability, I argue, is derived from her acknowledgement that in her earlier work she had attributed to women's character and activities an importance that could no longer be claimed in the changed political climate of the 1830s. Henceforth, political representation in parliament was to become the key to power. Women of all classes were therefore excluded from direct influence over the 'political subjects' whose importance Lady Davenant refers to, but only women who had ever had a consciousness of influence were likely to perceive the change in this early stage. In *Helen*, Edgeworth registers the same sense of women's sudden loss of significance that Staël had expressed with regard to France and the French revolution in *De la littérature*.

The drama of personal relationships in *Helen* thus takes place in a very specific context. It is not so much that there is an absence of political content that is replaced by emotional and psychological concerns, as some critics have suggested, but that the perception of the increased scope of the political and women's increasing exclusion from it determines an unusually pessimistic and interior perspective. There is nowhere for Helen to turn: the estate, which for so long in Edgeworth's fiction had been presented as the utopian space in which public and private meet, is reconceived as the site of an implicitly masculine tradition, from which Helen is in any case banished. Esther Clarendon's home in Llansillen bears a resemblance to Edgeworth's early image of the female-dominated estate, but it is a world which has come to seem chillingly remote from society, rather then representing society at its best. Ultimately Helen has no role, and cares for no role, other than that of Beauclerc's wife. *Helen* settles for a conservative (in all senses of the word) resolution of the plot, but it is a resolution that acknowledges the final loss of Edgeworth's optimism.

In 1837 the *Dublin University Magazine* published an article entitled 'Past and present state of literature in Ireland', which W. J. Mc Cormack has described as constituting, 'in effect, the first attempt at a theory of Anglo-Irish literature'.[45] The essay, whose authorship has been attributed by Mc Cormack to Isaac Butt, reveals the pervasive influence of Samuel Taylor Coleridge. The evidence of this influence lies in the contrast established by Butt between the literature of England and that of Ireland. Literature in England is imagined as an organic growth, which 'shed its early light on the foundations of the British constitution', and which has 'grown with its growth'.[46] The literature of Ireland, by contrast, has been 'recently engrafted'.[47] In both a British and an (Anglo)-Irish context, Coleridge represents an important medium for the nineteenth-century transmission of Burkean perspectives on culture: not least among these is the emphasis on nationality as a guarantor of social stability and of the preservation of culture from factional interests.[48] In his *Biographia Literaria*, Coleridge expresses the link between nineteenth-century conservatism and nationalism and the controversy surrounding the French Revolution:

> The youthful enthusiasts who, flattered by the morning rainbow of the French revolution, had made a boast of *expatriating* their hopes and fears, now, disciplined by the succeeding storms and sobered by increase of years, had been taught to prize and honour the spirit of nationality as the best safeguard of national independence, and this again as the absolute pre-requisite and necessary basis of popular rights.[49]

Here, Coleridge makes very clear that the assertion of norms, explicitly moral and political but also implicitly aesthetic (Wordsworth having been one of the very prominent 'youthful enthusiasts' of the French Revolution) associated with the principle of nationality is connected with the final defeat of the French Revolution as an ideal in England. The appearance of Isaac Butt's very Coleridgean account of literature in Ireland just three years after the publication of Edgeworth's last novel thus underlines the fact that this novel belongs to a decisively new moment in Irish and British culture. By the time *Helen* was published, the long struggle for the meaning of the French Revolution was over, and it had been decided in such a way as to guarantee the marginalisation of women writers such as Edgeworth. For most of her career she engaged in the contest over the meanings of national identity, and questioned and qualified the terms by which British and Irish identity was defined. The striking reversals in *Helen* throw this critique into sharp relief. *Helen*'s embrace of an Englishness defined by masculinity and aristocracy, and its location of these qualities in the implicitly threatened seclusion of the country estate suggest Edgeworth's belated acceptance of a Coleridgean view of culture and its relationship to nationality. Rather than simply signifying Edgeworth's silence on the matter of Ireland in the 1830s and 1840s, *Helen* therefore provides an essential insight into that silence.

As previous chapters have argued, Edgeworth's writing shows an awareness of the ways in which post-revolutionary constructions of French character could be used to limit women's access to education and influence, whilst facilitating stereotypes of Irish character dominated by comic stupidity and criminality. As a result, many of Edgeworth's texts envision an Irish identity which is in permanent transit. Although the novels end with 'homecomings', the Irish identity of the characters is constructed through journeys, changes of name, assumptions of false names and false nationalities. Colambre pretends to be Welsh and is usually assumed to be English; Grace Nugent thinks she's Irish but turns out to be English; Mr Henry, likewise, thinks he's Irish and turns out to be half-English and half-Italian; while behaving so like a Frenchman, Ormond is confirmed as 'Irlandais'; and, of course, 'Glenthorn-O'Donoghue-Delamere' realises that he has to choose what and who he is to be. Unlike Lady Morgan, Edgeworth never presented herself as a defenceless victim or a criminal, but there is a fugitive quality to the national identities of the characters in her novels. These 'fugitives' often cross over the borders between 'English' and 'Irish'. Crucially, moreover, the permeability of borders is associated with a society in which some power and influence is retained in what she constitutes as 'domestic' life, where women and men can meet on some kind of equal footing. Her last novel, therefore, is an eloquent statement on the transformations of the period, as it registers the conclusive end of a political system which was characterised by an elite cosmopolitan culture, in favour of a bourgeois democracy from which women were excluded and which vested its power in a new concept called the nation.

'Big House Novelist' or 'Irish Woman Writer'?

-→->-<-←-

Kathryn Kirkpatrick has commented that 'in Ireland, as in all states, reclaiming women's literature helps transform a national culture by including the voices of more of its citizens'.[1] This is a curious remark to make about the position of women writers in Ireland. In the eighteenth and nineteenth centuries in particular, Irish women writers were doubly distanced from the concepts of 'nation' and 'citizen', given that Ireland's status as a nation was compromised by its political subordination to Britain, concluding in its incorporation within the United Kingdom, and in view of the fact that citizenship, based on the models of the French revolutionaries, was specifically designed to exclude women. The effect of Kirkpatrick's comments is to appear retrospectively to confer Irish citizenship on these earlier writers, implying a rather unfortunate endorsement of the Irish nation as a transcendent body, existing timelessly but emerging into political form in the twentieth century. It is in fact precisely this construction of Ireland that has resulted in the relegation of women writers to the margins of the nation, at best. This construct requires the creation of a continuous nationalist history designed to counter actual historical and political discontinuities. This historical national community is one into which women can be admitted only on very limited grounds, because their presence disrupts the fiction of continuity.

The term 'Irish woman writer', when unpacked, suggests the nature of the problem. It suggests a commonality between Maria Edgeworth and, say, Kate O'Brien or Nuala Ní Dhomhnaill, which strains under differences such as language and religion. Irish writing as a whole is of course characterised to a certain extent by such fissures – what does Seán Ó Riordáin have in common with Richard Brinsley Sheridan, after all? The difference lies in the fact that traditions can be traced between men on the basis on public discourses centred on the nation. As I argued in the introduction to this book, the tendency to see women positioned in an inaccessible sphere of privacy and domesticity has made them more or less invisible to history; it has also resulted in an inability to read their work in terms of any form of tradition. By 'tradition' I mean simply the ability to take individual writers and *group* them, whether as women, as Irish, or – even – as Irish women. The lack of a public identity which has been enforced on Irish women over centuries makes it extremely difficult to conceive of them in any kind of group. As a result, it is difficult to conceptualise the idea of the 'Irish woman writer'. This is, however, a productive difficulty and one which should be taken very seriously, as it can illuminate the limitations of the 'group identity' that is signified in the term 'Irish'.

It is indicative of the uncomfortable place that women writers occupy within Irish literary culture that the only Irish women's 'tradition' that has been identified is that of the 'Big House' novel, which is usually described as beginning with Edgeworth's *Castle Rackrent* and including Somerville and Ross, Elizabeth Bowen and Molly Keane.[2] This category is impressively transhistorical, spanning almost 200 years – quite a feat, given Ireland's fractured literary history. The writers are of course all Anglo-Irish, and they do emanate from the upper echelons of Protestant society, although some are far more socially elite than others. The differences in their positions are however striking. How can one compare, for instance, Edgeworth, from an improving landed family in the immediate post-Union period, with Elizabeth Bowen, whose experiences were those of the War of Independence, the Free State and the Second World War? Margot Gayle Backus highlights the double edge of this category when she observes that 'the term "Big House novel" has served [. . .] simultaneously to invoke and to dismiss' the writers included within it, and that 'rather than inaugurating serious critical analysis, this term can operate as a shorthand invocation of unspecified but presumed political, intellectual, and aesthetic deficiencies'.[3]

Backus focuses on the recuperation of the radical and subversive meanings of these Anglo-Irish women's texts, previously smothered in this assumption-laden category. What I want to argue, however, is that the construction of this category as a singular example of an Irish women's tradition implies that *all* Irish women's writing is somehow tangential to mainstream concerns. The kind of transhistorical claims that are made for the 'Big House' tradition imply that it is only here that the great movements of history can somehow fail to register. This impenetrable isolation is of course projected onto the members of the Ascendancy class, but more particularly onto the women of that class. The assertion of this tradition of Anglo-Irish women's writing effectively serves as a warning to Irish women writers in general, to remind them to 'affiliate' their claims to those of the nation in order to avoid this kind of redundancy and marginality. A specific instance of this phenomenon can be observed in a fascinating account given by Eavan Boland of her meeting with Kate O'Brien.

Boland's *A Kind of Scar: The Woman Poet in a National Tradition* was a landmark articulation of the ways in which the Irish literary tradition had been constituted so as to exclude women, *by definition* rather than through any accidental oversight. In this context, Boland's comments on O'Brien are initially surprising. Rather than see in O'Brien a potential literary foremother, Boland emphasises the lack of connection between the two women, using signs and cues of class to suggest the gulf between them. She refers to her newly built, standard suburban home, to the as-yet unpacked boxes, to her anxiety about what to serve for dinner. In spite of the fact that Boland herself is from an upper-middle class background and that there is therefore no real distinction of class between them, Boland manages to suggest that, meeting Kate O'Brien, she felt like a social inferior, thus pushing certain buttons in the mind of the late twentieth-century reader: 'I was puzzled and deferential', she writes.[4] Boland is on one level simply being honest about her inability to relate to a much older woman, one with whom she clearly struggled to find common ground. This inability is *not*, however, diagnosed in terms of the journey that Boland had yet to make as she came to an increasing awareness of herself as a woman writer within a national tradition. Instead she continues to insist on distinguishing herself from O'Brien by emphasising her own ordinariness while making O'Brien seem foreign and strange. She ultimately represents O'Brien as a visitor from a past that is now irrecoverable:

> I sat in the white kitchen, the window facing out on newly-planted poplars, and took the book up and set it down. The breviary of another womanhood, another Ireland.
>
> The Ireland from which Kate O'Brien emerged was not the Catholic Ireland of nineteenth-century lore; of hand-to-mouth hardship and bleak survival. Her people must have known these things once; then it changed. By the end of the century they had advanced from handcarts and evictions to a settled prosperity. The characters in her novels have a certain worldly pride. They can tell the difference between Carrickmacross and Guipure lace. They send their children to school in Dublin. They furnish their long tables with silver and ivory-handled cutlery and their minds with all kinds of strivings which were unknown to their less fortunate compatriots.[5]

Boland's initial contrast of 'Kate O'Brien's Ireland' with 'the Catholic Ireland of nineteenth-century lore', that of poverty, hunger, oppression and emigration, raises the possibility that neither Ireland has absolute status as truth, the word 'lore' suggesting an image as much mythical as factual. She goes on to insist, however, that the other nineteenth-century Ireland is the more 'real', and issues in the present:

Kate O'Brien's world was perishing almost as soon as she had discovered it. It was an ethos and a mythos that would vanish completely with the First World War, absorbed into the shriek of steam-trains and the bright chrome of touring cars; whose pretensions to grace and separateness fell at Ypres and the Somme. It was a world whose outward gestures masked an inward yearning for certainty and structure: qualities which the modern world would dispense with; and not always politely.

I sat reading Kate O'Brien in another Ireland.[6]

Kate O'Brien has never seemed quite so like a member of the Ascendancy. I have dwelt on this particular encounter at some length because it seems to me to suggest very powerfully that Irish women writers feel a need to portray their female predecessors as always vanishing into a history that is lost to and disconnected from the present moment. The reasons for this lie in the dominance of the historical narrative of the nation, from which women have been excluded but which makes inclusion within it a precondition for recognition and visibility.

In this context the particular qualities and themes of Maria Edgeworth's last novel, *Helen*, emerge both as characteristic of the positioning of the Irish women writer, but also as oddly clear-sighted as to the mechanisms whereby Edgeworth herself would be edged out of the national tradition established in the late nineteenth century. As I pointed out in the previous chapter, the novel expresses socially conservative ideals which are clearly grounded in Edgeworth's reactions to the growth of democratic politics in general and to the emergence of what has been called 'the Catholic nation' in Ireland specifically. As we have seen, this has led virtually all commentators on Irish writing of this period to the conclusion that Edgeworth is, ultimately, fatally compromised as an 'Irish novelist' because her capacity to represent Ireland does not extend to the changed (the 'real', it is implied) Ireland that emerged in the aftermath of emancipation. I argue, however, that given the insistence on denying women in Ireland anything other than a private identity, women are in any case prevented from occupying this representative role once the possibility of a nation occupying a public sphere became a possibility. The emphasis on privacy and on troubled and painful personal relationships in *Helen*, together with its evocation of an idealised estate, the description of which evokes the past rather than the present, and which is presided over by a General who is 'English decidedly [. . .] of the old school', thus expresses with extraordinary poignancy the repeated banishment of the Irish woman writer to a past construed as foreign and remote.

Other women writers did emerge in the nineteenth century: Somerville and Ross, Rosa Mulholland, Emily Lawless, Lady Gregory, to name just a few. No one could claim that any of these writers, or any other women writers of the nineteenth century, were ever accorded the cultural centrality that Edgeworth enjoyed, however briefly. Rather than interpreting the end of Edgeworth's career as an Irish novelist as an indication of her limited conception of the nation, one could instead read it as an indication of the extent to which the newly emerging bourgeois Catholic nation was constructed along lines that precluded the visibility and cultural activity of women. This is not to say that women did not develop strategies to achieve visibility and a voice, but these strategies did not guarantee them a place at the national table.

Recent Irish feminist recovery and archival projects, such as the *Field Day Anthology*, volumes IV and V: *Women's Writing and Traditions* and the *Munster Women Writers Dictionary*, are bringing to light hundreds of writers and texts of which most Irish readers, even scholarly readers, are unaware. The task that confronts us is to attempt to understand how the work of these writers changes the received image of Irish writing. Margaret Kelleher has argued convincingly that the current work of recovery has many precedents in the work of nineteenth-century anthologists and critics of Irish women's writing, whose impressive achievements have passed almost completely from view, and advances some thoughtful and valuable ideas on the challenges peculiar to feminist recovery work in Ireland.[7] My own view is that it will not be possible to see meaningful and meaning-altering connections between Irish women writers until we realise the extent to which the concept of collective Irish identity which prevails and has prevailed since the nineteenth century is based on a fixation with the construction of identity in a national public sphere and thus on masculinity as a norm. With this in mind, we are perhaps at a moment in which it is possible to see Maria Edgeworth's writing for the unique achievement that it is, and to allow it to challenge us as readers today.

Notes

→>⊰⊹

INTRODUCTION

1   D. George Boyce, *Nineteenth-Century Ireland: The Search for Stability* (Dublin: Gill & Macmillan, 1990), p. 24.

2   Kevin Whelan, 'The republic in the village: the United Irishmen, the Enlightenment and popular culture', in his *The Tree of Liberty: Radicalism, Catholicism and the Construction of Irish Identity, 1760–1830* (Cork: Cork University Press, 1996), pp. 59–96.

3   Tom Dunne's *Rebellions: Memoir, Memory and 1798* (Dublin: Lilliput, 2004) is the most explicit and extensive rejoinder to Whelan. For his objection to Whelan's involvement in the 'politicised' commemoration of 1798, see for instance pp. 5–6. Dunne discusses revisionism and the applicability or otherwise of the term 'revisionist' to his own work, pp. 89–97.

4   R. F. Foster, 'Remembering 1798', in Ian McBride (ed.), *History and Memory in Modern Ireland* (Cambridge: Cambridge University Press, 2001), pp. 67–94, p. 88.

5   Oliver MacDonagh, *States of Mind: A Study of Anglo-Irish Conflict, 1780–1980* (London: George Allen & Unwin, 1983), p. 4.

6   See Jürgen Habermas, 'Modernity – an incomplete project?' and the response of Jean-François Lyotard, 'Answering the question: what is postmodernism?' in Peter Brooker (ed.), *Modernism/Postmodernism* (Harlow: Longman, 1992).

7   Mary O'Dowd, *A History of Women in Ireland, 1500–1800* (Harlow: Pearson Education, 2005), p. 1. The nineteenth century is slightly better served, with some key publications including Maria Luddy's *Women and Philanthropy in Nineteenth-Century Ireland* (Cambridge: Cambridge University Press, 1995) and also her *Women, Power and Consciousness in Nineteenth-Century Ireland: Eight Biographical Studies* (Dublin: Attic Press, 1996).

8   Maria Luddy's introductory essay to the new collected edition of the letters of William Drennan and Martha McTier is an excellent example of the kind of history that is required – but it remains an isolated example: 'Martha McTier and William Drennan: a "domestic history"', in Jean Agnew (ed.), *The Drennan–McTier Letters*, 3 vols (Dublin: Women's History Project/Irish Manuscripts Commission, 1998–9), I, pp. xxix–li.

9   Dáire Keogh and Nicholas Furlong, 'Preface', in *The Women of 1798* (Dublin: Four Courts, 1998), pp. 7–8, p. 7. Other publications which focus on women in the context of 1798 include the collections edited by John D. Beatty, *Protestant Women's Narratives of the Irish Rebellion of 1798* (Dublin: Four Courts, 2001) and *Women's Narratives of the Irish Rebellion of 1798* (Dublin: Four Courts, 2002).

10   Kevin Whelan, 'Section VI: Introduction', in Thomas Bartlett et al. (eds), *1798: A Bicentenary Perspective* (Dublin: Four Courts, 2003), pp. 469–77, p. 470.

11   Ibid., p. 470.

12 See for instance Lawrence E. Klein, 'Gender and the public/private distinction in the eighteenth century: some questions about evidence and analytic procedure', *Eighteenth-Century Studies* 29 (1995), pp. 97–109. For views on this question in a more specifically literary context see Elizabeth Eger et al. (eds), *Women, Writing and the Public Sphere, 1700–1830* (Cambridge: Cambridge University Press, 2001) and Anne Mellor, who writes that 'we can no longer assume that the doctrine of the separate spheres, the sexual division of labour into public/male and private/female realms, was universally accepted during the Romantic period'. 'A novel of their own: romantic women's fiction, 1790–1830', in John Richetti et al. (eds), *The Columbia History of the British Novel* (New York: Columbia University Press, 1994), pp. 327–5, p. 329.

13 See David Lloyd, 'Outside history: Irish new histories and the "subalternity effect"', in his *Ireland After History* (Cork: Cork University Press, 1999), pp. 77–88.

14 Colin Graham, 'Liminal spaces: postcolonialism and post-nationalism', in his *Deconstructing Ireland: Identity, Theory, Culture* (Edinburgh: Edinburgh University Press, 2001), pp. 81–101, p. 89.

15 Seamus Deane, *Strange Country: Modernity and Nationhood in Irish Writing since 1790* (Oxford: Clarendon, 1997), pp. 31, 32.

16 Luke Gibbons, *Edmund Burke and Ireland* (Cambridge: Cambridge University Press, 2003), pp. xii–xiii.

17 Ibid., p. 177.

18 Moynagh Sullivan, 'Feminism, postmodernism and the subjects of Irish and women's studies', in P. J. Mathews (ed.), *New Voices in Irish Criticism* (Dublin: Four Courts, 2000), pp. 243–51.

19 Cited in Gibbons, *Edmund Burke*, p. 211.

20 Ibid. Gibbons also dwells on the tension between this image and that of 'savage society' as somehow pre-social, pp. 211–12.

21 Mellor, 'A novel of their own', p. 330.

22 ME to Honora Edgeworth, 19 Aug. 1820, in Christina Colvin (ed.), *Maria Edgeworth in France and Switzerland: Selections from the Edgeworth Family Letters* (Oxford: Clarendon, 1979), p. 218.

23 Thomas Moore, 'Corruption', in *Poetical Works* (London: George Routledge & Sons, 1935), p. 495.

24 See Mary Campbell, *Lady Morgan: The Life and Times of Sydney Owenson* (London: Pandora, 1988), p. 71.

25 Cited in Jean Moskal, 'Gender, nationality and textual authority in Lady Morgan's travel books', in Theresa M. Kelley and Paula R. Feldman (eds), *Romantic Women Writers* (Hanover, NH: University Press of New England, 1995), pp. 171–93, p. 171.

26 Germaine de Staël, *De la littérature considérée dans ses rapports avec les institutions sociales*, ed. Axel Blaeschke (Paris: InfoMédia, 1998), p. 335.

27 See for instance Harriet Guest's *Small Change: Women, Learning, Patriotism, 1750–1810* (London: University of Chicago Press, 2000), which includes a discussion of Edgeworth's *Letters for Literary Ladies*.

28 Some of the key works in this field include Marianne Elliott, *The United Irishmen and France: Partners in Revolution* (London: Yale University Press, 1982); Hugh Gough and David Dickson (eds), *Ireland and the French Revolution* (Dublin: Irish Academic Press,

1990), Christopher Murray and Barbara Hayley (eds), *Ireland and France: A Bountiful Friendship* (Gerrard's Cross: Colin Smythe, 1992); Michael O'Dea and Kevin Whelan (eds), *Nations and Nationalisms: France, Britain, Ireland and the Eighteenth-Century Context* (Oxford: Voltaire Foundation, 1995); Graham Gargett and Geraldine Sheridan (eds), *Ireland and the French Enlightenment, 1700–1800* (Basingstoke: Macmillan, 1999); see also a number of essays in Eamon Maher and Grace Neville (eds), *France-Ireland: Anatomy of a Relationship* (Frankfurt: Peter Lang 2004).

29 See for instance Dáithí Ó hÓgáin, '"Said an elderly man …": Maria Edgeworth's use of folklore in *Castle Rackrent*', in Cóilín Owens (ed.), *Family Chronicles: Maria Edgeworth's Castle Rackrent* (Dublin: Wolfhound, 1987), pp. 62–70.

30 Mitzi Myers, '"Like the pictures in a magic lantern": gender, history and Edgeworth's rebellion narratives', *Nineteenth-Century Contexts* 19 (1996), pp. 373–412, p. 374.

31 Niall Ó Ciosáin, *Print and Popular Culture in Ireland, 1750–1850* (Basingstoke: Macmillan, 1997), see chapter 10, 'The ideology of status'.

32 Mitzi Myers, 'Goring John Bull: Maria Edgeworth's Hibernian high jinks versus the imperialist imaginary', in James E. Gill (ed.), *Cutting Edges: Postmodern Essays on Eighteenth-Century Satire* (Knoxville, TN: University of Tennessee Press, 1995), pp. 367–94, p. 369.

33 Tom Dunne, '"A gentleman's estate should be a moral school": Edgeworthstown in fact and fiction, 1760–1840', in Raymond Gillespie and Gerard Moran (eds), *Longford: Essays in County History* (Dublin: Lilliput, 1991), pp. 95–121, p. 101, p. 97.

34 Deane, *Strange Country*, p. 30.

35 Kevin Whelan, 'Foreword', in Sydney Owenson (Lady Morgan), *The Wild Irish Girl*, ed. Claire Connolly and Stephen Copley (London: Pickering & Chatto, 2000), p. xiv.

36 See *Belinda*, ed. Kathryn Kirkpatrick (Oxford: Oxford University Press, 1994) and *Harrington*, ed. Susan Manly (Peterborough, Ontario: Broadview Press, 2004). It is, however, unfortunate that the Penguin edition of *Ormond*, edited by Claire Connolly (Harmondsworth: Penguin, 2000), is no longer in print.

37 Sharon Murphy, *Maria Edgeworth and Romance* (Dublin: Four Courts, 2004), p. 42.

38 Claire Connolly, '"A big book about England?": public and private meanings in Maria Edgeworth's *Patronage*', in Jacqueline Belanger (ed.), *Facts and Fictions: Ireland and the Novel in the Nineteenth Century*, forthcoming.

39 Colin Graham, '"Staged quaintness": subalternity, gender and popular identity', in *Deconstructing Ireland*, pp. 102–31, p. 107.

CHAPTER ONE

1 Ian McBride, *Scripture Politics: Ulster Presbyterians and Irish Radicalism in the Late Eighteenth Century* (Oxford: Clarendon, 1998), p. 9.

2 Joep Leerssen, 'Monument and trauma: varieties of remembrance', in Ian McBride (ed.), *History and Memory in Modern Ireland* (Cambridge: Cambridge University Press, 2001), pp. 204–22, p. 214.

3 Harriet Guest, *Small Change: Women, Learning, Patriotism, 1750–1810* (London: University of Chicago Press, 2000), p. 15.

4   Mary Jean Corbett, *Allegories of Union in Irish and English Writing, 1790–1870: Politics, History and the Family from Edgeworth to Arnold* (Cambridge: Cambridge University Press, 2000), p. 39.

5   Ibid., p. 48.

6   Linda Colley, *Britons: Forging the Nation, 1707–1837* (London: Yale University Pres, 1992), p. 296.

7   Ibid., p. 296.

8   Ibid., p. 265.

9   Gary Kelly, *Women, Writing, Revolution, 1790–1827* (Oxford: Clarendon, 1993), p. 4.

10 Guest, *Small Change*, pp. 7–8.

11 Ibid., p. 5.

12 See Seamus Deane, *The French Revolution and Enlightenment in England, 1789–1832* (London: Harvard University Press, 1988).

13 Angela Keane, *Women Writers and the English Nation in the 1790s: Romantic Belongings* (Cambridge: Cambridge University Press, 2000), pp. 6–7.

14 Ibid., p. 5.

15 Ibid., p. 6.

16 Ibid., pp. 6–7.

17 Critics who emphasise conservative conjunctions of ideologies of gender and nation in Edgeworth include Elizabeth Kowaleski-Wallace, *Their Fathers' Daughters: Maria Edgeworth, Hannah More and Patriarchal Complicity* (New York: Oxford University Press, 1991); Nicola Watson, *Revolution and the Form of the British Novel, 1790–1825: Intercepted Letters, Interrupted Seductions* (Oxford: Clarendon, 1994); Seamus Deane, *Strange Country: Modernity and Nationhood in Irish Writing since 1790* (Oxford: Clarendon, 1997).

18 'Edgeworth's stern father: escaping Thomas Day, 1795–1801', in *Tradition in Transition: Women Writers, Marginal Texts and the Eighteenth Century* (Oxford: Clarendon, 1996), pp. 75–93, p. 80.

19 Richard Lovell Edgeworth and Maria Edgeworth, *Memoirs of Richard Lovell Edgeworth* [1820], 2 vols (Shannon: Irish University Press, 1969), I, p. 216.

20 Ibid., p. 217.

21 Dena Goodman has located the hostility to the 'feminised' Enlightenment culture of the salons in the writing of Rousseau, and specifically to his *Lettre à d'Alembert*. She traces the rise of men-only clubs in Paris in the 1780s, arguing that the men who formed them 'denied the need for women as a civilizing force, adopting Rousseau's position that men of letters would be better off without women'. Dena Goodman, *The Republic of Letters: A Cultural History of the French Enlightenment* (Ithaca, NY: Cornell University Press, 1994), p. 242.

22 See Madeleine R. Raaphorst, 'Adèle versus Sophie: the well-educated woman of Mme de Genlis', *Rice University Studies* 64 (1978), pp. 41–50. For a general account of French debates on women and education, see Jean H. Bloch, 'Women and the reform of the nation', in Eva Jacobs et al. (eds), *Woman and Society in Eighteenth-Century France* (London: Athlone, 1979), pp. 3–18.

23 Marilyn Butler, *Maria Edgeworth: A Literary Biography* (Oxford: Clarendon, 1972), p. 149.

24 Stéphanie-Félicité de Genlis, *Adelaide and Theodore; or, Letters on Education*, anon. trans., 3 vols (London: C. Bathurst & T. Cadell, 1783), I, p. 12.

25 Genlis, *Adelaide and Theodore*, I, p. 13.

26 Ibid.

27 Edgeworth, *Letters for Literary Ladies*, ed. Claire Connolly (London: J. M. Dent, 1993), p. 45.

28 Genlis, *Memoirs*, 8 vols (London: Henry Colburn, 1825), III, p. 139.

29 Ibid., p. 81.

30 Goodman, *The Republic of Letters*, p. 50.

31 Ibid., p. 39.

32 Genlis, *Memoirs*, III, pp. 268–9.

33 Mona Narain, 'A prescription of letters: Maria Edgeworth's *Letters for Literary Ladies* and the ideologies of the public sphere', *Journal of Narrative Technique* 28 (1998), pp. 266–86, p. 268.

34 Harriet Guest, *Small Change*, p. 18. Earlier assessments of *Letters for Literary Ladies* include those of Marilyn Butler, who describes it as 'earnest and stiff', and Jane Rendall, who concludes that it is 'a modest argument'. Marilyn Butler, *Jane Austen and the War of Ideas*, reissued with new introduction (Oxford: Clarendon, 1987), p. 127; Jane Rendall, *The Origins of Modern Feminism: Women in Britain, France and the United States, 1780–1860* (Basingstoke: Macmillan, 1985), p. 110.

35 Sylvana Tomaselli, 'The most public sphere of all: the family', in Elizabeth Eger et al. (eds), *Women, Writing and the Public Sphere, 1700–1830* (Cambridge: Cambridge University Press, 2001), pp. 239–56, p. 248.

36 Butler, *Maria Edgeworth*, p. 173.

37 Edgeworth, *Letters for Literary Ladies*, ed. Claire Connolly, p. xxvii. Except in the case of references to the 1795 edition, all further references are to this edition, and are given parenthetically in the text.

38 Deane, *Strange Country*, p. 7.

39 Edmund Burke, *Reflections on the Revolution in France* [1790], ed. Conor Cruise O'Brien (Harmondsworth: Penguin, 1986), p. 183.

40 See Mary Jean Corbett, *Allegories of Union*; Deirdre Lynch, 'Domesticating fictions and nationalising women: Edmund Burke, property and the reproduction of Englishness', in Alan Richardson and Sonia Hofkosh (eds), *Romanticism, Race and Imperial Culture, 1780–1834* (Bloomington, IN: Indiana University Press, 1996), pp. 40–71.

41 Edgeworth, *Letters for Literary Ladies* (London: J. Johnson, 1795), pp. 44–5.

42 Ibid., p. 57.

43 Ibid., p. 62–3.

44 Genlis, *A Short Account of the Conduct of Mme de Genlis since the Revolution* (Perth: R. Morison, 1796), pp. 4–5. An almost identical passage appears in *Memoirs*, IV, pp. 74–5.

45 A key text is John Millar's *Origin of the Distinction of Ranks* (1771), the first chapter of which is entitled 'Of the rank and condition of women in different ages'. See *The Origin of the Distinction of Ranks*, 3rd edn [1779], repr. in William C. Lehman, *John Millar of Glasgow: 1735–1801* (Cambridge: Cambridge University Press, 1960).

46 Mary Wollstonecraft, *A Vindication of the Rights of Woman* [1792], ed. Miriam Brody (Harmondsworth: Penguin, 1992), pp. 93, 80.

47 Dorinda Outram, *The Body and the French Revolution: Sex, Class and Political Culture* (London: Yale University Press, 1989), p. 126.

48 Neil McKendrick, John Brewer and J. H. Plumb, *The Birth of a Consumer Society: The Commercialisation of Eighteenth-Century England* (London: Europa, 1982), p. 19.

49 'Ask a Guinea Negro, and, with him, beauty is a greasy black skin, hollow eyes and a flat nose': Voltaire, *Philosophical Dictionary*, trans. Alex Holmes, 2 vols (London: B. Johnson, 1819), I, p. 39.

50 Quoted in McKendrick, Brewer and Plumb, *The Birth of a Consumer Society*, pp. 26–7. The use of the word 'tyrannized' in this quotation, with its connotations of 'eastern despotism' seems to suggest that the writer is engaged in a reversal of the usual hierarchy between east and west, achieved through the positioning of western women as symbols of an irrational tyranny.

51 Mitzi Myers, 'My art belongs to Daddy? Thomas Day, Maria Edgeworth and the pre-texts of *Belinda*: women writers and patriarchal authority', in by Paula Backscheider (ed.), *Revising Women: Eighteenth-Century 'Women's Fiction' and Social Engagement* (Baltimore, MD: Johns Hopkins University Press), pp. 104–46, p. 107.

52 Susan C. Greenfield, '"Abroad and at home": sexual ambiguity, miscegenation and colonial boundaries in Edgeworth's *Belinda*', *PMLA* 112 (1997), pp. 214–28, p. 215.

53 *Monthly Review*, Apr. 1802, repr. in *Belinda* ed. Eiléan ní Chuilleanáin (London: J. M. Dent, 1993), pp. 462–4, p. 462.

54 Colin B. Atkinson and Jo Atkinson, 'Maria Edgeworth, *Belinda* and women's rights', *Eire-Ireland* 19 (1984), pp. 94–118.

55 Greenfield, '"Abroad and at home"', p. 218.

56 Kowaleski-Wallace, *Their Fathers' Daughters*, p. 216.

57 Edgeworth, *Belinda*, ed. Kathryn Kirkpatrick (Oxford: Oxford University Press, 1994), p. 40. All subsequent references are to this edition and are given parenthetically in the text.

58 According to McKendrick, Brewer and Plumb, 'few modern copywriters can match the battery of advertising gimmicks unleashed on the British public by this single entrepreneur [George Packwood] in the space of less than two years'. *The Birth of a Consumer Society*, p. 153.

59 See Butler, *Maria Edgeworth*, p. 149. See also Butler, 'Edgeworth's stern father' and Myers, 'My art belongs to Daddy?'

60 *Memoirs of R. L. Edgeworth*, I, p. 214.

61 Ibid., p. 216.

62 Ibid., pp. 216–17.

63 Ibid., pp. 218–19.

64 Ibid., pp. 214–15.

65 Caroline Gonda, *Reading Daughters' Fictions, 1709–1834: Novels and Society from Manley to Edgeworth* (Cambridge: Cambridge University Press, 1996), p. 215.

66 See Greenfield, '"Abroad and at home"', pp. 219, 222.

67 Maria and her family were concerned that readers might assume these two tales to have been influenced by Hamilton's work – though they were in fact written before she had come across *Memoirs of Modern Philosophers*. See *The Novels and Selected Works of Maria Edgeworth*, 12 vols (London: Pickering & Chatto, 1999–2003), XII: *Early Lessons* and *Moral Tales*, ed. Elizabeth Eger and Clíona Ó Gallchoir.

68 Kathryn Kirkpatrick also concludes that Edgeworth 'giv[es] Lady Delacour, the reformed aristocrat, precedence', rather than the supposedly ideal Lady Anne Percival, and that she 'offers her as the alternative ideal woman even as she acknowledges this newly proffered choice as fictive': 'The limits of liberal feminism in Maria Edgeworth's *Belinda*', in Laura Dabundo (ed.), *Jane Austen and Mary Shelley and their Sisters* (Lanham, MD: University

Press of America, 2000), pp. 73–82, p. 80. Nicholas Mason, likewise, stresses that 'we need to be careful to read [Lady Delacour's] in terms of her position not only as a woman but as an aristocratic woman': 'Class, gender, and domesticity in Maria Edgeworth's *Belinda*', *Eighteenth-Century Novel* 1 (2001), pp. 271–85, p. 274.

69 William Drennan to Sam McTier, 1 Feb. 1793, in Jean Agnew (ed.), *The Drennan–McTier Letters*, 3 vols (Dublin: Irish Manuscripts Commission/Women's History Project, 1998–9), I, p. 476.

70 For a further discussion of Pamela Fitzgerald and Edgeworth's response to her see my 'Gender, nation and revolution: Maria Edgeworth and Stéphanie-Félicité de Genlis', in Eger et al. (ed.), *Women, Writing and the Public Sphere*, pp. 200–16, and 'Orphans, upstarts and aristocrats: Ireland and the idyll of adoption in the work of Mme de Genlis', in Oonagh Walsh (ed.), *Ireland Abroad: Politics and Professions in the Nineteenth Century* (Dublin: Four Courts, 2003), pp. 36–46.

CHAPTER TWO

1 William Drennan, *Glendalloch and Other Poems, by the late Dr Drennan, with additional Verses by his Sons* (Dublin: William Robertson, 1859), p. 13. For further discussion of Drennan see Norman Vance, *Irish Literature: A Social History. Tradition, Identity and Difference*, 2nd edn (Dublin: Four Courts, 1999), pp. 65–100. Vance offers some comment on 'Glendalloch'. See also Ian McBride, '"The son of an honest man": William Drennan and the dissenting tradition', in David Dickson, Dáire Keogh and Kevin Whelan (eds), *The United Irishmen: Republicanism, Radicalism and Rebellion* (Dublin: Lilliput, 1993), pp. 49–61. For information on Drennan's life and activities after the union, see McBride, *Scripture Politics: Ulster Presbyterians and Irish Radical Politics in the Late Eighteenth Century* (Oxford: Clarendon, 1998), pp. 210–14.

2 Joep Leerssen, *Remembrance and Imagination: Patterns in the Historical and Literary Representation of Ireland in the Nineteenth Century* (Cork: Cork University Press, 1996), p. 12.

3 R. B. McDowell, *Ireland in the Age of Imperialism and Revolution, 1760–1801* (Oxford: Clarendon, 1979), p. 260.

4 William Drennan, *Letters of Orellana* (Dublin: J. Chambers and T. Heery, 1785), p. 6.

5 Ibid., p. 8.

6 Ibid., p. 25.

7 Ibid., p. 10.

8 T. W. Tone, *An Argument on Behalf of the Catholics of Ireland*, in *The Writings of Theobald Wolfe Tone, 1763–1798*, vol. I: *Tone's Career in Ireland to June 1795*, ed. T. W. Moody, R. B. McDowell and C. J. Woods (Oxford: Clarendon, 1998), pp. 108–28, p. 117.

9 Leerssen, *Remembrance and Imagination*, p. 54.

10 See Mary Campbell, *Lady Morgan: The Life and Times of Sydney Owenson* (London: Pandora, 1988), pp. 94–5. Seamus Deane notes the connection briefly in *A Short History of Irish Literature* (London: Hutchinson, 1986), p. 91; for a brief discussion of Staël and the reception of her work in England, see Deane, *The French Revolution and Enlightenment in England 1789–1832* (London: Harvard University Press, 1988), pp. 27–31.

11 [Francis Jeffrey], *Edinburgh Review* 21 (1813), pp. 1–50, p. 9.

12 James Livesey, 'Acts of union and disunion: Ireland in Atlantic and European contexts', in Dáire Keogh and Kevin Whelan (eds), *Acts of Union: The Causes, Contexts and Consequences of the Act of Union* (Dublin: Four Courts, 2001), pp. 95–105, p. 101.

13 Thomas Bartlett, 'Britishness, Irishness and the Act of Union', in Keogh and Whelan (eds), *Acts of Union*, pp. 243–58, p. 243. Jim Smyth also takes this view, noting that '"dwarf states", principalities, free cities and medieval left-overs, like the papal enclave of Avignon, were absorbed into larger, territorially coherent, nation-states. The rebellion and the union were events in European history'. Jim Smyth, 'The 1798 Rebellion in its eighteenth-century contexts', in Smyth (ed.), *Revolution, Counter-Revolution and Union: Ireland in the 1790s* (Cambridge: Cambridge University Press, 2000), pp. 1–20, pp. 16–17.

14 Germaine de Staël, *De la littérature considérée dans ses rapports avec les institutions sociales*, ed. Axel Blaeschke (Paris: InfoMédia Communication, 1998), p. 129.

15 *Edinburgh Review* 21 (1813), p. 9.

16 See John Isbell, 'The painful birth of the romantic heroine: Staël as political animal, 1786–1818', *Romanic Review* 87 (1996), pp. 59–67.

17 Staël, *Considerations on the French Revolution*, 3 vols (London: Baldwin, Craddock & Joy, 1818), I, p. 267.

18 *De la littérature*, p. 192. The substance of Staël's ideas derives principally from Paul Henri Mallet's *Essay on the History of Denmark*, disseminated in Britain and Ireland in Bishop Percy's translation, entitled *Northern Antiquities* (1770), and also to an extent from Elizabeth Montagu's *Essay on Shakespear* [sic] (1769). The originality of the text lies in the political and ideological use to which she puts these ideas.

19 *De la littérature*, p. 180.

20 Ibid., p. 185.

21 Ibid., p. 330.

22 Ibid., p. 328.

23 *Considerations*, III, pp. 279–80.

24 Ibid., p. 280.

25 *De la littérature*, p. 213.

26 Ibid., p. 199.

27 Ibid., p. 222.

28 Ibid., p. 222.

29 Claire Connolly, Introduction to Sydney Owenson (Lady Morgan), *The Wild Irish Girl: A National Tale*, ed. Claire Connolly and Stephen Copley, with a Foreword by Kevin Whelan (London: Pickering & Chatto, 2000), p. xliv.

30 See Leerssen, *Remembrance and Imagination*, pp. 33–8.

31 Morgan, *The Wild Irish Girl*, p. 139. All subsequent references are to the edition in n. 29 above and are given parenthetically in the text.

32 See Thomas Bartlett, *The Fall and Rise of the Irish Nation: The Catholic Question, 1690–1830* (Dublin: Gill & Macmillan, 1992), pp. 271–4.

33 See McBride, *Scripture Politics*, chapter 9, 'Presbyterian radicalism in Irish history'.

34 For further discussion of Macpherson and the Ossian poems, see Fiona Stafford, *The Sublime Savage: A Study of James Macpherson and the Poems of Ossian* (Edinburgh: Edinburgh University Press, 1998); for the Irish dimension of the Ossian debate, see Clare O'Halloran,

Golden Ages and Barbarous Nations: Antiquarian Debate and Cultural Politics in Ireland (Cork: Cork University Press, 2004), 'Ossian and the Irish bards', pp. 97–124.

35 Ina Ferris acknowledges the 'troubling ambiguities of the project' initiated by Morgan in *The Wild Irish Girl*, and the extent to which the figure of Glorvina can be 'readily recuperated into metropolitan categories'; she argues, however, that in her later fiction Morgan shapes 'notions of female agency outside, though not directly opposed to, the domestic understanding that shaped most British fiction in the Romantic period'. *The Romantic National Tale and the Question of Ireland* (Cambridge: Cambridge University Press, 2002), pp. 71, 73.

36 Leerssen, *Remembrance and Imagination*, p. 38.

37 Ibid., p. 62.

38 Examples of this point of view include Elizabeth Harden: '*Castle Rackrent* is noticeably free from all the faults which were to mar Miss Edgeworth's later works'; and Joanne Altieri: 'Only [Edgeworth's] first novel, *Castle Rackrent* seems to have escaped her desire to "warn the generality of mankind … against lesser faults". The rest are normally and socially didactic in the extreme.' See *Family Chronicles: Maria Edgeworth's 'Castle Rackrent'*, ed. Cóilín Owens (Dublin: Wolfhound, 1987), p. 95, p. 97.

39 Robert Tracy, '"The cracked lookingglass of a servant": Inventing the colonial novel', in Shlomith Rimmon-Kenan, Leona Toker and Shuli Barzilai (eds), *Rereading Texts, Rethinking Critical Presuppositions: Essays in Honour of H. M. Daleski* (Frankfurt and New York: Peter Lang, 1997), pp. 197–212, p. 199.

40 Butler, 'General Introduction', *The Novels and Selected Works of Maria Edgeworth*, I, p. *XLIII*.

41 Willa Murphy inclines to this view in 'A queen of hearts or an old maid?: Maria Edgeworth's fictions of union', in Keogh and Whelan (eds), *Acts of Union*, pp. 187–201, see particularly pp. 198–201. Kathryn Kirkpatrick's interesting proposal is that there is a distinct difference between the earlier and later notes, particularly those in the Glossary: 'What appear in Edgeworth's early footnotes to *Castle Rackrent* as reservations in the margin of her essentially radical narrative are magnified exponentially into a competing narrative with the addition of the Glossary.' Kirkpatrick associates the Glossary very specifically with the voice and intervention of R. L. Edgeworth. 'Putting down the Rebellion: notes and glosses on *Castle Rackrent*', *Éire-Ireland* 30 (1995), pp. 77–90, p. 86.

42 Ann Owens Weekes, *Irish Women Writers: An Uncharted Tradition* (Lexington: University Press of Kentucky, 1990), p. 39.

43 Ibid., p. 40.

44 ME to Mrs Starke, 6 Sept. 1834, quoted in Marilyn Butler, *Maria Edgeworth: A Literary Biography* (Oxford: Clarendon, 1972), p. 241.

45 Marilyn Butler, 'Introduction', *Castle Rackrent* and *Ennui*, ed. Marilyn Butler (Harmondsworth: Penguin, 1992), p. 4.

46 Brian Hollingworth, *Maria Edgeworth's Irish Writing: Language, History, Politics* (Basingstoke: Macmillan, 1997), p. 71.

47 Ibid., p. 73.

48 See W. J. Mc Cormack, *The Pamphlet Debate on the Union between Great Britain and Ireland, 1797–1800* (Dublin: Irish Academic Press, 1996).

49 Daniel Hack, 'Inter-Nationalism: *Castle Rackrent* and Anglo-Irish Union', *Novel: A Forum on Fiction* 29 (1996), pp. 145–64, p. 150.

50 Patrick Geoghegan, 'The making of the Union', in Keogh and Whelan (eds), *Acts of Union*, pp. 34–45, p. 34. In an essay in the same volume James Kelly makes the case that proposals for legislative union had been a persistent, if fluctuating, feature of Anglo-Irish political relations throughout the eighteenth century, and in fact earlier: 'The Act of Union: its origins and background', in *Acts of Union*, pp. 46–66.

51 Claire Connolly, 'Writing the Union', in Keogh and Whelan, (eds), *Acts of Union*, pp. 171–86, p. 175.

52 See Mc Cormack, *The Pamphlet Debate on the Union*.

53 Connolly, 'Writing the Union', p. 175.

54 *The Novels and Selected Works of Maria Edgeworth*, I: *Castle Rackrent, An Essay on Irish Bulls* and *Ennui*, ed. Jane Desmarais, Tim McLoughlin and Marilyn Butler, p. 6. Subsequent references are to this edition and are given parenthetically in the text.

55 Kant's 'What is Enlightenment?' articulates this idea particularly clearly: '"Have courage to make use of your *own* understanding!" is [. . .] the motto of Enlightenment'. *The Cambridge Edition of the Works of Immanuel Kant: Practical Philosophy*, trans. and ed. Mary J. Gregor (Cambridge: Cambridge University Press, 1996), p. 17 (original emphasis).

56 Butler, General Introduction, *The Novels and Selected Works of Maria Edgeworth*, I, p. xlii. See also Weekes, *Irish Women Writers*.

57 Tom Dunne argues that Thady's servility is 'devious and false' in his *Maria Edgeworth and the Colonial Mind* (Dublin: National University of Ireland, 1985), p. 8.

58 Declan Kiberd, *Irish Classics* (London: Granta, 2000), p. 258.

59 Mitzi Myers, 'Goring John Bull: Maria Edgeworth's Hibernian High Jinks versus the imperialist imaginary', in James E. Gill (ed.), *Cutting Edges: Postmodern Essays on Eighteenth-Century Satire* (Knoxville, TN: University of Tennessee Press, 1995), pp. 367–94, p. 369.

60 *The Novels and Selected Works of Maria Edgeworth*, I: *Castle Rackrent, An Essay on Irish Bulls* and *Ennui*, ed. by Jane Desmarais, Tim McLoughlin and Marilyn Butler, p. 86. Subsequent references are to this edition and are given parenthetically in the text.

61 This passage can be found in the Textual Variants of *The Novels and Selected Works of Maria Edgeworth*, I, 376.

62 Butler, 'General Introduction', *The Novels and Selected Works of Maria Edgeworth*, I, p. *XLV*.

63 See Bartlett, *The Fall and Rise of the Irish Nation*, pp. 235–9.

64 Butler, 'General Introduction', *The Novels and Selected Works of Maria Edgeworth*, I, p. *XLV*.

CHAPTER THREE

1 ME to Charlotte Sneyd, 2 Apr. 1799. Edgeworth Papers, National Library of Ireland, MSS 13176. The Edgeworth papers from collections in both the National Library of Ireland and the Bodleian Library in Oxford are also available in a microfilm edition, *Women, Education and Literature: The Papers of Maria Edgeworth, 1768–1849* (Marlborough, Wiltshire: Adam Matthew, 1995).

2 Ian McBride emphasises the significance in the Catholic population of 'the sense of a past marked by collective loss and the often apocalyptic expectation of future deliverance',

expressed for instance in Jacobite poetry, and notes that the persistence of a 'dispossession mentality' was also remarked on in the writings of foreign travellers in Ireland: 'Memory and national identity in modern Ireland', in McBride (ed.), *History and Memory in Modern Ireland* (Cambridge: Cambridge University Press, 2001), pp. 1–42, p. 28.

3   See Kevin Whelan, *The Tree of Liberty: Radicalism, Catholicism and the Construction of Irish Identity, 1760–1830* (Cork: Cork University Press, 1996).

4   See Tom Dunne, *Rebellions: Memoir, Memory and 1798* (Dublin: Lilliput, 2004). See also Roy Foster's 'Remembering 1798' in *History and Memory in Modern Ireland*, pp. 67–94, which is supportive of Dunne's position.

5   See Tom Dunne, 'Subaltern voices? Poetry in Irish, popular insurgency and the 1798 rebellion', *Eighteenth-Century Life* 22 (1998), pp. 31–44.

6   Jim Smyth, '1798 in its eighteenth-century contexts', in Jim Smyth (ed.), *Revolution, Counter-Revolution and Union: Ireland in 1798* (Cambridge: Cambridge University Press, 2000), pp. 1–20, p. 9.

7   Joep Leerssen, 'Monument and trauma: varieties of remembrance', in Mc Bride (ed.), *History and Memory in Modern Ireland*, pp. 204–22, p. 217.

8   Ibid., p. 215.

9   T. W. Tone, 'Circular letter announcing the foundation of the Society of United Irishmen of Dublin, 30 September 1791', in *The Writings of Theobald Wolfe Tone, 1763–1798*, 1: *Tone's Career in Ireland to June 1795*, ed. T. W. Moody, R. B. McDowell and C. J. Woods (Oxford: Clarendon, 1998), p. 156.

10   See Helen Mary Thuente, *The Harp Re-Strung: The United Irishmen and Literary Nationalism* (Syracuse, NY: Syracuse University Press, 1994) and Luke Gibbons, 'Republicanism and radical memory: the O'Conors, O'Carolan and the United Irishmen', in Smyth (ed.), *Revolution, Counter-Revolution and Union: Ireland in 1798*, pp. 211–37. Ian McBride, however, disputes this particular linkage between politics and culture, saying that 'for the United Irishmen, the [romantic] rhetoric of nationalism was always subordinated to the pursuit of their republican goals'. 'The harp without the crown: nationalism and republicanism in the 1790s', in S. J. Connolly (ed.), *Political Ideas in Eighteenth-Century Ireland* (Dublin: Four Courts, 2000), pp. 159–84, p. 183.

11   Katie Trumpener, *Bardic Nationalism: The Romantic Novel and the British Empire* (Princeton, NJ: Princeton University Press, 1997), p. 12.

12   Mary Jean Corbett, *Allegories of Union in Irish and English Writing, 1790–1870* (Cambridge: Cambridge University Press, 2000), p. 61.

13   Tom Dunne, '"A gentleman's estate should be a moral school": Edgeworthstown in fact and fiction, 1760–1840', in Raymond Gillespie and Gerard Moran (eds), *Longford: Essays in County History* (Dublin: Lilliput, 1991), pp. 95–121, p. 97.

14   Niall Ó Ciosáin, *Print and Popular Culture in Ireland, 1750–1850* (Basingstoke: Macmillan, 1997), p. 170.

15   Ibid., p. 171.

16   John P. Farrell, *Revolution as Tragedy: The Dilemma of the Moderate from Scott to Arnold* (London: Cornell University Press, 1980), p. 76.

17   Ibid., pp. 76, 77.

18   Butler, *Castle Rackrent* and *Ennui* (Harmondsworth: Penguin, 1992), p. 24. See also *The Novels and Selected Works of Maria Edgeworth* 12 vols (London: Pickering & Chatto,

1999–2003), V: *The Absentee, Madame de Fleury, Emilie de Coulanges*, ed. Heidi Van de Veire and Kim Walker, with Marilyn Butler, for a detailed chronology of the composition of the two series of *Tales of Fashionable Life*.

19 Edgeworth said of Mme Pastoret's school that she 'never saw any charitable institution that seemed to me so useful or that was half so touching'. Christina Colvin (ed.), *Maria Edgeworth in France and Switzerland: Selections from the Edgeworth Family Letters* (Oxford: Clarendon, 1979), p. 39; see also Introduction, p. xvii.

20 *The Novels and Selected Works of Maria Edgeworth*, V, 253. All subsequent references are to this edition and are given parenthetically in the text.

21 Christopher Hill, 'Robinson Crusoe', *History Workshop Journal* 10 (1980), pp. 7–24, p. 12.

22 Mitzi Myers suggests that the notes on 'revolutionary education' in Edgeworth's Paris notebook find fictional form in *Madame de Fleury*. See 'The erotics of pedagogy: historical intervention, literary representation, the "gift of education" and the agency of children', *Children's Literature* 23 (1995), pp. 1–30, p. 4.

23 *The Novels and Selected Works of Maria Edgeworth*, V, p. xxxiv.

24 Myers, 'The erotics of pedagogy', p. 4.

25 *The Novels and Selected Works of Maria Edgeworth*, V, p. 261. All subsequent references are to this edition and are given parenthetically in the text.

26 Seamus Deane, *The French Revolution and Enlightenment in England, 1789–1832* (London: Harvard University Press, 1988), p. 22.

27 Frances Burney, *Brief Reflections Relative to the Emigrant French Clergy*, with an Introduction by Claudia L. Johnson (London, 1793; repr. Los Angeles: William Clark Memorial Library, 1990), p. 12.

28 *The Poems of Charlotte Smith*, ed. Stuart Curran (Oxford: Oxford University Press, 1993), p. 133.

29 Martin Thom, *Republics, Nations and Tribes* (London: Verso, 1995), p. 196. Thom is, however, sceptical of the grand claims made for the significance of the Emigration by Chateaubriand, and advises that 'the phenomenon may be both exaggerated and misinterpreted' (p. 197). The *perception* of the emigration as a force for cosmopolitanism remains important, however.

30 *The Novels and Selected Works of Maria Edgeworth*, V, p. xxxvii.

31 See *ME in France and Switzerland*, pp. xvii–xviii. Suard's *Mélanges de littérature* were published in 1803–4, and consist of a collection of short pieces written from the 1760s onwards for journals and periodicals. I have not been able to trace the extract reproduced in *Emilie de Coulanges*, however. J. B. Suard, *Mélanges de littérature*, 5 vols in 3 (Paris, 1803–4; Geneva: Slatkind Reprints, 1971).

32 *The Novels and Selected Works of Maria Edgeworth*, I: *Castle Rackrent, An Essay on Irish Bulls, Ennui*, ed. Jane Desmarais, Tim McLoughlin and Marilyn Butler, p. 161. Subsequent references are to this edition and are given parenthetically in the text.

33 Dunne, 'Edgeworthstown in fact and fiction', p. 107.

34 Trumpener, *Bardic Nationalism*, p. 142.

35 Joep Leerssen, *Remembrance and Imagination: Patterns in the Historical and Literary Representation of Ireland in the Nineteenth Century* (Cork: Cork University Press, 1996), p. 37.

36 Thomas Flanagan, *The Irish Novelists, 1800–1850* (New York: Columbia University Press, 1959), p. 83.

37 Seamus Deane, *A Short History of Irish Literature* (London: Hutchinson, 1986), p. 96.

38 Dunne, 'Edgeworthstown in fact and fiction', p. 102.

39 *The Novels and Selected Works of Maria Edgeworth*, I, p. xliii.

40 Flanagan, *The Irish Novelists*, p. 83.

41 This is the case in Tom Dunne's 'Edgeworthstown in fact and fiction'. Seamus Deane, however, acknowledges Hardcastle's role, characterising him as 'the local squire-bigot'. *A Short History of Irish Literature*, p. 95.

42 Dunne, 'Edgeworthstown in fact and fiction', p. 113.

43 Elizabeth Kowaleski-Wallace, *Their Fathers' Daughters: Hannah More, Maria Edgeworth and Patriarchal Complicity* (New York: Oxford University Press, 1991), p. 162.

44 Ibid., p. 165.

45 See Robert Tracy, 'Maria Edgeworth and Lady Morgan: legality versus legitimacy', *Nineteenth-Century Fiction* 40 (1985), pp. 1–22.

46 Sharon Murphy provides the most recent reiteration of this argument: 'To facilitate her ambition to produce an image of Ireland where [. . .] uncomfortable reminders of the nation's (rebellious) past are effaced, or disguised, Edgeworth consequently sends Lady Geraldine off to India with Cecil Devereux, and thus clears the way for Glenthorn's and Cecilia's eventual marriage. In effecting this union in her narrative, Edgeworth thus ostensibly satisfies the colonial imperatives that impel all her writing.' *Maria Edgeworth and Romance* (Dublin: Four Courts, 2004), p. 166.

47 Tracy, 'Maria Edgeworth and Lady Morgan', p. 5.

48 Thomas Moore, *The Life and Death of Lord Edward Fitzgerald*, 2 vols (London: Longman, Hurst, Rees, Orme & Brown, 1831), I, pp. 1–2.

49 *The Novels and Selected Works of Maria Edgeworth*, I, p. 10.

50 Edmund Burke, *Tracts Relating to Popery Laws*, in *The Writings and Speeches of Edmund Burke*, gen. ed. Paul Langford (Oxford: Clarendon, 1991), vol. IX, pt 1: *The Revolutionary War 1794–7*, pt 2: *Ireland*, ed. R. B. McDowell, p. 438.

51 Ibid., pp. 441–2.

52 Luke Gibbons acknowledges the gender implications of the *Tracts Relating to Popery Laws*, saying that the laws produce 'a transgression of gender relations which, in Burke's eyes, can only lead to profound social instability, if not to revolution itself'. Gibbons suggests, though, that Burke may have gained from 'this erosion of male authority', given for instance his investment in the 'renewed interest in sentimentalism which was informing contemporary aesthetic debates'. *Edmund Burke and Ireland* (Cambridge: Cambridge University Press, 2003), p. 71. The appropriation of femininity in an aesthetic context does not, however, address the very deep level at which Burke's social and political vision is bound up with a desire to maintain a strictly gendered hierarchy.

53 Thomas Bartlett, *The Fall and Rise of the Irish Nation: The Catholic Question, 1690–1830* (Dublin: Gill & Macmillan, 1992), p. 23.

CHAPTER FOUR

1 Marilyn Butler, *Maria Edgeworth: A Literary Biography* (Oxford: Clarendon, 1972), p. 230.

2 ME to Sophy Ruxton, 16 May 1813, in *Maria Edgeworth: Letters from England, 1813–44*, ed. Christina Colvin (Oxford: Clarendon, 1971), p. 49.

3 [Francis Jeffrey], *Edinburgh Review* 21 (1813), pp. 1–50, p. 2.

4 John Claiborne Isbell, *The Birth of European Romanticism: Truth and Propaganda in Staël's 'De l'Allemagne', 1810–1813* (Cambridge: Cambridge University Press, 1994), pp. 35–6.

5 David Simpson, *Romanticism, Nationalism and the Revolt Against Theory* (London: University of Chicago Press, 1993), p. 103. In general, see ch. 4, 'The image of Germany' for a useful account of changing English perceptions of German character and culture from the eighteenth to the nineteenth centuries.

6 Robert Escarpit, *L'Angleterre dans l'œuvre de Madame de Staël* (Paris: Marcel Didier, 1956), p. 45.

7 ME to C. Sneyd Edgeworth, 26 Feb. 1814, quoted in *The Novels and Selected Works of Maria Edgeworth*, 12 vols (London: Pickering & Chatto, 1999–2003), VI: *Patronage*, vols I and II, ed. Connor Carville and Marilyn Butler, p. xxii.

8 Naomi Schor, 'The portrait of a gentleman: representing men in (French) women's writing', *Representations* 20 (1987), pp. 113–33, p. 120.

9 Mc Cormack notes that the 'relationship (by contrast as well as resemblance) between *The Absentee* and this later "English" novel could be demonstrated in various ways': *The Absentee*, ed. W. J. Mc Cormack and Kim Walker (Oxford: Oxford University Press, 1988), Appendix III, p. 284.

10 Germaine de Staël, *Germany*, 3 vols (London: John Murray, 1813), I, p. xii. Subsequent references are to this edition and are given parenthetically in the text.

11 For an account of the complex writing and publication history of *Germany*, see Isbell, *The Birth of European Romanticism*.

12 Quoted in Butler, *Maria Edgeworth*, p. 440.

13 See ibid., p. 496n., and John Dinwiddy, 'Jeremy Bentham as a pupil of Miss Edgeworth's', *Notes and Queries* (1982), pp. 208–10.

14 Butler, *Maria Edgeworth*, p. 337.

15 James Newcomer, *Maria Edgeworth the Novelist, 1767–1849: A Bicentennial Study* (Fort Worth, TX: Christian University Press, 1967), p. 81.

16 W. J. Mc Cormack, 'The tedium of history: an approach to Maria Edgeworth's *Patronage*', in Ciaran Brady (ed.), *Ideology and the Historians* (Dublin: Lilliput, 1991), pp. 77–98.

17 Newcomer, *Maria Edgeworth the Novelist*, p. 81.

18 Louis Bonaparte became King of Holland in June 1806, but abdicated in 1810, after which the Netherlands was annexed to France.

19 *The Novels and Selected Works of Maria Edgeworth*, VI: *Patronage*, vols I and II, ed. Connor Carville and Marilyn Butler, p. 17. Subsequent references to *Patronage* are to volumes VI and VII of *Novels and Selected Works*, and are given parenthetically in the text as follows: (VI, 17).

20 Richard Lovell Edgeworth and Maria Edgeworth, *Memoirs of Richard Lovell Edgeworth* [1820], 2 vols (Shannon: Irish University Press, 1969), II, p. 208.

21 Frank O'Gorman, *The Long Eighteenth Century: British Political and Social History, 1688–1832* (London: Arnold, 1997), p. 248.

22 Clive Emsley, *British Society and the French Wars, 1793–1815* (Basingstoke: Macmillan, 1979), pp. 99–101.

23 See A. D. Harvey, *English Literature and the Great War with France* (London: Nold Jonson, 1981), pp. 116–21.

24 [John Ward], *Quarterly Review* 10 (1814), pp. 301–22, p. 312.

25 [Francis Jeffrey], *Edinburgh Review* 22 (1814), pp. 416–34, p. 432.

26 Emsley, *British Society and the French Wars*, p. 143; see also Linda Colley, *Britons: Forging the Nation, 1707–1837* (London: Yale University Press, 1992), p. 231.

27 O'Gorman, *The Long Eighteenth Century*, p. 249.

28 Dinwiddy, 'Jeremy Bentham as a Pupil of Miss Edgeworth's', p. 209.

29 Ibid.

30 Marilyn Butler provides summaries of the reception of *Patronage*, and the politics of that reception, in her 'Introductory note', *The Novels and Selected Works of Maria Edgeworth*, VI: *Patronage*, vols I and II, ed. Connor Carville and Marilyn Butler, pp. xxi–xxix. She comments that '[a] book which Bentham praised in a radical weekly for meeting his own progressive standards of justice and veracity was not likely to please reviewers across the general run of commercial journals', p. xxiv.

31 See Jean Mistler, *Madame de Staël et Maurice O'Donnell, 1805–1817, d'après des lettres inédites* (Paris: Calmann-Lévy, 1926).

32 Germaine de Staël, *De l'Allemagne*, ed. Jean de Pange, 5 vols (Paris: Hachette, 1958–60), I, pp. 93–4.

33 *De l'Allemagne*, I, p. 94 (own translation): 'On pourroit se représenter un caractère fier sans être sévère, qui ne blâmât rien d'après les règles reçues, mais seulement d'après l'impulsion du cœur.'

34 *De l'Allemagne*, I, p. 95.

35 Mc Cormack, 'The tedium of history', p. 85.

36 [Ward], *Quarterly Review* 10 (1814), p. 310.

37 *The Novels and Selected Works of Maria Edgeworth*, V: *The Absentee, Madame de Fleury, Emilie de Coulanges*, ed. Heidi Van de Veire and Kim Walker, with Marilyn Butler, p. 59. All subsequent references are to this edition and are given parenthetically in the text.

38 Marilyn Butler, 'Introduction' to *Castle Rackrent* and *Ennui*, ed. Marilyn Butler (Harmondsworth: Penguin, 1992), p. 51.

39 *Corinne, or Italy*, trans. Avriel H. Goldberger (London: Rutgers University Press, 1987), p. 32. All subsequent references are to this edition and are given parenthetically in the text.

40 Tom Dunne, '"A gentleman's estate should be a moral school": Edgeworthstown in fact and fiction, 1760–1840', in Raymond Gillespie and Gerard Moran (eds), *Longford: Essays in County History* (Dublin: Lilliput, 1991), pp. 95–121, p. 98

41 See for instance Charlotte Brooke's *Reliques of Irish Poetry*, in which she observes that 'the British muse is not yet informed that she has an elder sister in this isle [Ireland]; let us introduce them to each other! Together let them walk abroad from their bowers, sweet ambassadresses of cordial union between two countries that seem formed by nature to be joined by every bond of interest, and of amity.' *Reliques of Irish Poetry* (Dublin: George Bonham, 1789), pp. viii–ix.

42 Thomas Campbell, 'Ye mariners of England', in *The Complete Poetical Works of Thomas Campbell*, ed. J. Logie Robertson (London: Oxford University Press, 1907), pp. 187–8.

43 Thomas Campbell, 'Exile of Erin', in *The Complete Poetical Works of Thomas Campbell*, pp. 240–1, p. 240.

44 Details of McCann's activities as a United Irishman are given in Marianne Elliott, *Partners in Revolution: The United Irishmen and France* (London: Yale University Press, 1982), pp. 160, 269.

45 For a recent study of the connection between the United Irishmen and Hamburg, see Paul Weber, *On the Road to Rebellion: The United Irishmen and Hamburg, 1796–1803* (Dublin: Four Courts, 1997).

46 Newcomer, *Maria Edgeworth the Novelist*, p. 94.

47 Mc Cormack, 'The tedium of history', p. 95.

48 Mc Cormack has provided an exhaustive account of the Jacobite resonances of Grace's names – both that of her adoptive father, Nugent, and her real father, Reynolds, an officer who died in the Austrian service, suggesting (English) Jacobite sympathies. See W. J. Mc Cormack, *Ascendancy and Tradition in Anglo-Irish Literary History from 1789 to 1939* (Oxford: Clarendon, 1985), pp. 141–52.

CHAPTER FIVE

1 *The Novels and Selected Works of Maria Edgeworth*, 12 vols (London: Pickering & Chatto, 1999–2003), I: *Castle Rackrent, An Essay on Irish Bulls, Ennui*, ed. Jane Desmarais, Tim McLoughlin and Marilyn Butler, p. 86.

2 Brian Hollingworth, *Maria Edgeworth's Irish Writing: Language, History, Politics* (Basingstoke: Macmillan, 1997), p. 29.

3 'The intention to record in an objective scientific manner, is arguably facilitated by an assumption of superiority in the person who does the recording.' Hollingworth, *Maria Edgeworth*, p. 29.

4 John Edwards, *Multilingualism* (London: Routledge, 1994), p. 2.

5 Katie Trumpener, *Bardic Nationalism: The Romantic Novel and the British Empire* (Princeton, NJ: Princeton University Press, 1997), p. 64.

6 Susanne Hagemann, 'Tales of a nation: territorial pragmatism in Elizabeth Grant, Maria Edgeworth and Sydney Owenson', *Irish University Review* 33 (2003), pp. 263–78. See also Esther Wohlgemut, 'Maria Edgeworth and the question of national identity', *Studies in English Literature* 39 (1999), pp. 645–58.

7 An example which suggests the possibilities for a broader discussion of this kind can be found in Siobhán Kilfeather's remarks on the use of French in Elizabeth Griffith's *The History of Lady Barton* (1771) in 'Origins of the Irish female gothic', *Bullán* 1 (1994), pp. 35–45, p. 40.

8 Maria Edgeworth, *Letters for Literary Ladies*, ed. Claire Connolly (London: J. M. Dent, 1993), p. 36.

9 Sylvie Kleinman, 'Pardon my French: the linguistic trials and tribulations of Theobald Wolfe Tone', in Eamon Maher and Grace Neville (eds), *France-Ireland: Anatomy of a Relationship: Studies in History, Literature and Politics* (Frankfurt: Peter Lang, 2004), pp. 295–310, p. 310.

10 Maria Edgeworth, *The Novels and Selected Works of Maria Edgeworth*, V: *The Absentee*, p. 16.

11 Marianne Elliott, *Wolfe Tone: Prophet of Irish Independence* (London: Yale University Press, 1989), p. 387.

12 Ibid., p. 388.

13 Hollingworth, *Maria Edgeworth's Irish Writing*, p. 114.

14 Ibid., p. 113.

15 Butler, 'Introductory note', *The Novels and Selected Works of Maria Edgeworth*, III: *Leonora* and *Harrington*, ed. Marilyn Butler and Susan Manly, pp. ix–xi.

16 This reading can be found in Nicola Watson, *Revolution and the Form of the British Novel, 1790–1825: Intercepted Letters, Interrupted Seductions* (Oxford: Clarendon, 1994), pp. 78–82.

17 *The Novels and Selected Works of Maria Edgeworth*, III: *Leonora* and *Harrington*, ed. Marilyn Butler and Susan Manly, p. 125. All subsequent references are to this edition and are given parenthetically in the text.

18 Margaret Anne Doody, 'Missing *Les Muses*: Madame de Staël and Frances Burney', *Colloquium Helveticum* 25 (1997), pp. 81–117, p. 92.

19 Watson, *Revolution and the Form of the British Novel*, p. 81.

20 Michèle Cohen, *Fashioning Masculinity: National Identity and Language in the Eighteenth Century* (London: Routledge, 1996), p. 39.

21 Cohen, *Fashioning Masculinity*, p. 41.

22 Hagemann, 'Tales of the nation', p. 270.

23 See 'Introduction', in *Ormond*, ed. Claire Connolly (Harmondsworth: Penguin, 2000).

24 *The Novels and Selected Works of Maria Edgeworth*, VIII: *Ormond*, ed. Claire Connolly, p. 11. All subsequent references are to this edition and are given parenthetically in the text.

25 Edwards, *Multilingualism*, pp. 72–3.

26 Hollingworth, *Maria Edgeworth's Irish Writing*, p. 208.

27 See Stella Tillyard, *Citizen Lord: Edward Fitzgerald, 1763–1798* (London: Vintage, 1998), pp. 13–21.

28 Hollingworth, *Maria Edgeworth's Irish Writing*, p. 212.

29 Jeffrey Merrick, 'Introduction' in *André Morellet (1727–1819) in the Republic of Letters and the French Revolution*, ed. Jeffrey Merrick and Dorothy Medlin (New York: Peter Lang, 1995), pp. 1–3, p. 1. For ME's meeting with Morellet, see Christina Colvin (ed.), *Maria Edgeworth in France and Switzerland* (Oxford: Clarendon, 1979); Colvin remarks that 'the Edgeworths shared his interest both in the nuances of language and in political economy', p. xviii. See also p. 17 and pp. 23–4.

30 For an account of the events which led to Tone's departure from Ireland (from where he initially travelled to America, before embarking for France, 1 January 1796), see Elliott, *Wolfe Tone*, pp. 246–59.

31 Niall Ó Ciosáin, 'The Irish rogues', in James S. Donnelly Jr. and Kerby A. Miller (eds), *Irish Popular Culture, 1650–1850* (Dublin: Irish Academic Press, 1998), pp. 78–96, p. 79.

32 Cited in ibid., p. 86.

33 Cited in ibid., p. 86.

34 Meredith Cary also draws attention to the positive effects of Ormond's Parisian experiences: 'His experience of French courtesy enables him to bring the grace of orderliness to King Corny's cobbled-up court'. 'Privileged assimilation: Maria Edgeworth's hope for the Ascendancy', *Éire-Ireland* 26 (1991), pp. 29–37, p. 36.

35 Thomas Flanagan, *The Irish Novelists, 1800–1850* (London: Columbia University Press, 1959), p. 99.

36 Hollingworth, *Maria Edgeworth's Irish Writing*, p. 219.

37 See Trumpener, *Bardic Nationalism*, pp. 63–6.

38 Cary, 'Privileged assimilation', p. 33.

CHAPTER SIX

1 ME to Michael Pakenham Edgeworth, letter begun 14 Feb. 1834. Cited in Marilyn Butler, *Maria Edgeworth: A Literary Biography* (Oxford: Clarendon, 1972), p. 452.

2 According to the bibliography of the Modern Languages Association, only two articles have been published on *Helen* since 1961. A modest revival of interest may be detected in treatments of the novel in Elizabeth Kowaleski-Wallace's *Their Fathers' Daughters: Hannah More, Maria Edgeworth and Patriarchal Complicity* (Oxford: Oxford University Press, 1991), and Caroline Gonda's *Reading Daughters' Fictions, 1709–1834: Novels and Society from Manley to Edgeworth* (Cambridge: Cambridge University Press, 1996), pp. 226–38.

3 Margaret Kelleher, '"Philosophick views"? Maria Edgeworth and the Great Famine', *Éire-Ireland* (32) 1997, pp. 41–62, p. 42.

4 Butler, *Maria Edgeworth*, pp. 450–1.

5 Michael Hurst, *Maria Edgeworth and the Public Scene: Intellect, Fine Feeling and Landlordism in the Age of Reform* (London: Macmillan, 1969), p. 69.

6 Butler, *Maria Edgeworth*, p. 456.

7 Marilyn Butler, *Romantics, Rebels and Reactionaries: English Literature and its Background, 1760–1830* (Oxford: Oxford University Press, 1981), p. 178.

8 *The Novels and Selected Works of Maria Edgeworth*, 12 vols (London: Pickering & Chatto, 1999–2003), III: *Leonora* and *Harrington*, ed. Marilyn Butler and Susan Manly, p. 15.

9 ME to Rachel Mordecai Lazarus, 2 May 1825. Cited in Hurst, *Maria Edgeworth and the Public Scene*, p. 42.

10 Cited in Thomas Bartlett, *The Fall and Rise of the Irish Nation: The Catholic Question, 1690–1830* (Dublin: Gill & Macmillan, 1992), p. 329.

11 Edgeworth's views of O'Connell do not acknowledge what Oliver MacDonagh has called his 'deep-set anti-revolutionism', and the fact that he 'was always to distance himself from bloodshed, revolutionary disorder and conspiracy'. MacDonagh, *The Hereditary Bondsman: Daniel O'Connell, 1775–1829* (London: Weidenfeld & Nicolson, 1988), p. 94, p. 26. However, Edgeworth's perception that O'Connell was in the process of reshaping the location of power in Ireland was accurate, given that, according to MacDonagh, O'Connell's leadership 'may be categorized as a sort of controlled and contingent alienation of the Catholic body from the state'. *The Hereditary Bondsman*, p. 261.

12 Oliver MacDonagh, 'The age of O'Connell, 1830–45', in W. E. Vaughan (ed.), *A New History of Ireland*, V: *Ireland under the Union I, 1801–70* (Oxford: Clarendon, 1989), pp. 158–68, p. 160.

13 Cited in Hurst, *Maria Edgeworth and the Public Scene*, p. 58. The account given here is based on that of Hurst.

14 Cited in ibid., p. 59.

15 ME to Mrs Edgeworth, [fragment, ?18 May 1831], in Christina Colvin (ed.), *Maria Edgeworth: Letters from England, 1813–44* (Oxford: Clarendon, 1971), p. 543.

16 ME to Fanny Wilson, 22 Dec 1832, cited in Hurst, *Maria Edgeworth and the Public Scene*, p. 71.

17 Marilyn Butler remarks on 'how closely her last novel compares with her real-life perceptions of Whig high society': *Maria Edgeworth*, p. 465.

18 ME to Fanny Wilson, 2 July 1831, in Colvin (ed.), *Letters from England*, p. 565.

19 The phrase is used by Norman Gash, *Aristocrats and People: Britain, 1815–1865* (London: Edward Arnold, 1979), Chapter 5.

20 See ME to Mrs Frances Edgeworth, 30 April 1831, in Colvin (ed.), *Letters from England*, p. 531. The number referred to is *Quarterly Review* 44 (1831). Mahon later reviewed Lord John Russell's *The Causes of the French Revolution* for the *Quarterly* in 1833, remarking that 'we can observe in two countries like France and England, so intent upon each other's political movements, and so much affected by them, – the false system which leads to a revolution is always the opposite to that which produced the last in either country': *Quarterly Review* 49 (1833), pp. 152–74, p. 169.

21 ME to Mrs Frances Edgeworth, 30 Apr. 1831, in Colvin, (ed.), *Letters from England*, p. 530.

22 ME to Sophy Ruxton, [21 Mar. 1831], in ibid., p. 495.

23 ME to Mrs Frances Edgeworth, 17 Nov. 1830, in ibid., p. 429.

24 ME to Harriet Butler, 29 Mar. 1831, in ibid., p. 508.

25 ME to Mrs Frances Edgeworth, 17 Nov. 1830, in ibid., pp. 428–9.

26 For other contemporary accounts of these events see E. A. Smith, *Reform or Revolution? A Diary of Reform in England, 1830–2* (Stroud: Alan Sutton, 1992). See particularly ch. 3 'Winter of discontent, November–December 1830', pp. 38–46.

27 ME to Mrs Frances Edgeworth, 17 Nov. 1830, in Colvin (ed.), *Letters from England*, p. 429.

28 Ibid.

29 Cited in Hurst, *Maria Edgeworth and the Public Scene*, p. 71.

30 Cited in ibid., p. 77.

31 ME to Fanny Wilson, 11 June 1831, in Colvin (ed.), *Letters from England*, p. 549.

32 'State and prospects of the country', *Dublin University Magazine* 3 (1834), p. 14.

33 Ibid.

34 *The Novels and Selected Works of Maria Edgeworth*, IX: *Helen*, ed. Susan Manly and Clíona Ó Gallchoir, p. 17. All references are to this edition and are given parenthetically in the text.

35 For a discussion of the first Earl of Clarendon see Irene Coltman, *Private Men and Public Causes: Philosophy and Politics in the English Civil War* (London: Faber, 1962).

36 Maggie Gee, Introduction to *Helen* (London: Pandora, 1987), p. x.

37 Gonda, *Reading Daughters' Fictions*, p. 34.

38 Lady Davenant here follows the text of the *Considerations* very closely; the passage she cites concludes with tributes to Edgeworth and other British women novelists, in which Staël remarks that the influence of these female novelists is confined to their books. In her habitually allusive manner, therefore, Edgeworth reflects here on the social role of her fiction. See Germaine de Staël, *Considerations on the French Revolution*, 3 vols (London: Baldwin, Craddock & Joy, 1818), III, p. 296–7.

39 The vocabulary of factionalism derives from Edgeworth's first-hand experiences in Paris in 1820: 'But I should observe that in general a great change has taken place and the

men huddle together now in France as they used to do in England talking politics with their backs to the women in a corner or even in the middle of the room without minding them in the least and the ladies complain and look very disconsolate and ask themselves if this be Paris and others scream *ultra* nonsense or *libérale* nonsense to make themselves of consequence and to attract the attention of the gentlemen'. ME to Mrs Frances Edgeworth, 4 June 1820, in Christina Colvin (ed.), *Maria Edgeworth in France and Switzerland* (Oxford: Clarendon, 1979), p. 145.

40 Auguste de Staël, *Letters on England* (London: Treuttel & Wurtz, 1825), p. 129. Auguste de Staël was the son of Germaine de Staël. Prior to the writing of *Helen*, Edgeworth had corresponded with Auguste de Staël and had met him while visiting Coppet, Germaine de Staël's former home in Switzerland. In *Letters on England* Staël recommends reform of Parliament, and states that 'the end which ought to be sought in England is, to increase the influence of the middle classes'. *Letters on England*, p. 274. *Letters on England* is also referred to specifically during an exchange between Clarendon and Beauclerc in *Helen*, pp. 82-3.

41 W. J. Mc Cormack, *From Burke to Beckett: Ascendancy, Tradition and Betrayal in Literary History* (Cork: Cork University Press, 1994), p. 39.

42 See W. J. Mc Cormack, *Sheridan Le Fanu and Victorian Ireland* (Oxford: Clarendon, 1980) for a full treatment of Le Fanu's place in Anglo-Irish literature.

43 Butler, *Maria Edgeworth*, p. 478.

44 Ibid., pp. 477, 478.

45 W. J. Mc Cormack, 'Isaac Butt', in Seamus Deane (ed.), *The Field Day Anthology of Irish Writing*, 3 vols (Derry: Field Day, 1991), I, p. 1200.

46 Isaac Butt, 'Past and present state of literature in Ireland', in Seamus Deane (ed.), *The Field Day Anthology of Irish Writing*, I, pp. 1200-12, p. 1201.

47 Ibid., p. 1202.

48 See Mark Parker, 'The Institutionalization of a Burkean–Coleridgean literary culture', *Studies in English Literature* 31 (1991), pp. 693-711.

49 Samuel Taylor Coleridge, *Biographia Literaria*, in *The Collected Works of Samuel Taylor Coleridge*, vol. VII: *Biographia Literaria* vol. 1, ed. James Engell and W. Jackson Bate (Princeton, NJ: Princeton University Press, 1983), p. 190.

AFTERWORD

1 Kathryn Kirkpatrick, 'Introduction', in Kirkpatrick (ed.), *Border Crossings: Irish Women Writers and National Identities* (Tuscaloosa, AL: University of Alabama Press, 2000), pp. 1-12, p. 6.

2 Edgeworth is located as the originator of the Big House tradition in more critical works than it is possible to list, but an example would be in Joep Leerssen's *Remembrance and Imagination: Patterns in the Historical and Literary Imagination of Ireland in the Nineteenth Century* (Cork: Cork University Press, 1996), p. 65.

3 Margot Gayle Backus, *The Gothic Family Romance: Heterosexuality, Child Sacrifice and the Anglo-Irish Colonial Order* (London: Duke University Press, 1999), p. 174.

4 Eavan Boland, 'Continuing the encounter', in Eibhear Walshe (eds), *Ordinary People Dancing: Essays on Kate O'Brien* (Cork: Cork University Press, 1993), pp. 15-23. p. 16.

5   Ibid., p. 17.
6   Ibid.
7   See Margaret Kelleher, 'Writing Irish women's literary history', *Irish Studies Review* 9 (2001), pp. 5–14.

Bibliography

-+->-<+-

PRIMARY SOURCES

Abrantès, Laure Junot, Duchess d', *Memoirs of the Duchess d'Abrantès*, 8 vols (London: R. Bentley, 1833–5).

Barbauld, Anna Laetitia, *Selected Poetry and Prose*, ed. William McCarthy and Elizabeth Kraft (Peterborough, Ontario: Broadview Press, 2002).

Blair, Hugh, 'A critical dissertation on the poems of Ossian, son of Fingal', in *Poems of Ossian, Translated by James Macpherson*, 2 vols (London: W. Strahan & T. Beckett, 1773).

Brooke, Charlotte, *Reliques of Irish Poetry* (Dublin: George Bonham, 1789).

Burke, Edmund, *Reflections on the Revolution in France* [1790], ed. Conor Cruise O'Brien (Harmondsworth: Penguin, 1986).

—— *The Writings and Speeches of Edmund Burke*, gen. ed. Paul Langford: vol. IX, pt 1: *The Revolutionary War 1794–7*, pt 2: *Ireland*, ed. R. B. McDowell (Oxford: Clarendon, 1991).

Burney, Frances, *Brief Reflections Relative to the Emigrant French Clergy*, with an Introduction by Claudia L. Johnson (London, 1793; repr. Los Angeles: William Andrews Clark Memorial Library, 1990).

Butt, Isaac, 'Past and present state of literature in Ireland', in Seamus Deane (ed.), *The Field Day Anthology of Irish Literature*, 3 vols (Derry: Field Day, 1991), II, pp. 1200–12.

Campbell, Thomas, *The Complete Poetical Works of Thomas Campbell*, ed. J. Logie Robertson (London: Oxford University Press, 1907).

Coleridge, Samuel Taylor, *Biographia Literaria*, in *The Collected Works of Samuel Taylor Coleridge*, VII and VIII: *Biographia Literaria*, ed. James Engell and W. Jackson Bate (Princeton, NJ: Princeton University Press, 1983).

Davies, Sir John, *Discovery of the True Causes why Ireland was never Entirely Subdued* (1612; repr. Shannon: Irish University Press, 1969).

Drennan, William, *Letters of Orellana* (Dublin: J. Chalmers & T. Heery, 1785).

—— *Glendalloch, and Other Poems, by the late Dr Drennan, with Additional Verses by his Sons* (Dublin: William Robertson, 1859).

—— *The Drennan–McTier Letters*, ed. Jean Agnew, 3 vols (Dublin: Irish Manuscripts Commission/Women's History Project, 1998–9).

Edgeworth, Frances Anne, *A Memoir of Maria Edgeworth*, 3 vols (London: privately printed, 1867).

Edgeworth, Maria, *The Novels and Selected Works of Maria Edgeworth*, 12 vols, ed. Marilyn Butler et al. (London: Pickering & Chatto, 1999–2003).

—— *Women, Education and Literature: The Papers of Maria Edgeworth, 1786–1849* (Marlborough, Wiltshire: Adam Matthew, 1995.)

—— *Letters for Literary Ladies* (London: J. Johnson, 1795).

—— *Letters for Literary Ladies*, ed. Claire Connolly (London: J. M. Dent, 1993).

—— *Castle Rackrent* and *Ennui*, ed. Marilyn Butler (Harmondsworth: Penguin, 1993).

—— *Belinda*, ed. Kathryn Kirkpatrick (Oxford: Oxford University Press, 1994).

—— *Belinda*, ed. Eiléan Ní Chuilleanáin (London: J. M. Dent, 1993).

—— *The Absentee*, ed. W. J. Mc Cormack and Kim Walker (Oxford: Oxford University Press, 1988).

—— *Ormond*, ed. Claire Connolly (Harmondsworth: Penguin, 2000).

—— *Helen*, with an Introduction by Maggie Gee (London: Pandora, 1987).

—— [and R. L. Edgeworth], *Practical Education*, 2 vols (London: J. Johnson, 1798).

—— [and R. L. Edgeworth], *Memoirs of Richard Lovell Edgeworth* [1820], 2 vols (Shannon: Irish University Press, 1969).

Genlis, Stéphanie-Félicité de, *Adelaide and Theodore; or, Letters on Education*, 3 vols (London: C. Bathurst & T. Cadell, 1783).

—— *A Short Account of of the Conduct of Madame de Genlis since the Revolution* (Perth: R. Morison, 1796).

—— *De l'influence des femmes sur la littérature française, comme protectrices des lettres et comme auteurs; ou, précis de l'histoire des femmes françaises les plus célèbres*, 2 vols (Paris: Maradan, 1811).

—— *Memoirs*, 8 vols (London: Henry Colburn, 1825).

Godwin, William, *A Memoir of the Author of a Vindication of the Rights of Woman*, in *A Short Residence in Sweden, Norway and Denmark* and *A Memoir of the Author of a Vindication of the Rights of Woman*, ed. Richard Holmes (Harmondsworth: Penguin, 1987).

Hamilton, Elizabeth, *Memoirs of Modern Philosophers* [1800], ed. Claire Grogan (Peterborough, Ontario: Broadview, 2000).

Hare, Augustus, *Life and Letters of Maria Edgeworth*, 2 vols (London: Edward Arnold, 1894).

Kant, Immanuel, *The Cambridge Edition of the Works of Immanuel Kant: Practical Philosophy*, trans. and ed. Mary J. Gregor (Cambridge: Cambridge University Press, 1996).

Locke, John, *An Essay Concerning Human Understanding*, ed. Peter H. Nidditch (Oxford: Oxford University Press, 1988).

Macpherson, James, *The Poems of Ossian and related works*, ed. Howard Gaskill, with an Introduction by Fiona Stafford (Edinburgh: Edinburgh University Press, 1996).

Mallet, Paul-Henri, *Northern Antiquities*, trans. Thomas Percy, 2 vols (London: T. Carnan & Co., 1770).

Millar, John, *The Origin of the Distinction of Ranks*, 3rd edn [1779], in William C. Lehmann, *John Millar of Glasgow, 1735–1801* (Cambridge: Cambridge University Press, 1960).

Montagu, Elizabeth, *An Essay on the Writings and Genius of Shakespear* (London, 1769; repr. London: Frank Cass, 1970).

Montesquieu, Charles-Louis de Secondat, baron de, *The Spirit of the Laws*, trans. Thomas Nugent (New York: Hafner, 1949).

Moore, Thomas, *The Life and Death of Lord Edward Fitzgerald*, 2 vols (London: Longman, Hurst, Orme, Rees & Brown, 1831).

—— *Poetical Works* (London: George Routledge, 1935).

More, Hannah, *Strictures on Female Education* (London, 1799; repr. Oxford: Woodstock, 1995).

Morgan, Lady [Sydney Owenson], *The Wild Irish Girl: A National Tale* [1806], ed. Claire Connolly and Stephen Copley, with a Foreword by Kevin Whelan (London: Pickering & Chatto, 2000).

—— *France*, 4th edn (London: Henry Colburn, 1818).

—— *Lady Morgan's Memoirs: Autobiography, Diaries and Correspondence*, 2 vols (London: W. H. Allen & Co., 1863).

Musgrave, Richard, *Memoirs of the Different Rebellions of Ireland* [1802], 4th edn, ed. Steven W. Myers and Delores E. McKnight (Fort Wayne, IN: Round Tower Books, 1995)

Renan, Ernest, 'What is a nation?', in Homi K. Bhabha (ed.), *Nation and Narration* (London: Routledge, 1990), pp. 8–22.

Rousseau, Jean-Jacques, [*La nouvelle Héloïse*, 1761] *Eloisa, or a Series of Original Letters*, trans. William Kenrick (London, 1803; repr. Oxford: Woodstock, 1989).

—— *Emile* [1762], trans. Barbara Foxley (London: J. M. Dent, 1992).

Saussure, Albertine Necker de, 'Notice sur le caractère et les écrits de Madame de Staël', in *Oeuvres complètes de Madame de Staël*, 18 vols (Paris: Treuttel & Würtz, 1820–1), I, pp. i–ccxxi.

Scott, Walter, *Waverley; or, Tis Sixty Years Since* [1814], ed. Claire Lamont (Oxford: Oxford University Press, 1986).

Smith, Adam, *An Inquiry into the Nature and Causes of the Wealth of Nations*, ed. R. H. Campbell, A. S. Skinner and W. B. Todd, 2 vols (Oxford: Clarendon, 1976).

—— *The Theory of Moral Sentiments*, ed. D. D. Raphael and A. L. Macfie (Oxford: Clarendon, 1976).

Smith, Charlotte, *The Poems of Charlotte Smith*, ed. Stuart Curran (Oxford: Oxford University Press, 1993).

Spenser, Edmund, *A View of the Present State of Ireland* [1598], ed. W. L. Renwick (Oxford: Clarendon, 1970).

Staël, Auguste de, *Letters on England* (London: Treuttel & Wurtz, 1825).

Staël, Germaine de, *Delphine*, 6 vols (London: J. Mawman, 1803).

—— *The Influence of Literature upon Society*, 2 vols (London: H. Colburn, 1812).

—— *Germany*, 3 vols (London: J. Murray, 1813).

—— *Considerations on the French Revolution*, 3 vols (London: Baldwin, Craddock & Joy, 1818).

—— *De la littérature considérée dans ses rapports avec les institutions sociales*, ed. Axel Blaeschke (Paris: InfoMédia Communication, 1998).

—— *De l'Allemagne*, ed. by Jean de Pange and Simone Balayé, 5 vols (Paris: Hachette, 1958–60).

—— *Corinne, or Italy*, ed. and trans. Avriel H. Goldberg (London: Rutgers University Press, 1987).

Suard, J. B., *Mélanges de littérature*, 5 vols in 3 (Paris, 1803–4; Geneva: Slatkind Reprints, 1971).

Tone, Theobald Wolfe, *The Writings of Wolfe Tone, 1763–1798*, I: *Tone's Career in Ireland to June 1795*, ed. T. W. Moody, R. B. McDowell and C. J. Woods (Oxford: Clarendon, 1998).

Voltaire, *Letters Concerning the English Nation* [1733], ed. Nicholas Cronk (Oxford: Oxford University Press, 1994).

—— *Philosophical Dictionary*, trans. Alex Holmes, 2 vols (London: B Johnson, 1819).

Wollstonecraft, Mary, *A Vindication of the Rights of Woman* [1792] (Harmondsworth: Penguin, 1992).

—— *The Works of Mary Wollstonecraft*, ed. Marilyn Butler and Janet Todd, VI: *An Historical and Moral View of the French Revolution* (London: William Pickering, 1989).

Young, Arthur, *A Tour in Ireland*, 2 vols (London: T. Cadell & J. Dodsley, 1780).

SECONDARY SOURCES

Atkinson, Colin B., and Jo Atkinson, 'Maria Edgeworth, *Belinda* and women's rights', *Eire-Ireland* 19 (1984), pp. 94–118.

Backus, Margot Gayle, *The Gothic Family Romance: Heterosexuality, Child Sacrifice and the Anglo-Irish Colonial Order* (London: Duke University Press, 1999).

Balayé, Simone, *Madame de Staël: lumières et liberté* (Paris: Klincksieck, 1979).

—— (ed.), *Madame de Staël: écrire, lutter, vivre* (Geneva: Librairie Droz, 1994).

Bartlett, Thomas, *The Fall and Rise of the Irish Nation: The Catholic Question 1690–1830* (Dublin: Gill & Macmillan, 1992).

—— and David Dickson, Dáire Keogh and Kevin Whelan (eds), *1798: A Bicentenary Perspective* (Dublin: Four Courts, 2003).

Beatty, John D., *Protestant Women's Narratives of the Irish Rebellion of 1798* (Dublin: Four Courts, 2001).

—— *Women's Narratives of the Irish Rebellion of 1798* (Dublin: Four Courts, 2002).

Beckett, J. C., *The Making of Modern Ireland, 1603–1923* (London: Faber & Faber, 1966).

—— *The Anglo-Irish Tradition* (London: Faber & Faber, 1976).

—— 'The Irish writer and his public in the nineteenth century', *Yearbook of English Studies* 11 (1981), pp. 102–16.

Bhabha, Homi K. (ed.), *Nation and Narration* (London: Routledge, 1990).

Bloch, Jean H., 'Women and the reform of the nation', in Eva Jacobs, W. H. Barber, Jean H. Bloch, F. W. Leakey and Eileen Le Breton (eds), *Woman and Society in Eighteenth-Century France* (London: Athlone, 1979), pp. 3–18.

Boland, Eavan, 'Continuing the encounter', in Eibhear Walshe (ed.), *Ordinary People Dancing: Essays on Kate O'Brien* (Cork: Cork University Press, 1993), pp. 15–23.

Bosse, Monika, 'La Révolution de l'héroisme féminin: une œuvre de jeunesse de Madame de Staël', in Marie-France Brive (ed.), *Les femmes et le Révolution Française*, 3 vols (Toulouse: Université de Toulouse, 1989–91), I, pp. 279–84.

Boyce, D. George, *Nineteenth-Century Ireland: The Search for Stability* (Dublin: Gill & Macmillan, 1990).

Bowman, Frank P, 'La polémique sur les *Considérations sur la Révolution Française*', in *La Groupe de Coppet et la Révolution Française* (Lausanne: Institut Benjamin Constant, 1988), pp. 225–41.

Broglie, Gabriel de, *Madame de Genlis* (Paris: Librairie Académique Perrin, 1985).

Brooker, Peter (ed.), *Modernism/Postmodernism* (Harlow: Longman, 1992).

Brown, Malcolm, *The Politics of Irish Literature, from Thomas Davis to W. B. Yeats* (London: George Allen & Unwin, 1972).

Butler, Marilyn, *Maria Edgeworth: A Literary Biography* (Oxford: Clarendon, 1972).

—— 'The uniqueness of Cynthia Kirkpatrick: Elizabeth Gaskell's *Wives and Daughters* and Maria Edgeworth's *Helen*', *Review of English Studies* 23 (1972), pp. 278–90.

—— *Romantics, Rebels and Reactionaries* (Oxford: Oxford University Press, 1981).

—— *Jane Austen and the War of Ideas*, reissued with a new introduction (Oxford: Clarendon, 1987).

—— 'Telling it like a story: the French Revolution as narrative', *Studies in Romanticism* 28 (1989), pp. 345–64.

—— 'Edgeworth's stern father: escaping Thomas Day, 1795–1801', in Alvaro Ribero and James G. Basker (eds), *Tradition in Transition: Women Writers, Marginal Texts and the Eighteenth-Century Canon* (Oxford: Clarendon, 1996), pp. 75–93.

—— and Christina Colvin, 'Maria Edgeworth et *Delphine*', *Cahiers Staëliens* 26 (1979), pp. 77–9.

Butler, H. J. and H. E. (eds), *The Black Book of Edgeworthstown and Other Edgeworth Memories 1585–1817* (London: Faber & Gwyer, 1927).

Campbell, Mary, *Lady Morgan: The Life and Times of Sydney Owenson* (London: Pandora, 1988).

Cary, Meredith, 'Privileged assimilation: Maria Edgeworth's hope for the Ascendancy', *Eire-Ireland* 26 (1991), pp. 29–37.

Clemit, Pamela, *The Godwinian Novel: The Rational Fictions of Godwin, Brockden Brown, Mary Shelley* (Oxford: Clarendon, 1993).

Cohen, Michèle, *Fashioning Masculinity: National Identity and Language in the Eighteenth Century* (London: Routledge, 1996).

Colley, Linda, *Britons: Forging the Nation 1707–1837* (London: Yale University Press, 1992).

Coltman, Irene, *Private Men and Public Causes: Philosophy and Politics in the English Civil War* (London: Faber & Faber, 1962).

Colvin, Christina (ed.), *Maria Edgeworth: Letters from England 1813–1844* (Oxford: Clarendon, 1971).

—— *Maria Edgeworth in France and Switzerland: Selections from the Edgeworth Family Letters* (Oxford: Clarendon, 1979).

Connolly, Claire, 'Gender, nation and Ireland in the early novels of Maria Edgeworth and Lady Morgan' (PhD thesis, University of Wales, Cardiff, 1995).

—— 'Writing the Union' in Dáire Keogh and Kevin Whelan (eds), *Acts of Union: The Causes, Contexts and Consequences of the Act of Union* (Dublin: Four Courts, 2001), pp. 171–86.

—— '"A big book about England"? Public and private meanings in Maria Edgeworth's *Patronage*', in Jacqueline Belanger (ed.), *Facts and Fictions: Ireland and the Novel in the Nineteenth Century*, forthcoming.

Connolly, S. J. (ed.), *Political Ideas in Eighteenth-Century Ireland* (Dublin: Four Courts, 2000).

Coulet, Henri, 'Révolution et roman selon Madame de Staël', *Revue d'histoire littéraire de la France* 87 (1987), pp. 638–60.

Corbett, Mary Jean, *Allegories of Union in Irish and English Writing, 1790–1870: Politics, History and the Family from Edgeworth to Arnold* (Cambridge: Cambridge University Press, 2000).

Coulter, Carol, *The Hidden Tradition: Feminism, Women and Nationalism in Ireland* (Cork: Cork University Press, 1993).

Crawford, Robert, *Devolving English Literature* (Oxford: Clarendon, 1992).

Cronin, John, *The Anglo-Irish Novel.* 1 *The Nineteenth Century* (Belfast: Apppletree, 1980).

Cullen, Mary, (ed.), *1798: 200 Years of Resonance* (Dublin: Irish Reporter Publications, 1998).

Curtin, Nancy J., *The United Irishmen: Popular Politics in Ulster and Dublin, 1791–1798* (Oxford: Clarendon, 1994).

Davidoff, Leonore and Catherine Hall, *Family Fortunes: Men and Women of the English Middle Class, 1780–1850* (London: Routledge, 1992).

De Man, Paul, 'Madame de Staël et Jean-Jaques Rousseau', *Preuves* 190 (1966), pp. 35–40.

Deane, Seamus, 'Edmund Burke and the ideology of Irish liberalism', in Richard Kearney (ed.), *The Irish Mind: Exploring Intellectual Traditions* (Dublin: Wolfhound, 1985), pp. 141–56.

—— *A Short History of Irish Literature* (London: Hutchinson, 1986).

—— 'Irish national character 1790–1900', in Tom Dunne (ed.), *The Writer as Witness: Literature as Historical Evidence* (Cork: Cork University Press, 1987), pp. 90–113.

—— *The French Revolution and Enlightenment in England, 1789–1832* (London: Harvard University Press, 1988).

—— (ed.), and Andrew Carpenter and Jonathan Williams (assoc. eds), *The Field Day Anthology of Irish Writing*, 3 vols (Derry: Field Day, 1991).

—— 'Montesquieu and Burke', in Christopher Murray and Barbara Hayley (eds), *Ireland and France: A Bountiful Friendship* (Gerrards Cross: Colin Smythe, 1992), pp. 17–29.

—— *Strange Country: Modernity and Nationhood in Irish Writing since 1790* (Oxford: Clarendon, 1997).

De Jean, Joan, *Tender Geographies: Women and the Origins of the Novel in France* (New York: Columbia University Press, 1991).

Delon, Michel, 'Germaine de Staël and other possible scenarios of the Revolution', in Madelyn Gutwirth, Avriel H. Goldberger and Karen Smzurlo (eds), *Germaine de Staël: Crossing the Borders* (New Brunswick, NJ: Rutgers University Press, 1991), pp. 22–30.

Dinwiddy, J. R, 'Jeremy Bentham as a Pupil of Miss Edgeworth's', *Notes and Queries* 29 (1982), pp. 208–11.

Donnelly, James S., Jr, and Kerby A. Miller (eds), *Irish Popular Culture, 1650–1850* (Dublin: Irish Academic Press, 1998).

Doody, Margaret Anne, 'Missing les muses: Madame de Staël and Fanny Burney', *Colloquium Helveticum* 25 (1997), pp. 81–117.

Dunne, Tom, *Maria Edgeworth and the Colonial Mind*, O'Donnell Lecture (Dublin: National University of Ireland, 1984).

—— 'Haunted by history: Irish romantic writing, 1800–1850', in Roy Porter and Mikulas Teich (eds), *Romanticism in National Context* (Cambridge: Cambridge University Press, 1988), pp. 68–91.

—— "'A gentleman's estate should be a moral school": Edgeworthstown in fact and fiction 1760–1840', in Raymond Gillespie and Gerard Moran (eds), *Longford: Essays in County History* (Dublin: Lilliput, 1991), pp. 95–121.

—— 'Subaltern voices? Poetry in Irish, popular insurgency and the 1798 rebellion', *Eighteenth-Century Life* 22 (1998), pp. 31–44.

—— *Rebellions: Memoir, Memory and 1798* (Dublin: Lilliput, 2004).

Durand-Serail, Béatrice, 'Madame de Staël et la condition post-révolutionnaire', *Romanic Review* 82 (1991), pp. 36–48.

Eagleton, Terry, *Heathcliff and the Great Hunger: Studies in Irish Culture* (London: Verso, 1995).

Eagles, Robin, *Francophilia in English Society, 1748–1815* (Basingstoke: Macmillan, 2000).

Edwards, John, *Multilingualism* (London: Routledge, 1994).

Eger, Elizabeth, and Charlotte Grant, Clíona Ó Gallchoir and Penny Warburton (eds), *Women, Writing and the Public Sphere, 1700–1830* (Cambridge: Cambridge University Press, 2001).

Elliott, Marianne, *Partners in Revolution: The United Irishmen and France* (London: Yale University Press, 1982).

—— *Wolfe Tone: Prophet of Irish Independence* (London: Yale University Press, 1989).

Emsley, Clive, *British Society and the French Wars, 1793–1815* (Basingstoke: Macmillan, 1979).

Escarpit, Robert, *L'Angleterre dans l'œuvre de Madame de Staël* (Paris: Marcel Didier, 1956).

Farrell, John P., *Revolution as Tragedy: The Dilemma of the Moderate from Scott to Arnold* (London: Cornell University Press, 1980).

Ferris, Ina, *The Romantic National Tale and the Question of Ireland* (Cambridge: Cambridge University Press, 2002).

Flanagan, Thomas, *The Irish Novelists, 1800–1850* (New York: Columbia University Press, 1959).

Foster, R. F., *Modern Ireland 1600–1972* (London: Allen Lane/Penguin, 1988).

—— 'Remembering 1798' in Ian McBride (ed.), *History and Memory in Modern Ireland* (Cambridge: Cambridge University Press, 2001), pp. 67–94.

Gargett, Graham, and Geraldine Sheridan (eds), *Ireland and the French Enlightenment, 1700–1800* (Basingstoke: Macmillan, 1999).

Gash, Norman, *Aristocracy and People: Britain 1815–1865* (London: Edward Arnold, 1979).

Gaskill, Howard (ed.), *Ossian Revisited* (Edinburgh: Edinburgh University Press, 1991).

Geoghegan, Patrick, 'The making of the Union', in Dáire Keogh and Kevin Whelan (eds), *Acts of Union: The Causes, Contexts and Consequences of the Act of Union* (Dublin: Four Courts, 2001), pp. 34–45.

Gibbons, Luke, 'Republicanism and radical memory: the O'Conors, O'Carolan and the United Irishmen', in Jim Smyth (ed.), *Revolution, Counter-Revolution and Union: Ireland in the 1790s* (Cambridge: Cambridge University Press, 2000), pp. 211–37.

—— *Edmund Burke and Ireland* (Cambridge: Cambridge University Press, 2003).

Godechot, Jaques, 'Nation, patrie et nationalisme en France au XVIIIe siècle', *Annales Historiques de la Révolution Française* 43 (1971), pp. 81–501.

Gonda, Caroline, *Reading Daughters' Fictions, 1709–1834: Novels and Society from Manley to Edgeworth* (Cambridge: Cambridge University Press, 1996).

Goodman, Dena, *The Republic of Letters: A Cultural History of the French Enlightenment* (Ithaca, NY: Cornell University Press, 1994).

Graham, Colin, *Deconstructing Ireland: Identity, Theory, Culture* (Edinburgh: Edinburgh University Press, 2001).

Greenfield, Susan, 'Abroad and at home: sexual ambiguity, miscegenation and colonial boundaries in *Belinda*', *PMLA* 1997 (112), pp. 214–28.

Guest, Harriet, *Small Change: Women, Learning, Patriotism, 1750–1810* (Chicago and London: University of Chicago Press, 2000).

Gutwirth, Madelyn, *Madame de Staël, Novelist: The Emergence of the Artist as Woman* (London: University of Illinois Press, 1978).

—— 'La *Delphine* de Madame de Staël: femme, Révolution at mode épistolaire', *Cahiers Staëliens* 26 (1979), pp. 151–65.

—— Avriel H. Goldberger, and Karen Szmurlo (eds), *Germaine de Staël: Crossing the Borders* (New Brunswick, N.J.: Rutgers University Press, 1991).

Hack, Daniel, 'Inter-nationalism: *Castle Rackrent* and Anglo-Irish union', *Novel: A Forum on Fiction* 29 (1996), pp. 145–64.

Hagemann, Susanne, 'Tales of a nation: territorial pragmatism in Elizabeth Grant, Maria Edgeworth and Sydney Owenson', *Irish University Review* 33 (2003), pp. 263–78.

Harmand, Jean, *The Keeper of Royal Secrets: Being the Private and Political Life of Madame de Genlis* (London: Eveleigh Nash, 1913).

Harvey, A. D., *English Literature and the Great War with France* (London: Nold Jonson, 1981).

Häusermann, H. W., *The Genevese Background: Studies of Shelley, Francis Danby, Maria Edgeworth, Ruskin, Meredith and Joseph Conrad in Geneva* (London: Routledge & Kegan Paul, 1952).

Herold, J. Christopher, *Mistress to an Age: A Life of Madame de Staël* (London: Hamish Hamilton, 1959).

Hill, Christopher, 'Robinson Crusoe', *History Workshop Journal* 10 (1980), pp. 7–24.

Hobsbawm, E. J. *Nations and Nationalism since 1780: Programme, Myth, Reality* (Cambridge: Cambridge University Press, 1990).

Hollingworth, Brian, *Maria Edgeworth's Irish Writing: Language, History, Politics* (Basingstoke: Macmillan, 1997).

—— 'Completing the Union: Edgeworth's *The Absentee* and Scott the novelist', in J. H. Alexander and David Hewitt (eds), *Scott in Carnival* (Aberdeen: University of Aberdeen, 1993), pp. 502–11.

Hurst, Michael, *Maria Edgeworth and the Public Scene: Intellect, Fine Feeling and Landlordism in the Age of Reform* (London: Macmillan, 1969).

Isbell, John Claiborne, *The Birth of European Romanticism: Truth and Propaganda in Staël's 'De l'Allemagne', 1810–1813* (Cambridge: Cambridge University Press, 1994).

—— 'The painful birth of the romantic heroine: Staël as political animal, 1786–1818', *Romanic Review* 87 (1996), pp. 59–67.

Keane, Angela, *Women Writers and the English Nation in the 1790s: Romantic Belongings* (Cambridge: Cambridge University Press, 2000).

Kearney, Richard (ed.), *The Irish Mind: Exploring Intellectual Traditions* (Dublin: Wolfhound, 1985).

Kelleher, Margaret, '"Philosophick views"? Maria Edgeworth and the Great Famine', *Eire-Ireland* 32 (1997), pp. 41–62.

—— 'Writing Irish women's literary history', *Irish Studies Review* 9 (2001), pp. 5–14.

Kelly, Gary, *English Fiction of the Romantic Period, 1789–1830* (Harlow: Longman, 1989).

—— *Revolutionary Feminism: The Mind and Career of Mary Wollstonecraft* (Basingstoke: Macmillan, 1992).

—— *Women, Writing, Revolution, 1790–1827* (Oxford: Clarendon, 1993).

Kelly, James, 'The Act of Union: its origins and background', in Dáire Keogh and Kevin Whelan (eds), *Acts of Union: The Causes, Contexts and Consequences of the Act of Union* (Dublin: Four Courts, 2001), pp. 46–66.

Keogh, Dáire and Nicholas Furlong, eds., *The Women of 1798* (Dublin: Four Courts, 1998).

Kennedy, Máire 'Nations of the mind: French culture in Ireland and the international booktrade', in Michael O'Dea and Kevin Whelan (eds), *Nations and Nationalisms: France, Britain, Ireland and the Eighteenth-Century Context* (Oxford: Voltaire Foundation, 1995), pp. 147–58.

Kidd, Colin, *British Identities before Nationalism: Ethnicity and Nationhood in the Atlantic World, 1600–1800* (Cambridge: Cambridge University Press, 1999).

Kiberd, Declan, *Irish Classics* (London: Granta, 2000).

Kilfeather, Siobhán, '"Strangers at home": political fictions by women in eighteenth-century Ireland' (PhD thesis, Princeton University, 1989).

—— 'Origins of the Irish female gothic', *Bullán* 1 (1994), pp. 35–45.

Kirkpatrick, Kathryn, 'Putting down the rebellion: notes and glosses on *Castle Rackrent*', *Éire-Ireland* 30 (1995), pp. 77–90.

—— 'The limits of liberal feminism in Maria Edgeworth's *Belinda*', in Laura Dabundo (ed.), *Jane Austen and Mary Shelley and their Sisters* (Lanham, MD: University Press of America, 2000), pp. 73–82.

—— (ed.), *Border Crossings: Irish Women Writers and National Identities* (Tuscaloosa, AL: University of Alabama Press, 2000).

Kitchen, Johanna, 'La littérature et les femmes selon l'ouvrage *De la Littérature* de Madame de Staël', in *Benjamin Constant, Madame de Staël et la groupe de Coppet* (Lausanne: Institut Benjamin Constant, 1982), pp. 401–25.

Klein, Lawrence E., 'Gender and the public/private divide in the eighteenth century: some questions about evidence and analytic procedure', *Eighteenth-Century Studies* 29 (1995), pp. 97–109.

Kleinmann, Sylvie, 'Pardon my French: the linguistic trials and tribulations of Theobald Wolfe Tone', in Eamon Maher and Grace Neville (eds), *France-Ireland: Anatomy of a Relationship* (Frankfurt: Peter Lang, 2004), pp. 295–310.

Kowaleski-Wallace, Elizabeth, *Their Father's Daughters: Hannah More, Maria Edgeworth and Patriarchal Complicity* (New York: Oxford University Press, 1991).

Landes, Joan B., *Women and the Public Sphere in the Age of the French Revolution* (London: Cornell University Press, 1988).

Lawless, Emily, *Maria Edgeworth* (London: Macmillan, 1904).

Leerssen, J. Th., *Mere Irish and Fíor-Ghael: Studies in the Idea of Irish Nationality, its Development and Literary Expression Prior to the Nineteenth Century*, 2nd edn (Cork: Cork University Press, 1996).

—— 'On the treatment of Irishness in romantic Anglo-Irish fiction', *Irish University Review* 20 (1990), pp. 254–84.

—— *Remembrance and Imagination: Patterns in the Historical and Literary Representation of Ireland in the Nineteenth Century* (Cork: Cork University Press, 1996).

Livesey, James, 'Acts of union and disunion: Ireland in Atlantic and European contexts', in Dáire Keogh and Kevin Whelan (eds), *Acts of Union: The Causes, Contexts and Consequences of the Act of Union* (Dublin: Four Courts, 2001), pp. 95–105.

Lloyd, David, *Anomalous States: Irish Writing and the Post-Colonial Moment* (Dublin: Lilliput, 1993).

—— *Ireland After History* (Cork: Cork University Press, 1999).

Longley, Edna, *The Living Stream: Literature and Revisionism in Ireland* (Newcastle-upon-Tyne: Bloodaxe, 1994).

Lynch, Deirdre, 'Domesticating fictions and nationalising women: Edmund Burke, property and the reproduction of Englishness', in Alan Richardson and Sonia Hofkosh (eds), *Romanticism, Race and Imperial Culture, 1780–1834* (Bloomington, IN: Indiana University Press, 1996), pp. 40–71.

Mason, Nicholas, 'Class, gender, and domesticity in Maria Edgeworth's *Belinda*', *Eighteenth-Century Novel* 1 (2001), pp. 271–85.

May, Georges, *Le Dilemme du roman au XVIIIᵉ siècle* (Paris: Presses Universitaires de France, 1963).

McBride, Ian, '"The son of an honest man": William Drennan and the dissenting tradition', in David Dickson, Dáire Keogh, and Kevin Whelan (eds), *The United Irishmen: Republicanism, Radicalism and Rebellion* (Dublin: Lilliput, 1993), pp. 49–61.

—— *Scripture Politics: Ulster Presbyterians and Irish Radicalism in the Late Eighteenth Century* (Oxford: Clarendon, 1998).

—— '"The common name of Irishman": Protestantism and patriotism in eighteenth-century Ireland', in Tony Claydon and Ian McBride (eds), *Protestantism and National Identity: Britain and Ireland, c.1650–c.1850* (Cambridge: Cambridge University Press, 1998), pp. 236–61.

—— (ed.), *History and Memory in Modern Ireland* (Cambridge: Cambridge University Press, 2001).

Mc Cormack, W. J., *Sheridan Le Fanu and Victorian Ireland* (Oxford: Clarendon, 1980).

—— *Ascendancy and Tradition in Anglo-Irish Literary History from 1789 to 1939* (Oxford: Clarendon, 1985).

—— 'French Revolution ... Anglo-Irish literature ... beginnings? The case of Maria Edgeworth', in Hugh Gough and David Dickson (eds), *Ireland and the French Revolution* (Dublin: Irish Academic Press, 1990). pp. 229–43.

—— 'The tedium of history: an approach to Maria Edgeworth's *Patronage*', in Ciaran Brady (ed.), *Ideology and the Historians* (Dublin: Lilliput, 1991), pp. 77–98.

—— *From Burke to Beckett: Ascendancy, Tradition and Betrayal in Literary History* (Cork: Cork University Press, 1994).

—— *The Pamphlet Debate on the Union between Great Britain and Ireland, 1797–1800* (Dublin: Irish Academic Press, 1996).

MacDonagh, Oliver, *States of Mind: A Study of Anglo-Irish Conflict, 1780–1980* (London: George Allen & Unwin, 1983).

—— *The Hereditary Bondsman: Daniel O'Connell, 1775–1829* (London: Weidenfeld & Nicolson, 1988).

—— 'Introduction: Ireland and the Union 1801–70', in W. E. Vaughan (ed.), *A New History of Ireland*, v: *Ireland under the Union, I: 1801–1870* (Oxford: Clarendon, 1989), pp. xlvii–lxv.

—— 'The age of O'Connell, 1830–45', in W. E. Vaughan (ed.), *A New History of Ireland*, v: *Ireland under the Union, I: 1801–70* (Oxford: Clarendon, 1989), pp. 158–68.

McDowell, R. B., *Ireland in the Age of Imperialism and Revolution, 1760–1801* (Oxford: Clarendon, 1979).

McKendrick, Neil, John Brewer and J. H. Plumb, *The Birth of a Consumer Society: The Commercialisation of Eighteenth-Century England* (London: Europa, 1982).

Meaney, Gerardine, *Sex and Nation: Women in Irish Culture and Politics* (Dublin: Attic Press, 1991).

Mellor, Anne K., *Romanticism and Gender* (London: Routledge, 1993).

—— 'A novel of their own: romantic women's fiction, 1790–1830', in John Richetti (ed.), *The Columbia History of the British Novel* (New York: Columbia University Press, 1994), pp. 327–51.

Merrick, Jeffrey, and Dorothy Medlin (eds), *André Morellet (1727–1819) in the Republic of Letters and the French Revolution* (New York: Peter Lang, 1995).

Miller, Nancy K., 'Men's reading, women's writing: gender and the rise of the novel', in Joan DeJean and Nancy K. Miller (eds), *Displacements: Women, Tradition, Literatures in French* (London: Johns Hopkins University Press, 1991), pp. 37–54.

Mistler, Jean, *Madame de Staël et Maurice O'Donnell, 1805–1817, d'après des lettres inédites* (Paris: Calmann-Lévy, 1926).

Moody, T. W., F. X. Martin and F. J. Byrne (eds), *A New History of Ireland*, iii: *Early Modern Ireland, 1534–1691* (Oxford: Clarendon, 1976).

—— and W. E. Vaughan (eds), *A New History of Ireland*, iv: *Eighteenth-Century Ireland, 1691–1800* (Oxford: Clarendon, 1986).

Moskal, Jeanne, 'Gender, nationality and textual authority in Lady Morgan's travel books', in Theresa M. Kelley and Paula R. Feldman (eds), *Romantic Women Writers* (Hanover, NH: University Press of New England, 1995), pp. 171–93.

Murphy, Sharon, *Maria Edgeworth and Romance* (Dublin: Four Courts, 2004).

Murphy, Willa, 'A Queen of Hearts or an old maid?: Maria Edgeworth's fictions of Union', in Dáire Keogh and Kevin Whelan (eds), *Acts of Union: The Causes, Contexts and Consequences of the Act of Union* (Dublin: Four Courts, 2001), pp. 187–201.

Myers, Mitzi, 'Reform or ruin: "a revolution in female manners"', *Studies in Eighteenth-Century Culture* 11 (1982), pp. 199–216.

—— 'De-romanticizing the subject: Maria Edgeworth's "The Bracelets", mythologies of origin, and the daughter's coming to writing', in Theresa M. Kelley and Paula R. Feldman (eds), *Romantic Women Writers* (Hanover, NH: University Press of New England, 1995), pp. 88–110.

—— 'Goring John Bull: Maria Edgeworth's Hibernian high jinks versus the imperialist imaginary', in James E. Gill (ed.), *Cutting Edges: Postmodern Essays on Eighteenth-Century Satire* (Knoxville, TN: University of Tennessee Press, 1995), pp. 367–94.

—— 'The erotics of pedagogy: historical intervention, literary representation, the "gift of education", and the agency of children', *Children's Literature* 23 (1995), pp. 1–30.

—— '"Like the pictures in a magic lantern": gender, history, and Edgeworth's rebellion narratives', *Nineteenth-Century Contexts* 19 (1996), pp. 373–412.

—— 'War correspondence: Maria Edgeworth and the en-gendering of revolution, rebellion and union', *Eighteenth-Century Life* 22 (1998), pp. 74–91.

—— 'My art belongs to Daddy? Thomas Day, Maria Edgeworth and the pre-texts of *Belinda*: women writers and patriarchal authority', in Paula Backscheider (ed.), *Revising Women: Eighteenth-Century 'Women's Fiction' and Social Engagement* (Baltimore, MD: Johns Hopkins University Press, 2000), pp. 104–46.

Narain, Mona, 'A prescription of letters: Maria Edgeworth's *Letters for Literary Ladies* and the ideologies of the public sphere', *Journal of Narrative Technique* 28 (1998), pp. 266–86.

Newby, Percy Howard, *Maria Edgeworth* (Denver: Swallow, 1950).

Newcomer, James, *Maria Edgeworth the Novelist, 1767–1849: A Bicentennial Study* (Fort Worth, TX: Texas Christian University Press, 1967).

—— *Maria Edgeworth* (Lewisburg, PA: Bucknell University Press, 1973).

Ní Chuilleanáin, Eiléan, 'Women as writers: Dánta Grá to Maria Edgeworth', in Eiléan Ní Chuilleanáin (ed.), *Irish Women: Image and Achievement* (Dublin: Arlen House, 1985), pp. 111–26.

O'Brien Johnson, Toni, and David Cairns (eds), *Gender in Irish Writing* (Milton Keynes: Open University Press, 1991).

Ó Ciosáin, Niall, *Print and Popular Culture in Ireland, 1750–1850* (Basingstoke: Macmillan, 1997).

—— 'The Irish rogues', in James S. Donnelly Jr and Kerby Miller (eds), *Irish Popular Culture, 1650–1850* (Dublin: Irish Academic Press, 1998), pp. 78–96.

O'Dea, Michael, and Kevin Whelan (eds), *Nations and Nationalisms: France, Britain, Ireland and the Eighteenth-Century Context* (Oxford: Voltaire Foundation, 1995).

O'Dowd, Mary, *A History of Women in Ireland, 1500–1800* (Pearson Education, 2005).

Ó Gallchoir, Clíona, 'Gender, nation and revolution: Maria Edgeworth and Stéphanie-Félicité de Genlis', in Elizabeth Eger et al. (eds), *Women, Writing and the Public Sphere, 1700–1830* (Cambridge: Cambridge University Press, 2001), pp. 200–16.

—— 'Orphans, upstarts and aristocrats: Ireland and the idyll of adoption in the work of Mme de Genlis', in Oonagh Walsh (ed.), *Ireland Abroad: Politics and Professions in the Nineteenth Century* (Dublin: Four Courts, 2003), pp. 36–46.

O'Gorman, Frank, *The Long Eighteenth Century: British Political and Social History, 1688–1832* (London: Arnold, 1997).

O'Halloran, Clare, *Golden Ages and Barbarous Nations: Antiquarian Debate and Cultural Politics in Ireland, c.1750–1800* (Cork: Cork University Press, 2004).

Ó Tuathaigh, Gearóid, 'The role of women in Ireland under the new English order', in Margaret MacCurtain and Donncha Ó Corráin (eds), *Women in Irish Society* (Dublin: Arlen House, 1978), pp. 26–36.

Outram, Dorinda, *The Body and the French Revolution: Sex, Class and Political Culture* (London: Yale University Press, 1989).

—— *The Enlightenment* (Cambridge: Cambridge University Press, 1995).

Owens, Cóilín (ed.), *Family Chronicles: Maria Edgeworth's 'Castle Rackrent'* (Dublin: Wolfhound, 1987).

Parker, Mark, 'The institutionalization of a Burkean–Coleridgean literary culture', *Studies in English Literature* 31 (1991), pp. 693–711.

Perera, Suvendrini, *Reaches of Empire: The English Novel from Edgeworth to Dickens* (New York: Columbia University Press, 1991).

Poovey, Mary, *The Proper Lady and the Woman Writer: Ideology as Style in the Works of Mary Wollstonecraft, Mary Shelley and Jane Austen* (London: University of Chicago Press, 1984).

Porter, Roy, *Enlightenment: Britain and the Creation of the Modern World* (London: Allen Lane, 2000).

Poulet, Georges, 'La pensée critique de Madame de Staël', *Preuves* 190 (1966), pp. 27–35.

Raaphorst, Madeleine R., 'Adèle versus Sophie: the well-educated woman of Mme de Genlis', *Rice University Studies* 64 (1978), pp. 41–50.

Rafroidi Patrick, *Irish Literature in English: the Romantic Period, 1789–1850*, 2 vols (Gerrards Cross: Colin Smythe, 1980).

Rendall, Jane, *The Origins of Modern Feminism: Women in Britain, France and the United States, 1780–1860* (Basingstoke: Macmillan, 1985).

Rice, Adrian, 'The lonely rebellion of William Drennan', in *The Poet's Place: Ulster Literature and Society. Essays in Honour of John Hewitt, 1907–87* (Belfast: Institute of Irish Studies, 1991), pp. 77–95.

Richardson, Alan, *Literature, Education and Romanticism: Reading as Social Practice, 1780–1832* (Cambridge: Cambridge University Press, 1994).

Rogers, Katherine, *Feminism in Eighteenth-Century England* (Brighton: Harvester, 1982).

Rubel, Mary Margaret, *Savage and Barbarian: Historical Attitudes in the Criticism of Homer and Ossian in Britain, 1760–1800* (Amsterdam: North Holland, 1978).

Schofield, Mary Anne, and Cecilia Macheski (eds), *Fetter'd or Free? British Women Novelists, 1670–1815* (London: Ohio University Press, 1986).

Schor, Naomi, 'The portrait of a gentleman: representing men in (French) women's writing', *Representations* 20 (1987), pp. 113–30.

Simpson, David, *Romanticism, Nationalism and the Revolt against Theory* (London: University of Chicago Press, 1993).

Smith, E. A., *Reform or Revolution? A Diary of Reform in England, 1830–2* (Stroud: Alan Sutton, 1992).

Smyth, Jim (ed.), *Revolution, Counter-Revolution, Rebellion: Ireland in the 1790s* (Cambridge: Cambridge University Press, 2000).

Spencer, Jane, *The Rise of the Woman Novelist: From Aphra Behn to Jane Austen* (Oxford: Basil Blackwell, 1987).

Stafford, Fiona J., *The Sublime Savage: A Study of James Macpherson and the Poems of Ossian* (Edinburgh: Edinburgh University Press, 1988).

Stewart, Joan Hinde, *Gynographs: French Novels by Women of the late Eighteenth Century* (London: University of Nebraska Press, 1993).

Sullivan, Moynagh, 'Feminism, postmodernism and the subjects of Irish and women's studies', in P. J. Mathews (ed.), *New Voices in Irish Criticism* (Dublin: Four Courts, 2000), pp. 243–51.

Thom, Martin, *Republics, Nations and Tribes* (London: Verso, 1995).

Thuente, Mary Helen, *The Harp Re-strung: The United Irishmen and the Rise of Literary Nationalism* (Syracuse: Syracuse University Press, 1994).

Tieghem, Paul van, *Ossian en France*, 2 vols (Paris: F. Rieder & Cie, 1917).

Tillyard, Stella, *Aristocrats: Caroline, Emily, Louise and Sarah Lennox, 1740–1832* (London: Vintage, 1995).

—— *Citizen Lord: Edward Fitzgerald, 1763–1798* (London: Vintage, 1998).

Todd, Janet, *Feminist Literary History: A Defence* (Cambridge: Polity, 1988).

Tracy, Robert, 'Maria Edgeworth and Lady Morgan: legality versus legitimacy', *Nineteenth Century Fiction* 40 (1985), pp. 1–22.

—— '"The cracked lookingglass of a servant": inventing the colonial novel', in Shlomith Rimmon-Kenan, Leona Toker and Shuli Barzilai (eds), *Rereading Texts, Rethinking Critical Presuppositions: Essays in Honour of H. M. Daleski* (Frankfurt and New York: Peter Lang, 1997), pp. 197–212.

Trumpener, Katie, *Bardic Nationalism: The Romantic Novel and the British Empire* (Princeton, NJ: Princeton University Press, 1997).

Vance, Norman, *Irish Literature, A Social History: Tradition, Identity and Difference*, 2nd edn (Dublin: Four Courts, 1999).

Vaughan, W. E. (ed.), *A New History of Ireland*, v: *Ireland under the Union I: 1801–1870* (Oxford: Clarendon, 1989).

Vickery, Amanda, 'Historiographical review: golden age to separate spheres? A review of the categories and chronology of English women's history', *Historical Journal* 36 (1993), pp. 383–414.

Watson, Nicola J, *Revolution and the Form of the British Novel, 1790–1825: Intercepted Letters, Interrupted Seductions* (Oxford: Clarendon, 1994).

Weber, Paul, *On the Road to Rebellion: The United Irishmen and Hamburg, 1796–1803* (Dublin: Four Courts, 1997).

Weekes, Ann Owens, *Irish Women Writers: An Uncharted Tradition* (Lexington: University Press of Kentucky, 1990).

Weinbrot, Howard D., 'Enlightenment canon wars: Anglo-French views of literary greatness', *English Literary History* 60 (1993), pp. 79–100.

Whelan, Kevin, *The Tree of Liberty: Radicalism, Catholicism and the Construction of Irish Identity, 1760–1830* (Cork: Cork University Press, 1996).

Wilson, Kathleen, *The Sense of the People: Politics, Culture and Imperialism in England, 1715–1785* (Cambridge: Cambridge University Press, 1995).

—— *The Island Race: Englishness, Empire and Gender in the Eighteenth Century* (London: Routledge, 2003).

Wohlgemut, Esther, 'Maria Edgeworth and the question of national identity', *Studies in English Literature* 39 (1999), pp. 645–58.

Woodward, Llewellyn, *The New Oxford History of England*, xii: *The Age of Reform, 1815–1870* (Oxford: Clarendon, 1962).

Index

✦